GOING PLAID IN A SOLID GRAY WORLD

GOING PLAID IN A SOLID GRAY WORLD

Collected Columns

Tamra Wilson

REDHAWK
PUBLICATIONS

Redhawk Publications
2550 US Hwy 70 SE
Hickory NC 28602

ISBN: 978-1-952485-34-3

Library of Congress Control Number: 2021943816

Robert Canipe, Publisher and Senior Editor
Tim Peeler, Editor
Patty Thompson, Project Coordinator

Each of these essays, in slightly different form, first appeared in the column, "A Fork in the Road," published by the *Hickory Daily Record*, the *Observer-News-Enterprise*, and/or the *Lincoln Herald*.

Photo credits:
Special thanks to Reggie Thomas, Candace Tippett, Renee Potter, and Carlie Stevenson for the image from The Sea Captain's House.

For Tym

CONTENTS

NATURAL FARE

GUESTS

OTHER COURSES

HOLIDAY FARE

ON THE ROAD

COVID TAKE-AWAYS

A LA CARTE

Acknowledgments

Sincere appreciation to all who have helped get this project into the oven and onto the table. Thanks to Gayle Coyne for her encouragement; to Sylvia Bajorek, Janet Ford, and Candace Tippett for editorial excellence; to the *Hickory Daily Record*, *Lincoln Herald* and *Observer-News-Enterprise* for agreeing to see these pieces morph into a book; and to the fine folks at Redhawk Publications for taking this fledgling under their wings.

I am forever indebted to my husband Tym, who figured into many of the essays and proofread many of them as early drafts. I miss him more than we could ever imagine.

Foreword

Since 2015, Tammy Wilson has offered readers a unique perspective of life in Catawba County through her column "A Fork in the Road." Through her writing, Tammy captures the essence of what it means to be fully human in our time and place.

These 135 essays offer commentary on such topics as greeting-card glitter, going plaid in a solid gray world and wearing white shoes after Labor Day. But there are weightier subjects too: storms, COVID, slave narratives and war casualties. Interspersed throughout are slices of humor that feel as if you're chatting over the backyard fence.

As executive director of The Corner Table, Inc. I am pleased to partner with Tammy, who is an honoree of this year's Bakers Dozen Women's Society—local women charged with raising vital funds to support our mission of feeding the hungry. Proceeds from the sale of this book will help provide hope for the less fortunate in our community. Opinions expressed in the essays are the author's alone; they do not necessarily reflect the opinions or policies of The Corner Table or its affiliates.

The Corner Table provides free meals in a family-friendly restaurant setting through our soup kitchen program, as well as to-go bags each Friday for our guests to cover another meal. We also coordinate the county-wide backpack program for local school children and prepare and distribute frozen meals throughout the county to individuals who are homebound or need additional meals outside of our lunch service. Last year alone, The Corner Table served nearly 32,000 guests and 1,569 school children. That's no small potatoes.

I hope that you will savor these collected essays from "A Fork in the Road."

Summer Lee Jenkins
Executive Director
The Corner Table, Inc.

122 N. Main Avenue
P.O. Box 1051
Newton, NC
828-464-0355
www.thecornertable.org

Using a Smartphone or other device, scan the code to visit The Corner Table.

When you come to a fork in the road, take it.
                                        Yogi Berra

STARTERS

Three winters that sent us packing

My parents' front porch, January 1979. The snow stayed; we did not.

January 2018

The recent cold snap reminds me of why I live in North Carolina. Six degrees Fahrenheit sounds extreme, but it could be worse. The other day a Facebook friend posted a photograph from Central Illinois back in 1979. It showed a winter scape of a rural highway buried in twelve-foot drifts.

I replied, "Thanks for reminding me what prompted Tym and me to move South."

This same topic came up a few weeks earlier when I noticed that Catawba County Museum of History was seeking artifacts for a display about "local immigrants."

I asked museum director Amber Clawson Albert if people from other parts of the United States would qualify.

She had never thought of that. Turns out she had never heard of the three horrific winters that sent us South.

Since moving to Catawba County as newlyweds, we have tried to describe what sent us packing from the Midwest. Our winter weather memories are so unbelievable, we ourselves have a hard time believing what we're saying until compatriots from Chicago and Erie and Cleveland and

Pittsburgh chime in.

The winters of 1977, 1978 and 1979 smashed records for prolonged cold, snowfall and misery for much of the Midwest and Northeast. If you lived there during the late 1970s, you know what I'm talking about.

Winter came brutally harsh by mid-January. It snowed and snowed again—so much so that equipment operators in our small town plowed the state highways closed at sunset. You could not get in and out of town because emergency personnel did not wish to risk having to go find you in a ditch.

Whiteouts were common. When the wind picked up, which it did regularly, it was impossible to see the highway edge or oncoming traffic. If you lived on a farm, you had better have supplies on hand.

I'm sure there are those who have lived in harsher climates—the High Sierras or the Yukon—but Central Illinois had seen nothing like it in living memory. In our little town south of Decatur, water pipes were freezing. I remember as a young reporter taking a photo of a matchstick next to a stream of water to show readers how far a tap should be turned on to ensure free-flowing water in the morning.

More than once, I drove into rural areas, mindful of where the last farmhouse was located in case I ran off the road and had to seek shelter. Motorists were warned to carry a water jug, food, blankets, a snow shovel, ice scraper and kitty litter or sand to help traction if they got stuck.

Overheated flues and stovepipes posed fire danger. As the snow piled up over the weeks, country intersections became particularly hazardous. Snowbanks were higher than the roofs of cars, making it impossible to see oncoming cross traffic.

Meanwhile, sports arenas and other free-span roofs were not designed to withstand the weight of epic snows. Collapses were common.

In 1978-79, we lived in Bloomington, about one hundred miles southwest of Chicago. An excerpt from weather.gov tells it all:

Back-to-back brutal winters occurred in the late 1970s. These were three of the five coldest winters on record. 1976-77 had 54.1 inches of snow and was the third coldest winter ever. January 1977 was the coldest January on record with an average temperature of 10.1. There were 12 days below zero in January 1977. December 28, 1976, to February 8, 1977, has the distinction of being the longest continuous string of sub-freezing weather in Chicago history: 43 days.

Winter 1977-78 was the fifth coldest. The 82.3 inches of snow that fell was the second highest seasonal total. Winter 1978-79 was the second coldest. The 89.7 inches of snow that fell is the all-time season record. One of Chicago's worst blizzards occurred January 13-14, 1979. The storm total was 18.8 inches of snow. Roofs collapsed from the weight of the snow, people fought over parking spaces and a mayor lost his job.

I remember Chicago's winter of 1979. I had ordered my wedding gown from Marshall Field's downtown store. One of my fittings was scheduled on a snowy Saturday in March. What should have been a two-and-a half-hour train ride took four.

Yankees and their snow stories. Things get worse with the telling, but what's been called a "whiteout" and "blizzard" in North Carolina has never come close to what we saw up north.

In Catawba County, I have never been trapped inside my home because there are three-foot snow drifts blocking the door. I've never seen roofs cave in from the weight of snow.

Even though the extreme weather pattern hasn't returned in thirty-nine years, Tym and I have never entertained the idea of moving back to the Midwest. When we left Illinois in 1979 for a Southern place called Catawba County, we told ourselves if we ever went back and complained about winter, it would be our own fault.

Those winters marked us for life. When looking at property to rent—and later buy—our thoughts were often about insulation, water pipes, the steep grade of driveways, the strength of the roof, how far to shovel a sidewalk. After nearly 40 years of Southern living, we still think of stuff like that.

When I spoke to Dr. Albert about the museum display, she asked if we had any iconic things brought with us. No, I said. The down coats are long gone with the bent snow shovel, and we aren't complaining about it. We have snow photographs, but these days people would assume they were Photoshopped.

Family and friends who stayed in Illinois have made fun of us over the years, pointing out that such weather was an aberration. We were weenies to leave, but what they forget is that back then, scientists warned of coming bad times. Global cooling, they said, was caused by the accumulation of air pollution blotting out the sun. The earth would become colder, the winters harsher.

Those same friends and family have conveniently forgotten a couple of other record-breaking chills that came to Illinois a few years after we left. Again, weather.gov tells the story.

"From December 22-25, 1983, the temperature plunged below zero for one hundred consecutive hours, a record. It was the coldest Christmas ever in Chicago. December 24 had a low of -25 and a high of -11, an average of -18, making it the coldest day in Chicago history."

Then on January 20, 1985, the temperature plummeted to -27, and a wind chill of -93 was recorded, thus setting a new coldest temperature for Chicago.

Nope. Not moving back.

My fork in the road

February 2015

I love the quips of Yogi Berra. One of my favorites is, "When you come to a fork in the road, take it."

I did just that when I retired from Catawba County Library System. On January 28, I packed up my office and headed out to a new adventure. Then some of you in Readerland asked if I'd ever write a column again, now that I was no longer writing for the library. Which put me at another fork in the road, and heaven knows you shouldn't stand in the fork very long.

Picking a Word of the Year can change your life. This year I decided to focus on "fun." I chose that word because it's better to have it than not.

To prove how serious I am about fun, I've ridden two roller coasters, and allowed myself to not finish a book I didn't like. I've introduced myself to a new grocery store, toured a farmer's market just to take pictures, and gone to three first-run movies.

I've taken time to savor a cup of hot tea and shortbread on chilly afternoons. I've taken time to remark about the crocus peeping out of the mulch. I've ridden down the highway listening to Jan & Dean with the windows rolled down. All this and it's only February.

A writer friend has a goal to get rid of anything in her house that annoys her. Cleaning out drawers and closets can be their own kind of fun I suppose, reminiscing over objects you've forgotten you had and, obviously, could do without. It's fun to get things in order, to repurpose the excess—pass it along to charity or give as gag gifts, a ticket to uproarious fun. The best part of the purge is the exhilaration of the clean sweep, knowing you have helped others instead of feeding the landfill.

I suppose this means I should sort through those four boxes of office stuff I brought home. They annoy me because they've been sitting in the middle of the room for almost a month now. If it would have rained or snowed or sleeted, I'd have an excuse to sort through them and check that task off the list.

Panglossian is a fifty-cent word meaning "excessive optimism." Such people choose their path to the happy place, in spite of heartache and disappointment.

That outlook was put to the test last week I was having a lovely evening out with friends when I accidentally dropped my new cellphone on the sidewalk. Five weeks into owning this phone, it now has a tiny chip and a cracked screen. It's very annoying, but I can't throw it out. My whole life is tied up in that little flat square with its absurd glass face.

The Panglossian in me says to overlook the damage. My phone now has character because I chose fun over staying at home on a rare balmy night in February. The phone still works. It's no longer new or perfect, but neither am I.

Panglossians can talk themselves into anything.

New day, new adventure

A recent retiree told me she has a goal to do something new every day. So far, she has visited Central America, learned how to open a bottle of champagne with a butter knife and gone zip lining, so she's off to a good start.

Why not expand our world a bit, stretch our minds? Why not improve our skill set, as people call abilities these days?

Trying something new could be reading a new author, learning a new dance, visiting a place you've never been before. It could be browsing a new store, traveling down a new street, learning how to use a Smartphone app, learning a different language. It could mean getting artsy. Going to the movies, seeing a new play, taking an art class, skipping over to a new radio station, visiting a new exhibit at the museum.

A writer friend says every story is a food story. Your "something new" could be trying a new recipe. It could be dining at a restaurant you've never tried, ordering a new dessert at your old faithful. You could pick up the latest copy of *Southern Living* or check out a cookbook from the library.

Jack Nicholson and Morgan Freeman pushed new stuff to the max in the hit movie, *The Bucket List*. The 2007 film depicts the two actors about to kick the bucket. They circle the globe to see the Great Pyramid, Mount Everest and Hong Kong. Nice if you can afford it.

I don't have an actual bucket list, but I do have some things I hope to accomplish— research projects, writing projects, cleaning closets and drawers, organizing my scrapbooks and photographs…and visiting Norway. When I was thirteen, I wrote in my diary that I wanted to see Norway, and the thought has stuck with me. Now's the time to make it happen.

The Norway thing was reinforced by riding the Maelstrom attraction in the Norway pavilion at EPCOT. It was a ride I could never get enough of. A gentle rollercoaster boat with splashes in mini fjords, views of big oil rigs and Vikings, narration with a Norwegian accent: "You are not the first to pass this way, nor shall you be the last. Those who seek the spirit of Norway face peril and adventure but more often find beauty and charm."

On a hot day in Orlando, Norway's air conditioning was worth the long wait. This ride is a good substitute until the real thing comes along.

Beach, mountains identify us

Home is where the buoys are: Yes, I'm a beach person.

October 2015

Do you prefer the beach or the mountains?

The question forces you to answer where you stand, literally. The question reminds me of *The Wizard of Oz*, when Glinda, the witch of the North, asked Dorothy, "Are you a good witch or a bad witch?"

"I'm not a witch at all," Dorothy replies.

And the munchkins titter. They know there's no such thing as middle ground.

Choosing sides is part of life. Liberal or conservative, traditional or modern, up or down, left or right. As we become more polarized, we can't not have an opinion on things…immigration, Planned Parenthood, candidates. A society of extremes doesn't allow middle of the road.

Our beloved Piedmont, the half-way point, doesn't count, either. If it were, I'd have to answer "Piedmont" because it's actually the place my husband

and I picked. We came to Catawba County through a job offer and said we'd try it out. That was more than 37 years ago.

Growing up on the prairie, we had never been asked the beach vs. mountain question because both places were too far away. Many Midwesterners live their entire lives without seeing either.

I've since learned that I'm a beach person. I've actually lived briefly on two bodies of water: Tampa Bay and the English Channel. Ocean breezes trump the mountains every time. Surf and sand have a way of calling me home. The beach is a summer place.

For me and others of my ilk, I feel claustrophobic on winding mountain roads.

I know. You mountaineers have a point rooting for crisp air, breathtaking vistas and daredevil overlooks. You imagine being an eagle soaring over valleys. Some of you do that on snow skis. Mountains are winter and fall places.

Maybe that's what I am, a warm-weather person—warm weather with a breeze. For me the choice is easy. Send me out on a spit of land with the waves crashing, gulls calling overhead. Send me shelling or hunting for sea glass.

Ocean people say they like looking out at the edge of the world. Mountain people say they're looking out over it, like a bird. Or God.

Statistically there are far more coastal people than mountain people, which could be a source of pride for those who favor higher altitudes. Mountaineers are a rarer lot. Then again, being a beach person means we see things the way most do, which is probably why the beach is often crowded. If we're not already there, we're trying to get there as soon as we can.

I want my 'saved' hour back

The Bakelite clock.

November 2019

Is there anything more annoying than Daylight Savings Time?

I woke up Sunday to realize that the rest of the world had fallen back and left me behind, or ahead, or…whatever.

My dogs, meanwhile, operate on the sun and belly time: when the sun comes up, it's time to fill their bellies.

After tending to breakfast, I spent the next hour adjusting clocks. Until now, my husband handled most mechanical and digital gadgetry, so Sunday's wakeup call was another unpleasant adventure on the high lonesome. Both of my watches and my alarm clock involve old-fashioned dials. Just pull out the little side knob and twist.

The hallway wall clock was a simple fix too. Just move the hour hand.

Digital oven clocks were another matter. No knobs to twist and no arrows pointing up or down. It takes a secret decoder to figure out how to reset them, and my husband is no longer around to share it.

I rifled through the stash of owner's manuals for the microwave and found instructions for adjusting the clock, but the convection oven had me stumped. There are no "up" and "down" arrows described by the online reference guide, and heaven knows where the owner's manual is.

I skipped the oven clock for an easier target: the vintage Bakelite clock over the kitchen sink. I bought this charmer of a timepiece from the trash heap of the Great Depression. It came with a crumbling electrical cord and rusted works, but I was in love with its lime green case and Art Deco numerals.

Back in 1931, manufacturers weren't very concerned with the aesthetics of an electrical cord snaking down the wall. Electrical cords would have been a status symbol for people who didn't have electricity, such as those in bread lines and most farm families. Far fewer folks would have been bothered with the time shuffle every spring and fall. There were weightier issues to worry about, such as their next meal.

Before I adjusted the Bakelite clock on Sunday, I searched the attic for a small screwdriver to open the back of the case. Then I carefully bent five flanges to remove the face and access the hour hand.

Twenty minutes later, I applauded myself for my can-do spirit as I re-hung the clock above the sink.

Meanwhile, two vehicles awaited me in the garage. Luckily, there were owner's manuals available, though I had no clue that instructions for the SUV were in a separate manual labeled "Infotainment System." That's how I learned to press "5" and then a series of other numbers to reset the clock.

But still, the onerous oven clock was taunting me with a time display that would be correct if I lived in Nova Scotia or New Brunswick.

We can thank Canadians for initiating Daylight Savings. Back in 1908, residents of Thunder Bay, Ontario decided it would be a brilliant to temporarily move their clocks ahead one hour to "save" artificial light. Others followed suit as World War I approached, thinking that the Daylight Savings would help them accomplish more for the war effort by saving electricity, or something like that. Merits of that argument have been argued for more than a century.

A total of seventy countries (or portions of them) now follow the Daylight Savings scheme, using various dates to switch back and forth, which adds to the confusion.

Meanwhile, there are some American holdouts. The states of Arizona and Hawaii do not observe Daylight Savings time. Neither does Puerto Rico.

And as for my stubborn oven clock, I suppose I could call the Frigidaire helpline or the appliance dealer we bought it from assuming anyone there remembers how to reset an eleven-year-old digital clock. I can hope that a friend may be able to divine the secret code.

Or I could continue to use masking tape to cover the display. There are three clocks in the kitchen and two of them tell correct time: Eastern Standard Time. The "standard" part should tell us something.

What I didn't tell these new parents

April 2017

B eing a parent is tough business.
I recently visited our six-month-old granddaughter Violet and her parents in California. She was generally all smiles when she wasn't hungry, tired or wet. She was, however, getting ready to cut her first teeth, so she spent a lot of time grumpily rubbing her bottom gums.

Her mom, mindful of my first-year calendar I'd kept when Violet's dad was a baby, asked questions about Lantz. When did he begin to crawl? Did he sleep through the night? Did he cut teeth at this stage?

As I rifled through my foggy memory bank, and a lot of it came back to me, like remembering almost-forgotten phrases from college French.

I watched Violet drool as she felt her bottom gums. Maybe she needs Baby Oragel, I said.

The name came to me quickly, though I haven't used the stuff in decades.

Diaper rash? Try Desitin ointment.

Diapers? A store brand will do. (They had already figured this out.)

It will be thirty years since I dealt with my own crying baby and learned how to care for him. Now that baby is caring for his own child.

I learned on an earlier Violet visit that today's diapers have a color strip that turns green when the baby is wet. No finger checking anymore.

We tried in vain to show Violet how to crawl, how to get those hands moving with the knees. But something else begged me to tell this new Mom and Dad that these are the "good ole days" before Violet can get into everything. This is when heavy-duty parenting begins. Be prepared to baby-proof the house, I told them. Cover electrical outlets, keep household cleaners out of reach, pick up splinters from firewood. Beware of dangling cords.

I didn't tell them about the time I had mindlessly turned my back from the ironing board. That day Lantz pulled the cord and the hot iron landed on his foot. He was lucky. No broken bones or scars.

I didn't mention the time he came running into the house yelling "Mama, there's a snake sticking his tongue out at me!"

That day I hurried to the driveway to see his toddler tricycle straddling a baby copperhead.

It's those forays into the darker side of parenting that still give me pause, as they should.

Violet's parents will make mistakes. All parents do. So what would I tell them?

Relax. I know, it's a cliché, but most of their concerns aren't big at all. Thirty years from now, what difference will it make if Violet crawled at six months or seven? Who will care if she ate sweet potatoes before she tried chicken? What will it matter if she learned to speak at eleven months or fifteen?

If I had it to do over, I wouldn't waste time comparing Lantz to others. Children learn and grow at their own rate. I would turn off the TV and read to him more—even more than I did. We'd take him on more walks and point out nature—even more than we did.

I would spend more time in the present than the future. I wouldn't sweat the small stuff, and it's mostly all small stuff.

Do you really know what time it is?

January 2019

It's 2019. Our vehicles are another model year older. We've inched another digit toward the Twenties.

I'm trying to absorb the fact that today's eighteen-year-olds were born in 2001, the year of 9-11. They have little if any memory of events before 2006—no memory of what life was like before the iPhone or Facebook. They've always written a current date with a "20" prefix when they write a check, if they write any at all.

The year 2019 will bring some anniversaries. It will be sixty years since 1959, the year of Fidel Castro's revolution and the death of rock legend Buddy Holly. You know, the day the music died.

This year will mark fifty years since Woodstock and the first moon landing. And a group called Chicago Transit Authority, aka Chicago, released a hit single, "Does Anybody Really Know What Time It Is?"

It will be forty years since 1979, the year fifty-two American diplomats and other citizens were taken hostage in Iran.

It's been thirty years since the Berlin Wall fell.

Twenty years ago, we were prepping for the Y2K disaster that never happened, and partying like it was well, 1999.

Ten years ago, Barack Obama was inaugurated as President. Less than a week earlier, Capt. "Sully" Sullenberger landed an American Airlines Airbus on the Hudson River after two bird strikes disabled the engines.

Was that really ten years ago? Time really does fly.

Today's thirty-somethings arrived when Ronald Reagan was president. They might remember what life was like before personal computers existed, but they probably don't.

The year I turned thirty, my employer offered early retirement to those fifty-five and older. I looked around and saw these gleeful people signing up for a pension and thought they were pretty darned old. Now, the youngest Baby Boomers are fifty-five, and I'm not sure how this happened.

When it comes to the topic of age and our role in history, I recall a talk by author Reynolds Price. When he was born in 1933, his sixty-five-year-old grandparents knew some ex-slaves.

I scratched my head until I realized that of course he was right. When I was born in the 1950s, at least one Civil War veteran was still living.

The last confirmed veteran from either side was a man named Albert Woolson who died in 1956. The year 2012 saw the last World War I veteran.

History touches us from all sides. Growing up I often heard that my grandparents had seen more change than I would ever see in my lifetime. Why they had gone from horse and buggy to Man on the Moon! Yet NASA sent Neil Armstrong to the moon using less computing power than what operates an automobile these days. Armstrong, by the way, is the topic of a movie *First Man* released late last year. *First Man* depicts ancient history to those under sixty.

My husband and I often discuss the changes that would shock our mothers, both of whom died in 2002. Neither of them ever took their shoes off to board a plane. Neither one ever heard of Smartphones or satellite radio or would have considered buying water in individual plastic bottles.

My mother, who grew up ordering clothes and supplies from the Sears & Roebuck catalog, loved receiving packages in the mail or picking up her order at the Sears store in town. Eventually the catalog agencies were considered old-fashioned. Big Box stores were the way to go.

Except now they aren't. Sears is going belly up and everyone has returned to mail-order, except we call it "ordering online." If Sears hadn't bailed out of the catalog business in 1993, they could have out-Amazoned Amazon.

What's new is old, including ideas…and us.

RESERVATIONS

Blame it on chevrons

Chevrons haunt me wherever I go.

March 2017

No design motif has irked me more than chevrons. Wherever there's a clean surface, a chevron will find a home.

I know exactly where I was when I knew the Chevron Era had arrived. It was way back in 2013. I saw two guests at the same wedding wearing the same orange-and-white chevron dress. They were seated at the same table, and I can only imagine what they said to one another.

"Oh, you're wearing the same ugly dress that I am," one says.

"No, mine's uglier," the other counters.

"No mine!"

Let's face it—wavy horizontal stripes do not flatter most figures. The lines are the jagged lines of the Richter scale; the result is even worse.

I have had a running joke with my friend Candace, who was actually with me the time I spotted my first chevron garment in a shop window. We both agreed that we were not fans.

Since then, we've turned chevrons into a torment, gifting each other chevron items, swapping chevron gift bags, sending emails of chevron photos.

Recently, I sent Candace a wedding picture from Facebook—the chevron dress distracted all attention from the bride.

About a year into this, I told Candace my ultimate chevron story.

"I suffered the ultimate chevron torment on Sunday," I told her. "The minister had a chevron pattern on his stole."

I was forced to look at it for an entire hour.

There is nothing soothing about the chevron. History teaches that the chevron design dates to 1,800 BC. Wikipedia reports that ancient Cretans designed pottery using those sharp wavy symbols. Cretins is more like it.

Clearly, we are not the first to be tormented with this motif. The symbol has been used for centuries on military uniforms and heraldic shields, particularly in Switzerland. Maybe the chevron mimics the jagged peaks of the Alps.

Now nearly every tunic has one of those odd dips in the back or to the side, an elongated "V" front or back that will shout "2016" or "2017" to fashion historians. I am not fooled. They're a chevron spinoff.

Why chevrons and why now?

We're a deeply divided world—not just a rocky sea, but discord of seismic proportions. Chevrons, I think, reflect gnashed teeth, the rocky waves, shaky ground.

Look at the lines of clashing pickets and signs, the body language of people who disagree. It's very angular. Reinforced by peaked hemlines of tunics and skirts, exclaim the fact that we're throwing ourselves a little off kilter, rocking the ship of state, not standing on the level.

Chevrons may well be the perfect sign of our times.

They've got your number

H i. It's Capitol One. Did you just spend $19.99 at iTunes?"
When I woke up to this text last Thursday, I knew it wasn't going to be a good day.

Someone had swiped my credit card data and run up some charges. They'd first tested the account with a .99 charge to iTunes. Then the crook made three more charges of $19.99 to iTunes within a few minutes—while I was asleep. Then came a fourth iTunes purchase of $20.98 before Capitol One got wise.

After more than 90 minutes on the phone, I learned more disturbing news. The thief had tried to buy equipment from Hometics for nearly $375, but that charge was declined. Capitol One's consumer tracking program realized that I don't ordinarily buy fancy massagers in the middle of the night. Before that, the fraudster had tried to purchase $1 in beauty supplies—another test to ensure that my account number was valid.

I spent the better part of two hours trying to straighten the mess out, going over my online statement, speaking to several customer service representatives at Capitol One and iTunes—dealing with the inevitable security drill. "Please state your name, the last four digits of your card number, your mother's maiden name, the name of your first pet, your mailing address with zip code."

The crook, meanwhile, didn't have to do any of this while making off with $80 in merchandise. The charges are technically still on my account, pending investigation by iTunes and Capitol One. That might take days or weeks.

So, who's really holding the bag here?

Ultimately, it's other customers, i.e. you and me. We'll pay with higher fees for goods and services, fancier technology to prevent fraud, more hassle when opening a credit account, more irritating security questions.

While I had the customer service rep on the line, I asked him what the chances of catching the crook were. His reply: "Less than one percent."

This one incident cost me and customer service representatives at least an hour of our time.

And then Fed Ex got in on the act. After I changed the passwords for my iTunes and credit card accounts, Capitol One shipped a new card overnight to the tune of $25.

I figure this incident essentially stole more than $100 in real goods and services plus time and inconvenience. I'm convinced that my card was electronically skimmed a day or two earlier. This would explain how the swindler had my number, expiration date and CVV code and was in such a hurry to run up a bill.

The good news is that the spree was caught early, and my credit card company covers the loss. And it could have been far worse. The crook could have stolen my card information while I was on an extended stay out of town and I had no other credit card to use, which is all the more reason to have more than one active card at all times.

Credit card theft is a multi-billion-dollar enterprise. And while consumers bemoan how companies track purchases and consumer behavior, few consider how that very technology can be their friend. Without tracking, this crook wouldn't have been caught until I reviewed my next statement. The thief would have run up a heftier bill for me, the merchants and my credit card company to sort out and ultimately pay for.

But I will pay for it. So will you. Merchants and credit card companies don't write off such losses and forget it.

Had I been a victim of identity theft, the stakes would have been far higher. According to the Federal Trade Commission, recovering from identity theft takes an average of six months and 200 hours of work. Think about that the next time you answer security questions and get caught in the phone loop with customer service.

Passwords a mission impossible

March 2015

L et's face it. We're drowning in passwords.
What used to be associated with secret clubs has crept into everyday life at an alarming clip. Passwords are required to open an account, pay a bill, retrieve your own money and place orders. Passwords are needed for things you merely want and those you don't: emails from your insurance company, your tax preparer, your banker, your doctor.

Passwords are the good guys in a world of sleepless hackers and identity thieves working behind every computer screen. Outsmarting them has given rise to twenty-first-century paranoia—discovery of your passwords.

Picking a password is something like playing Scrabble in Chinese or maybe Sudoku. It's too numerical for me. I follow the rules: no birth dates or obvious data like addresses or phone numbers. I use different passwords for different accounts, which gives rise to reams of passwords to remember. I've used nicknames, pet names, childhood nonsense, jumbled root words, foreign terms and different combinations for my passwords only to forget them the day they've been changed to something "safe." They are secure all right, from me.

Some setups require passwords that must be "used" within ninety days or they're no good. These are particularly annoying because they have a built-in fuse, like the one on "Mission Impossible."

Recently I ran out a paper copy of my passwords. It was eleven sheets of data to access everything from hotel reservation websites to reward cards, frequent flier accounts to retailers. Some of them are no doubt expired like a head of lettuce turned soupy in the back of the vegetable bin. I'll never know until I try to use them and learn the bad news. Access denied.

How to access and reset the password. The secret code can be sent to your email if you can remember what it is. Most of us don't normally email ourselves.

A recent data breach prompted me to go through my password list and update them. I knocked on the cybergates of my various credit card accounts, bank accounts, organizations and other places that require a password which is just about everything. I updated them.

In the process, I received snarky comments: Very weak, Weak or Medium. Only when I encrypted my password with a nonsensical combination of capitals, symbols numbers and letters did the messenger praise me with "Strong."

Trying to remember what I had just typed means I must write it down quick, before they dissolve into the black hole. Then hide it where I think I can find it again.

A friend told me recently that she bought an address book to store her passwords alphabetically. Brilliant, I thought. Organized, methodical, logical—assuming she can remember where she kept the address book.

Distress over the dress that got away

February 2020

Consider an episode at Marshall's in Charlotte. I went there on a lark, not looking for anything in particular. As most avid shoppers know, that's when good buys abound.

Sure enough, before I left the store, I'd found three must-have garments including a gray Anne Klein sweater dress with a stylish cowl collar. Not only was the price right ($29.99) but it fit perfectly.

I took this keeper to the checkout. Soon, the clerk was wrestling with the dress collar and a plastic ink tag. The more she tried, the less the security tag wanted to budge. The knit fabric had worked its way into the tag removal mechanism built into the counter.

"You need to stop. You're going to tear a hole in the fabric," I told her.

She kept tugging until she tore a hole in it. Did I mention that this was the only dress of that type in my size?

The store manager was willing to cut me a deal, but I refused. I know what happens to knits when the threads are cut. Think ladders in your tights and just say "no."

I left the store, fuming. If only I'd been more adamant, insisted the clerk stop jerking on the fabric. If only she'd listened to me.

The more I thought about this, the angrier I became. Who puts a security tag on a $30 dress? Shouldn't anti-theft devices be reserved for more expensive merchandise?

The next morning, I told myself that surely that wasn't the only bargain-priced Anne Klein sweater dress on the planet. Of course not! There must be another one at another Marshall's. In my crazed obsession, I checked online for Marshall's and Anne Klein. No luck. Then I drove to the new Marshall's in Lincolnton, imagining a clone of the sweater dress hanging enticingly from a rack.

Not only did they not have that dress, they had no dresses, period.

A friend who heard about my ink tag incident offered to do me a favor. She was going to Raleigh that week and would stop at Marshall's on the way.

Turned out there were two such stores on the route, but no gray sweater dresses to be had.

In the coming days, I checked other stores. The Hickory Belk had a similar dress on sale for $50. Belk didn't have my size in stock, but it could be ordered. Free shipping. I liked the free part.

Of course, I ordered the dress, but it wasn't the same as that perfect one in Charlotte. No, this dress ran a little large. I know, better than too snug. But this alternative cost $20 more.

Ink tags have been around for years. They presumably deter shoplifters by beeping if someone leaves the store with a tag attached. If you get home with the tagged merchandise and try to remove the device yourself, the tag will eject ink onto the garment.

Yes, I know you can remove the tag. I've seen the YouTube video, but why risk ruining the perfect garment?

A few days later over lunch, I told another friend about my dress fiasco. She could sympathize. She used to work in retail, so she's well aware of the ink tag aggravation and the shoplifting that we all pay for.

"The bottom line is, the crooks are in charge," I said. "They've been in charge for years."

Think about what thieves cost us. Higher prices at stores which are already struggling to compete with online retailers.

Yes, security is big business these days. We can barely afford all the gadgets and systems it takes to keep thieves at bay. The errant ink tag seems inconsequential, except for the heartburn and wasted time and the extra $20 I had to pay for a dress that doesn't fit as well as the first one.

Please don't make this grandma remember

Getting acquainted with Miss Violet.

October 2016

Recently a friend gave me a book of good intentions, titled *Grandmother Remembers: A Written Heirloom for my Grandchild.*

I call it a book of good intentions because few people ever fill them out. This one is as pristine as it was when it was published in 1983. But my friend is moving and it was going to Goodwill if I didn't take it.

She insisted I keep it. "You're a new grandma now."

True. Violet Rae Wilson was only a few weeks old.

I thumbed through the pages. There was the family tree and pages about my own family, the day I was born, my days as a young girl, my engagement, wedding and my memories of Violet's daddy, our son Lantz.

I know I should fill out the thing right now, except I, like the previous owner and giver/receiver, am not keen on exposition. I know that sounds odd coming from one who's written all her life.

Grandmother Remembers is full of writing prompts. I'm to list my schools, where my family lived, pets we had…but there are other prompts, too, such as "My parents were strict about…" and "At home I was expected to…."

How truthful should I be? This book will likely be passed down to Violet's children whom I may never know. "As a girl my favorite song was…"

Of course, they would bring music up! How do you pick just one song? What if you change your mind later? What if I say "Albatross" by Fleetwood Mac? Or "A Summer Song" by Chad & Jeremy and forget to mention "Sloop John B" by the Beach Boys or "Knights in White Satin" by the Moody Blues? What will those songs tell someone fifty years from now?

And what of some other favorites such as "Cara Mia" by Jay and the Americans or "There's a Kind of Hush" by Herman's Hermits or "Ashokan Farewell" by whoever recorded it for the Civil War miniseries? Or "Girls Just Wanta Have Fun" by Cyndi Lauper or "Faithful One" by Cliff Richard? I have such a crowded, disjointed list.

There are more open-ended questions, such as "My teenage years were…." And I wonder what kind of question is that? Who hasn't experienced some dopey years when they were a teenager?

I'm invited to share memories of my engagement. "When I Told My Parents They. …" I don't remember what they said after "Oh Lord."

Our most memorable wedding gift was… Should I write about the electric hot dog cooker that we traded for store credit?

Or how about "How the World Has Changed Since I was a Girl?" How many pages are there? The last line on that page is "I think a woman president would be…." I remind myself that this book was published in 1983.

And there's this "Today My Favorite" section. What if I say my favorite dessert is still coconut cream pie with toasted coconut flakes? Or what if I choose "There's a Kind of Hush" as my favorite song? Violet has heard it already, so she's tied to the Sixties by default. Come to think of it, we're all tied to the past by default.

Page 59 is reserved for "Treasures I Have Saved for You." How about a whole house full of stuff her parents won't want…china, silver, crystal, linens? It's high-maintenance stuff from my bridal registry to be displayed in a china cabinet. And then there are pictures of Victorian relatives, a four-drawer cabinet of family records. Will Violet care about all that?

Page 55 has the heading "The Future" with plenty of blanks for me to fill in my wish list. I'm still a teenager in many ways, and all said, that's what I hope for Violet. That she won't grow "old." She will graduate from high school in 2034. She will be my age now in 2078. Why does that frighten me?

The problem with *Grandmother Remembers* is that this grandparent remembers too much. Editing is hard work. Writing memoir is one of the toughest things to do. Our lives are so much more than a few sentences about favorites and names and dates.

I set the book aside. I'll get to it one of these days.

Why my interest isn't Pinterest

October 2017

I can't say when I became aware that I don't need Pinterest. Maybe at the beginning, when a friend warned me not to sign up. "Pinterest will take over your life," she said.

I have enough online addictions. The official Pinterest website described the site a place for "recipes, home ideas, style inspiration and other ideas to try." In other words, people who want to be Martha Stewart with a theme.

I get the theme part. When my husband and I moved into our house, we determined that it was to appear nautical. We took cues from that fabulous old restaurant in Myrtle Beach—The Sea Captain's House on Ocean Drive. I asked permission to take pictures of their décor, their architectural features, lighting and wall and window treatments.

A nautical house was something we could agree on—a seafaring house in the middle of the woods in Catawba County. Whenever we puzzled over what to put in our house, we asked what would the sea captain choose? Anything that appeared extraneous was explained simply: "The sea captain picked up some odd cargo."

Maybe I'm a wannabe Pinterest fan, but if given a choice of say, lobsters and anchors versus ladybugs and cute bees, I'm all in with the seashore. I don't need a cutesy website to know this.

My friend Patty says she "does" Pinterest but has managed to resist the creative temptation to become a true devotee. If she throws a party, she doesn't check Pinterest for cute party favors or recipes or clever table decorations. You know, the glitter that gets on everything, the Mardi Gras beads that drape around candle sticks and old books.

I've heard of people, all of them women, who can't host a gathering without Pinterest's cleverness. This amounts to mass quantities of extra stuff—matched tableware, color-coordinated food, toothpicks, napkins, you name it.

Such attention to detail seems out of place in our loose-fitting world. No one seems to obey the old rules of no white shoes after Labor Day, but woe be to the one who throws a bridal shower without Pinterest.

Millennials have embraced Pinterest in a big way, although they may not be matchy-matchy elsewhere. Try decorating their digs without consulting the pros at Pinterest!

Just dare.

Same goes for the gender reveal parties—a concept that still feels foreign to me.

Patty says that you can look at pictures without setting up an account. I've done some of this. I see picture-perfect rooms and blooms.

Thanks to Pinterest, there's been an uptick in home accessories and chalk boards with cute sayings on them.

I'm willing to bet we can thank Pinterest for the bumper crop of pillows on sofas and beds. They've invaded hotels to the point at every check in we have to harvest six pillows from the bed just to watch TV.

Gone are the down-to-earth days of home-baked, lop-sided birthday cakes and hand-written invitations.

Recently, I tried to buy a pack of those old-fashioned party invitations that let you fill in the blanks with an ink pen.

No luck. The only option was to buy themed computer-generated invitations to make them look slick and professional— and risk several paper jams in my temperamental printer. Or I could simply buy some nice blank note cards and handwrite them myself.

I chose the latter and went so far as to handwrite the envelopes because I know the first thing that gets opened in the mail is a hand-addressed envelope.

Take that, Pinterest.

Navigating our un-private world

November 2018

I'm convinced that my Smartphone is a two-way listening device.

I saw an intriguing interview a few months ago. News anchor and technology reporter Brett Larson discussed how smartphone apps are programmed to listen to their owners whenever the phone is turned on.

Tech industry leaders deny that phones actively listen to us without the voice assistant, "Siri" being activated. I believed them until a few days later when my son and daughter-in-law showed me a hard-shell suitcase they had just purchased. My phone was "on," as it usually is, and we were talking about that suitcase with the eye-catching tropical palm-leaf design. We had not asked for any help from Siri.

The next day my Instagram feed showed me an ad for a pink hard-shelled suitcase and in the photo—as if added for my benefit—was an image of a palm leaf. I know I didn't imagine it because I made a screenshot of the image. It's still in my photo archive.

Coincidence?

I know Smartphones are programmed to "help" you find merchandise you may be interested in. It's a marketing thing. What I don't get is how the phone heard our conversation. I never keyed in suitcases or palm leaves. I know this sounds wacky, but it appears my phone knew about the conversation because it heard it. It had the smarts to translate that chatter to direct us to a retailer who could sell me a suitcase like the one I was talking about in the privacy of my own living room.

We don't live in a private world anymore. Anyone who has ever traveled by air knows that. TSA notwithstanding, we have willingly given up private matters that our parents would have found shocking twenty years ago. The attacks on 9-11 prompted us to willingly stand for full-body scans, have agents rifle through our baggage, quiz us about artificial joints and to remove our shoes and empty our pockets.

The suitcase incident does raise questions. Who knows what permissions lurk within the fine print of those license agreements we agree to whenever we open Facebook for the first time? What are we signing up for when our Smartphone asks to access the microphone functions? What are we allowing when we download a new app?

The over-reach of technology and what we allow it to probe into our lives is creepy at best. Smartphones and their eavesdropping cousins, smart tower "Alexa" or "Echo" exist for eavesdropping. I don't own such a tower nor do I plan to buy one. The idea of a listening device hidden in plain sight, is a frill I don't need, and I suspect, you don't either. If I need to turn on my security system or adjust the thermostat, I can do it myself. And if I need to know the distance between Earth and Mars, I can look that up without a smart tower.

A few years ago, when we had purchased a new vehicle, it came with OnStar, GM's subscription service for navigation, communications, diagnostics and emergency services. We had not fully activated the service, and one night I was driving down Startown Road. When I adjusted the rear-view mirror, a woman's voice began talking about my "emergency." I was so startled I could have swerved into the ditch.

The mystery voice belonged to the "OnStar Lady" who had been summoned when I mistakenly pressed a button on the rear-view mirror. She insisted that I set up the system immediately, demanding my email address and phone number.

When I buy a new vehicle, I yearn for the old days when a customer signed the papers, shook hands with the salesman and drove off the lot. Things were simple. New auto owners didn't have to set computers, clocks and other gadgets or pay for a subscription.

There's something unsettling about driving a car that's being monitored by a computer system that tells me things I should know—that the oil needs changing or that my air bag has deployed. Or that my vehicle is under warranty.

The pitch is that I should feel less anxious with a remote entity following my every move. In case of emergency, OnStar will dispatch help right away.

What they're forgetting are all the other drivers with cellphones who want to be first to call 911 or Tweet news of my mishap. Or those who will post photos on Instagram and Facebook.

Or my cellphone that has been listening all along.

NATURAL FARE

When nature came calling

The buck stopped here.

October 2019

A deer came to visit last Monday.

We were heading out on our mid-morning dog walk and I turned around to see what was holding up Jolene, our Corgi mix.

It was a four-point buck in the middle of the road.

Deer are not an unusual site in our neighborhood, especially in fall and winter when they seek out acorn snacks. But on a drizzly August morning? A deer following me? That's odd.

Since we were heading toward a busy road, we turned around and walked back home. Mr. Four Point followed.

We had never seen a tamer deer outside a petting zoo. He let me pet his head and feel his fuzzy antlers. He sauntered up to the front door. Tym brought out a dish of dog food, which the animal much appreciated.

I know. We're not supposed to feed wildlife, but this fellow had apparently been around friendly humans before.

A spot on his left flank told me that he might have been injured and taken in as a fawn. Maybe he was a pet who had strayed or otherwise been dumped into our neighborhood. We see wildlife all the time—small herds of deer, rafters of wild turkeys, crows and red hawks, but until last Monday, no tame deer.

Social media is amazing when it comes to lost animals. Our neighbors marveled at the pictures of Mr. Four Point. One Facebooker said she had seen a video of him taken on Sigmon Dairy Road the day before.

I checked the image. Sure enough, it was the same deer. I could tell by the pattern of his rack.

Nearly everyone who's seen the pictures or heard our deer story has warned us about feeding him. When hunting season arrives, he could wind up as venison.

I know that as well as I know that someone, somehow has intervened to befriend him over the past couple of years.

I was amazed at how dog-like he was—like a Great Dane on stilts. His ears felt like pliable cardboard and his antlers were flocked with stubble. "Velvet" it's called.

Mr. Four Point moseyed outside the house Monday, to the patio, sniffed the door to the screened porch. I have no doubt he would have stepped inside, given the chance.

This animal has known only human kindness and he's roaming—at least two miles by my calculation.

But why did this animal show up at this time in this place?

The Internet offers symbolic meaning for animal totems. Native Americans and Celtic people have this figured out. Deer mean peace, innocence, the opening of new doors.

When deer are close by, so are the angels.

All I know is that if we'd opened a door, Mr. Deer would have likely come in. I can picture Mr. Four Point on the couch, nibbling snacks off the counter, then bedded down in a corner while the dogs look on, waiting for the next miraculous thing to happen.

Such a tale my DNA tells

July 2018

Testing DNA has become a national craze.

A while back I succumbed to the temptation. Like thousands of others, I ponied up the fee and mailed off my saliva sample to Ancestry.com.

A few weeks later, I learned that I am 43 % British, 34 % Irish and 12 % Scandinavian. The Scandinavian bit threw me. My family paper trail shows I'm decidedly German and Dutch, not Danish or Norwegian. So, I decided to test the test.

This time I used the 23 and Me company and opted for the health reports (more cash of course), though I was most interested in solving the riddle about being a Lady Viking.

Turns out 23 and Me categorized me as 62% British and Irish, 15% German-French and less than 1% Scandinavian. Another 17% of me was classified as "broadly European," which covers a lot of bases—possibly Norse heritage.

Vikings aside, my DNA experiences have been fun and thought-provoking. Every so often I receive email updates about DNA relatives who share matching bits of genetic material with me.

One of these relatives was a Fell, a surname I recognized from my mother's family tree. I ended up talking to this man in northwest Iowa. He told me when his great-grandfather Fell died in the 1880s. At that point his great-grandmother "fell" on hard times. She and her children became servants for a wealthy farmer. Years later, the farmer bequeathed much of his fortune to her children.

My DNA health-related reports have been impressive. The science accurately predicted details about my toes, my earlobes, my hairline, and chin. The results also predict the odds for me having dimples, fair skin and freckles. The science was spot on predicting whether I'm repulsed by "chewing sounds," whether I'm apt to sneeze in sunlight, whether I prefer a salty vs. sweet taste, whether I like cilantro (coriander). I don't know what the big deal is about cilantro…maybe it's the popularity of Mexican and Thai restaurants. Years ago, a lot of us didn't know what cilantro was.

23 and Me accurately suggested that I am not a deep sleeper, and that I am predisposed to wake up at 6:37 a.m. They have it down to the minute. And, like a self-fulfilling prophecy, I have checked the clock every morning

since, and 6:37 a.m. is correct within a few minutes.

One of the most intriguing reports claims that I have a specific genetic variant related to muscle tissue. It's the same variant possessed by elite power athletes such as sprinters, throwers and jumpers. Until now I have never considered myself athletic, but who knows? Maybe my destiny was to be an Olympian and I missed my calling.

23 and Me also claims that I share a Haplogroup with Benjamin Franklin. Haplogroups are comprised of people who share a cluster of genes from a single parent. Presumably my Haplogroup descends from a prehistoric mother who wandered into Europe around 10,000 years ago. Fittingly, my Haplogroup is most common among people from Northern Scandinavia, which brings me back to that Viking question.

I must point out that my DNA results have been "relatively" correct, which raises deeper questions. If DNA determines so much of our physical traits and abilities, how much free choice do we really have? How much of our life is pre-determined by ancestors who lived hundreds and thousands of years ago?

I think the answers are "not much" and "a lot."

A storm story to beat Hugo

September 2018

In September 2017, when we learned that Western North Carolina might be in the path of Hurricane Irma, thoughts of Hugo cropped up on the news and Facebook.

Call this the Storm of the Century if you will, but I pin that title on the ice storm of 1996.

My family missed Hugo by thirty hours. My brother had the good fortune of being married out of state on September 22, 1989. We returned days later to a dark house and five trees down on our property, the sound of chain saws and no running water. But September is a fairly warm month.

On February 2, 1996, the groundhog did not see his shadow. By early afternoon, freezing rain turned to wintry mix and sleet. An icy coating began to form on trees and power lines. I was working at Lenoir-Rhyne at the time, and offices closed early that Friday.

Our son Lantz, then a fifth grader, had gone to work with me since his school was cancelled. We rode home on a slow trek down Robinson Road.

Two things I learned to respect that day: black ice and wintry mix. We arrived to a house without electricity, no running water (we were on a well) and a cold woodstove. The temperature in the house had already dipped to sixty degrees.

Lantz helped me get the wood stove going and hang sheets to block off hallways and conserve as much heat as possible. The storm had come without a thought to power outages or the need to store water, light oil lamps and keep the wood stove banked.

That night, the three of us, our two dogs and our neighbor's dog that had been left behind, hunkered down on the sofa and a mattress in front of the stove, but our high ceilings kept most of the heat above us.

Life became eerily quiet except for the pop of burning firewood and the hiss of kerosene lanterns. Trees snapped in the weight of the ice and snow. It sounded like gunshots going off. We prayed the trees wouldn't block our driveway or fall on the house.

Catawba County was quickly divided into the haves and have-nots. Our main goal was to keep the house warm enough to keep the water pipes from freezing. Stores had long run out of generators and kerosene heaters and bottled water.

Meanwhile, Tym and I were expected to report to work on time, so we had to leave extra early. I took a duffle bag with towels and a change of clothes to take advantage of the showers in the L-R locker room.

Like nineteenth-century pioneers, our life revolved around sunlight. We banked the stove and hoped it didn't burn out before morning. The temperature in the room hovered in the 40s at night.

We were in survival mode—collecting water at work in Thermos jugs, buying enough supplies to hold us over. Surely the power would be on tomorrow.

Tomorrow turned into the next day and the next. We ran out of wood and had to borrow some from friends. Before sunset, I'd head to the creek on our property and lower a bucket on a rope to collect water to flush the toilet.

The temperature outside dropped to single digits; our deck became our ice box. I gained a new appreciation for what life would have been like one hundred years ago as I slogged in my boots to the creek to gather more water.

By the third day, the novelty had worn off. Driving home to the snowy landscape was beautiful, but driving past dark house after dark house made it eerie. In our development, there were a few families who toughed it out that week. Lanterns beckoned like they would have in pioneer days.

Neighbors who had a generator invited us to dinner in order to use steaks out of their freezer before the meat went bad. Another family offered to keep Lantz while we went to work.

In town it was still 1996. At home, it was 1896. No heat, no running water, no electricity. I came to resent those who came to work from warm homes, lights and warm showers, whining that the ice storm had disrupted their cable TV service.

Doing without is relative.

Duke Energy considers the ice storm of February 1996 as among the worst ever in terms of power outages. Some customers went as long as two weeks without power while temperatures plummeted to near zero. Road cleanup and repair costs alone exceeded $20 million.

Being without power after Hugo was no picnic. Being without electricity that week in February was something else again. Thanks to the wood stove, we survived. Our pipes didn't freeze, and we learned a lot about the importance of a backup heating system and essential supplies such as nonperishable food, bottled water, wood and lamp oil.

Lesson learned.

In search of quirky old stuff

Chalkware Dutch girl once hung in Aunt O's farm kitchen.

January 2017

My friend Gina is into chalkware, those funky wall plaques from the 1940s and 50s painted in glossy bright colors. She said she was looking on eBay for a fruit plaque to replicate one she remembered in her grandmother's house. A piece with bananas or apples or maybe grapes.

I knew exactly what she was talking about. My Aunt O had a chalkware Dutch boy and girl hanging by the kitchen sink in her farmhouse. After my aunt died, I rescued them from the resale box. The chalkware figures hadn't seen the light of day in forty-five years, but I remembered the colorful pair as a kid along with the well-scrubbed smell of castile soap, and O's red and white kitchen curtains.

Gina said so far she hadn't located chalkware fruits that are becoming quite collectible. A prime example can fetch $25 or more.

There we were at the lunch table, both of us products of the 1950s, trying to re-create something we'd seen in a relative's farm kitchen when we were growing up.

Gina's quest is tenuous because chalkware breaks easily. Once the chalkware fad subsided, most of it was discarded.

I snapped up my cousin's offer of the Dutch pair and found a perfect place for them in our laundry room. The boy still has the price written on his backside: $1.50—a considerable amount for a time when $1.50 would buy two bags of groceries.

Like my Aunt O and my mother, my kitchen curtains are white with red trim. I never considered that similarity until just now. Our tastes, our ideas of the way things ought to be are set at an early age. As we grow older, we yearn for the same feeling, the friendly coziness of eating Neapolitan ice cream at my Aunt's kitchen table, looking out over her horse lot and the giant weeping willow branches we kids dared to swing on when nobody was looking.

Gina told me that she's also into carved eggshells. She quickly showed me an example on her iPhone. They look like works of lacy art. I thought about how you might clean such a delicate object. You'd have to keep it under glass, out of the dust.

And then I told her about Aunt O's secret egg, the first egg laid on their farm. It was a small brown egg marked with the date hand-written by my uncle. October 8, 1938. Once we kids discovered the aging egg was hiding in a cup in O's kitchen cabinet, we would demand to see it during every visit. Crazy, I know.

Gina gasped when I told her about the egg. Turns out she has kept the first swan's egg found at her lake house. It's a large, lovely bluish egg. She has it kept in a basket with some other specimens gathered from ducks.

A preserved egg is like a first child, she said. It's special, and once something so delicate has been kept that long, it's a shame to get rid of it.

I agreed. In fact, after O died, I bought my cousin a container to hold the 1938 egg.

Gina and I marveled at these common stories. How many years could have passed without us talking about the eggs? It makes me wonder how many other things we share and don't realize.

If we stay long enough in another person's life, we can usually find some intriguing intersections if we're not too busy doing something else.

Caution: Tree butchers at large

May 2019

It's spring and the tree butchers are out in search of trees to scalp. Recently I saw their handiwork south of Newton: beautifully shaped hardwoods reduced to the shape of surgical gloves. Glorious trees with full canopies were ridiculously pruned in half or worse yet, cut to become a totem pole with arms. This butchery always provokes my stump speech.

Not only do the trees look deformed, but the severe trimming may cause the tree to die—and die more quickly. Think of a human body with all limbs and the head removed. The prognosis is never good.

I don't blame the tree surgeons entirely. Homeowners want to prevent damage to their roofs from falling limbs and trees. Large trees with overhanging limbs are unsettling though branches can be carefully and artfully trimmed to avoid damaging anything.

A friend recently told me about a tree disaster at her church in Taylorsville. A strong wind toppled a large tree onto the roof, leaving a hole the size of an automobile. It was the better part of a year before parishioners could use the building.

Then tree paranoia took hold. Several lovely old trees succumbed to the tree surgeon's blade and the street is now a parade of large stumps. Somehow those folks think stumps—the six- and ten-foot kind, are preferable to just cutting the trees down and being done with it.

Slow death is never attractive. The tree, unable to support itself with life-breathing leaves, may branch out a few green whiskers on its pitiful stumps. In a few years, the weakened tree will attract insects or become diseased. The root system will collapse. The tree is doomed.

Homeowners tend to freak out when a tree falls in the neighborhood. I understand. We live on a wooded lot and we've made a rule not to go out walking when strong winds pick up. Limbs can fall and crush what's under them.

Diseased and damaged trees need to be watched and, perhaps, removed, but why do the job in sections? And why take down a perfectly healthy tree just because an itinerant tree surgeon knocks on the door? It seems wise to check credentials and make sure the tree "experts" are insured and know what they're doing. Tree cutting is dangerous business and should be done only after careful deliberation.

Dr. Karen McDougal, our local "tree lady," taught botany many years at Lenoir-Rhyne University. One of her pet peeves is the "broccoli tree"—a butchered tree fit for a zombie apocalypse. You've seen those unsightly trunks with a few stubby limbs, or even worse, a trunk with a flat-top "haircut."

I remember these trimming crews coming through our old neighborhood, destroying every sapling along the front of our wooded lot. These trees weren't near the power lines, but they were headed in that direction. We wound up with an unsightly bare spot in front of our house and a huge mess to clean up.

I understand issues with power lines. Homeowners often don't have a clue how large that cute maple will grow.

For the life of me, I don't understand why people pay big money to have a perfectly good tree butchered into an unsightly mess with little more than fringe for branches and leaves.

Just cut the thing down and be done with it.

OK, I'm off my stump now.

The stink bug plague continues

September 2016

When a friend from Maine told me that she did not know what a stink bug was, I was incredulous until I realized that a few years ago I didn't know what one was either.

Think of the devil in insect form, I told her—a small gray shield buzzing around your home, alighting on white surfaces, hovering near windows. If threatened, they emit an unpleasant, lingering odor. Hence the name "stink bug."

To add to the insult, they leave an ugly brown residue on white lampshades and curtains and windowsills and carpet. If you miss out on the stench, brown calling cards will let you know they've been there.

Woe to those who suck one of these insects into a vacuum cleaner. You may be tempted to burn the machine and kick it to the curb. At least get rid of the vacuum bag. Stink bugs swirl their little smelly selves inside a hot vacuum cleaner bag with dust and hair and what-have you isn't their idea of a good time. They feel threatened, emit their obnoxious odor.

Stink bugs should have been one of the seven plagues of the Bible, up there with hordes of grasshoppers and locusts. They eat vegetables and fruit. Ask local farmers and gardeners. They'll tell you.

Stink bugs are the ugly stepsisters at the pageant, the flat latex version of the shiny Japanese beetles that destroy roses. I haven't seen stink bugs on my roses, but I wouldn't put it past them.

Stink bugs, I told my Mainer friend, invade each fall. They move in like squatters and take root. They hitch rides in suitcases and in cars. On one occasion, they appeared crawling across the Thanksgiving table, which proves how late the stink bug season can last.

Stink bugs annoy me even more because they remind me of the good old days that will never come again: PSB, or pre stink bug. Back then you could greet the fall, sit on your porch without being bombarded with these evil pests that march across the screen, slip through the cracks, burrow into boxes, corners, drawers, closets and claim your house as their own.

I understand there are stink bug deterrents on the market, though I haven't heard of any that are cheap or effective. One couple I know catches stink bugs in a Death Jar. Filled with Dawn detergent, the bugs are scooped into the liquid that helps neutralize the smell, one bug at a time.

My husband says to not let these pests bother me. There's no getting rid of them, they're here to stay, he says. And he's right, though ignoring them won't make them go away.

Count your blessings, I remind my Maine friend. If I were you, I'd set up a roadblock on I-95 North. Inspect luggage, vehicles, boats, everything coming into the beautiful Pine Tree State. Give these bugs the heave ho. Do it now, while there's still time, while you still have your sanity …and clean lampshades.

Before the hornworm cometh

To pick or not to pick, that is the question.

August 2015

The dreaded tomato hornworm. *Manduca quinquemaculata*—a wickedly long name for the gardener's Enemy Number One. Beware. He has designs on your tomato patch.

One day you have a picture-perfect tomato on the vine. You let it grow one more day, to get a little more juicy, vine-ripened tasty. And the next morning you wake to see the tomato half eaten, the vine stripped bare. And you know that Hornworm is back.

For several years now I've waited, or I've forgotten that Perfect Tomato and his relatives gracing the raised bed, waiting with their collars tinged with green. I'll wait until they're fully red, fully ripe. And the next day they are decimated along with the plant that stands as leafless as a miniature cell tower.

Hornworm hangs on the underside of whatever foliage is left, his pudgy green self swollen to size of my pinkie.

Get yourself some Sevin dust, you say. Fog the tomato patch, but the point of raising organic tomatoes is to avoid pesticides which is part of the whole reason for growing tomatoes in the first place. So I lie in wait, eyes peeled for Hornworm.

Growing tomatoes successfully is knowing when to harvest before you're sorry. The certainty of Hornworm is Murphy's Law in action. If anything can go wrong, it will. He's the diner who orders the last piece of pie while you debate, he's the driver who cuts into the prized parking spot, the Ticketmaster customer who snaps up the last Paul McCartney ticket before your fingers can press "buy."

This year will be different, you say.

I know I have said that. As my tomatoes blush into perfect globes, I will check each evening for a nibbled leaf, a sign that Hornworm has dropped by for happy hour.

He has gorged on the equivalent of three trips to the buffet at Golden Corral. Pulling him from the plant in mid-munch will make me shiver. I will don garden gloves because I can't stand the feel of his prickly little feet.

If I'm an early bird, I'll get the worm.

Carpe diem. I will pick the tomato now, while there's time.

April a gardener's clean slate

March 2015

If you're a gardener, you know the siren song of bedding plants and seed packets from the neighborhood garden center. Buy me! Plant me!

And you give in because you believe the colorful posters. You picture yourself in a wide-brimmed hat in a weed-free garden, holding enough produce to feed a small army.

April is the gardener's clean slate. That's why I like spring best—before it gets hot and buggy and weedy. This year will be different. This time I'll demand order. I'll weed, prune, dead-head, spray and otherwise tend to these precious baby plants, watching them grow into youths and adults with luscious fruit or roots or stalks or whatever the edible part may be. I won't wimp out. The rabbits and deer won't show up. Tomato worms and slugs will never appear. Aphids will never hatch.

I didn't grow up in farm country for nothing. So many tractors and planters and plows making slow processions along the county roads made me aware of what time it was: time to till large swaths of black soil, time to begin another cycle of corn and soybeans.

It was the natural order of things. Later, in my first apartment, I felt out of order not being up close with plants, and so I bought a pair of redwood flower boxes to plant impatiens and marigolds on my balcony. And it has been so every year since. I must plant something.

By mid-March this year I had my little raised bed spaded, raked. Onion sets and lettuce plants, then seeds for spinach, arugula and radishes. For a few precious weeks in May and June we can enjoy better-than-fresh produce, the satisfaction of putting my big toe into the realm of self-sufficiency.

Perennials may be my best friends. I've managed to establish an asparagus bed—with all the lime and sand I can muster to sweeten clay. And I've kept Mr. Rhubarb alive, that one faithful plant that shoots his crimson stalks outward before slugs chew his bold green leaves to lace.

I have best luck with chives and sage and rosemary. They come back every year without my help. Low-maintenance should be my middle name.

I know in the end things will shift. They always do. The weather will turn hot and dry and it will be too much of a pain to water things. Or I'll forget for a day or two, then three. The weeds will begin their death march, and the dreaded tomato worm will somehow strip my prized tomato plant bare in one night.

In April, all of that bad stuff is too far away. This is the clean-slate season. I am hopeful.

As Yellow Season ends, here come the cicadas

May 2021

If you've lived in Catawba County very long, you know that each spring, pollen coats everything from pets to porches, turning blue cars green and red cars orange.

This year's apex came around May 1, when pollen-laden fluff swept into the garage, collected on steps and corners. I dusted handfuls of it off my outdoor furniture, but somehow managed to not to tear, cough and sneeze as much I have in the past.

I've spent forty-one springs here. Back at the beginning, I don't remember sweeping fluff off the steps or watching pollen change the exterior color of my vehicle. Maybe my awareness of the torment is a function of my proximity to trees. Those early years were spent in a rather treeless housing development. I worked in downtown Hickory. I wasn't surrounded by woods.

What I do remember was the full glory of a Carolina spring—a parade of blooms starting with jonquils and redbud trees, moving on to forsythia, dogwood, iris, tulips, lilacs, the inevitable riot of azaleas in white, pink, lilac and red.

Since 1987 I've lived on wooded lots full of oak trees and their stringy blossoms. We can thank oak trees for much of what makes Yellow Season yellow. The stringies have an actual name—"catkins"—which may have something to do with the fact that they attach to cat fur. I have no idea.

Pine pollen is another major contributor to Yellow Season. And if there's one thing Western North Carolina has plenty of, it's pine trees.

Promotional brochures don't point out that our proximity at the foot of the Appalachians makes us sitting ducks for clouds of pollen bearing down each spring.

If you move here and don't already have allergies, give it time. Mine took about twelve years to kick in. Sneezy, itchy eyes came upon me at about the time I developed full-bore sensitivity to poison ivy and bee stings. Oh, and tick bites. These days, if one of those arachnids attaches itself to my skin, I will itch the "bite" into tomorrow.

I'm glad there's no Arachnid Season, but be forewarned: another scourge is coming—the seventeen-year cicadas. If predictions are true, this brood will make Yellow Season look bush league.

I remember the last cicada summer with its screaming insects buzzing around like a scourge from the book of Exodus. Cicadas—whether the annual variety or the seventeen-year screamers—are harmless unless you're a young sapling, which they find especially tasty.

For the rest of us, the menacing thought of cicadas taking over the outdoors creeps us out. Maybe it's the buzzing sound or the idea of being dive-bombed by large buzzing insects with beady red eyes. Or the fact that they remind us of a cheesy sci-fi movie.

"Brood Ten" or "Brood X" refers to one of the larger colonies of burrowed cicadas in North America. They're making their first appearance since 2004. The largest swarms are expected in Western North Carolina (that's us) and other parts of the Eastern United States.

Expect a cast of billions well into the month of June. Aside from a deafening roar, they won't create too much havoc. In a larger sense, their holes provide natural aeration for our clay-heavy soil; the damage caused by females laying eggs (called flagging) is a natural pruning for trees.

Their appearance involves their mating ritual. The males' loud buzzing is meant to be a love song to female cicadas. Think of a giant singles bar in the trees, and you get the idea.

Brood X hasn't been seen since 2004, when the parents of the current brood died off, leaving their young to hibernate underground, feeding on nutrients from roots of trees and shrubs.

2021 is their time in the sun.

The last time around, Brood X cicadas were blamed for causing highway accidents after drivers freaked over cicadas buzzing their way into open car windows.

Advice to the wise: keep your doors and windows closed. The wits you keep may be your own.

EDITOR'S NOTE: In spite all the hype, Catawba County was spared the Brood X onslaught.

I love washed-up bits of history

June 2017

I can tell you when I got the sea glass bug.

The year was 2002 when I read the Anita Shreve novel, *Sea Glass*. The historical romance focused on Honora Beecher, a young bride, and her husband starting out life amidst 1920s turmoil and how their fragmented life was mirrored by bits of sea glass collected near their home along the New Hampshire coast.

New Hampshire has less than twenty miles of coastline, so the locale was rather specific.

I was smitten by the idea of Honora collecting these beach jewels. Was that a bygone hobby in this age of plastic?

I found out later while studying in Maine. I met Mary, a fellow student. She took me on a hunt outside a seafood restaurant on Bailey Island. Sure enough, there were bits of brown and clear and green glass among the well-tumbled pebbles and broken sea shells.

"The trick is to look for something manmade," she said.

Manmade—an unusual color, something angular. After finding a few worn shards of drink bottles, I was hooked. It's the color, history, nature's work on manmade junk.

I don't know where I've been all these years. I could have been looking for sea glass instead of sea shells at my decades of beach trips, but better late than never.

Since Bailey Island, Mary and I have become good friends, and I try to visit her in Delaware every year or so. My last visit was last month. When I arrived at mid-day on Sunday, Mary said she'd already checked the tides. "Low tide is 3 p.m. and we have 45 minutes to get there."

We dropped everything and hustled on up to Woodland Beach on Delaware Bay. It helped to have Philadelphia and Trenton and Wilmington nearby. They mean busy sea lanes where plenty of things getting dropped or tossed into the water. There are heavy things such as cement pilings and bricks that have been tumbled into ovals, remnants of wooden barrels and even a fiberglass potty.

Hunting for bits of glass in such a place takes patience and a keen eye—and stretching to keep your neck and lower back from cramping up. After an hour of scouring that beach—with a few other sea glass hunters—I came upon a well-barnacled Nehi bottle. The pressed herringbone pattern told me it was probably pre-World War II. I found part of a square drink bottle I can't identify, several pieces of green, brown, aqua and white milk glass—all lost and found from ship to shore.

Yes, this is a trash dump of sorts, but the fact that the stuff has been well-washed and tumbled to a new shape puts these finds in a different category from trash.

Every time I pick a piece out of the sand, I wonder how long it's been in the ocean, and how it got there. I imagine boaters on a beautiful Sunday afternoon, sailors heading off to war, a long-ago shipwreck.

Mary had great luck that Wednesday at the old Indian River Lifesaving Station. We walked the beach with a good bit of luck, but the real discovery was later, in the ladies' restroom. On a shelf in one of the stalls, someone had left shells and two bits of rare rose-colored milk glass. My imagination went to work again. Such glass was popular in the 1950s, but it's been made since the 1600s.

Mary realized the rarity she'd found and tucked them away for safekeeping. She wants to have jewelry made from them.

Meanwhile, I've begun following some stellar sea glass hunters on Instagram. This finders' world involves all sorts of "mermaid loot" on the beach—sea plastic (parts of toys, Army men, dinnerware, etc.) sea pottery (shards of dinnerware and decorative pieces), and sea metal, for example. One collector recently posted a tiny lead pine tree that had been part of a toy ice skater set made in the 1890s.

Where was that piece all this time? Only the sea knows.

Cold snap a mild taste of 1816

May 2020

L ast weekend's cold snap had us gardeners scurrying to cover tender plants. Saturday's dip into the mid-30s was the coldest May reading I can recall in Catawba County.

Sunday morning, I saw 36 degrees. A friend saw frost on her car in Newton.

I checked the web to see the average last frost date for this area: April 15. A popular gardening website, Dave's Garden, put it this way for Hickory, NC: "Each winter, on average, your risk of frost is from October 23 through April 14. You are almost guaranteed that you will not get frost from April 30 through Oct. 9."

So much for Dave's guarantee.

But suppose this recent cold kept going for days or weeks, or even months?

This happened a little over 200 years ago. Known as the Year of No Summer, 1816-1817 was a mini-Ice Age. Talk about climate change! It began with the eruption of Mt. Tambora in Indonesia on April 15, 1815. Volcanic dust dispersed over the northern hemisphere. By 1816, the thick layer of ash lowered global temperatures to essentially erase the entire growing season.

I'm familiar with this story because it was part of an American history presentation that I've given about the decade 1810-1820. If you think we've got trouble, read on.

§

Signs of a possible cool summer were evident by spring. Mid-May brought unseasonable temperatures with frost as far south as Virginia. A strong cold front crossed New England on May 28 with light snow as far south as Pennsylvania. Those raising fruit or other farm crops were already in trouble.

Things warmed up a bit in June, but then a strong Nor'easter developed on the 6th when as much as a foot of snow fell on New England.

By July people began talking famine. Weather improved, though and hardy grains of wheat and rye and potatoes were doing well. In mid-August more frost arrived over New York and all of New England. Reports of temperatures below 30 degrees were common. Only 10 percent of the crop was harvested in some areas. Corn prices rose from $1 a bushel to nearly $3.

There were reports of people eating raccoons, pigeons and mackerel as farmers, unable to afford to feed their livestock, sold off their herds and flocks.

An account of the year's bizarre weather appeared in a newspaper in Brevard Station (Stanley), NC. "That year started out... so mild for the months "of January and February that many folks let their fires go out and burned wood only for cooking; however, March was very cold and windy. Showers started the month of April but ended with snow and ice.

"In May, the temperature was like that of winter. The young buds that began forming in April were stiff and frozen. Ice a half-inch thick formed on ponds and rivers in North and South Carolina. Crops failed to ripen, trees bore no fruit, corn died though it was planted over and over again."

An area landmark, Rosedale Plantation, figures into the period. Charlotte's oldest frame home was erected in 1815 by a man who died after losing the property and its 911 acres in the economic disaster that followed the calamity of 1816. Remarkably, Rosedale survives and is open to the public.

Locally, the white frame structure we know as Old St. Paul's Lutheran Church was completed in 1818, decidedly after—not during—the calamitous years preceding.

On a personal note, one of my ancestors was affected by the 1816 crop failure. Records from Adams County, Ohio, show that by 1819, he owed $249 to the local storekeeper—a fortune in those days, but far less than his neighbors whose individual debts mounted to as much as $1,800.

Hard times are nothing new.

Texas storm: History repeats itself

August 2017

Most of us watching the Hurricane Harvey recovery are horrified by the destruction and misery.

The few bright spots are seeing people and their pets brought to safety and Newton's own Brock Long, the newly appointed FEMA administrator, in charge of recovery efforts.

Meanwhile, breathless reporters claim this is a never-before-seen event. "Record-breaking," "unprecedented," "beyond anything experienced," they say.

To those who know American history, the drama unfolding in Southeast Texas is all too familiar. The Great Galveston Hurricane of 1900 was the deadliest natural disaster in U.S. history. Best-selling author Erik Larson described this shocking episode in his historical novel, *Isaac's Storm: A Man, A Time and the Deadliest Hurricane in History*. If you haven't read it, now would be an appropriate time.

Isaac Cline was the chief meteorologist for Galveston, Texas, in 1900. On September 7 of that year, most people were unaware of the monstrous storm brewing in the Gulf of Mexico that would flatten most of Galveston and its surroundings. Winds reached 145 mph when the Great Galveston Hurricane made landfall. Back then, hurricanes didn't have first names or category designations, though like Harvey, it would have been Category 4.

I remember the vivid episodes in Larson's book, about a family desperately trying to ride out the storm in their second floor, then their attic and roof, while waves collapsed walls and sent the building off its foundation. And I think of pathetic souls caught trying to escape in a passenger train swamped in rising water.

Isaac Cline was skeptical about his over-confident colleagues. He felt unease about atmospheric readings the night of September 7, and rightly so. A few years earlier, he had derided the idea of building a sea wall for Galveston, a measure that could have helped prevent some of the destruction of 1900.

In Cline's day, weather forecasting was in its infancy. Without modern communications systems, satellite imagery and hurricane-hunting aircraft, forecasters had scant knowledge of the immense hurricane brewing in the Caribbean. It had already blown across Cuba, and was intensifying over open water.

The Texas coast was full of tourists at the time, reveling in the last chance to enjoy summer as clouds thickened and wind began to pick up. Few wanted to be bothered with moving off the beach to higher ground.

In a saving grace, Cline bent the rules of convention to issue a hurricane warning to Galveston on September 8, but it was too little too late. The storm was already destroying everything in its path. Bodies washed ashore for days and weeks afterward. The final death toll was estimated between 6,000 to 8,000 people. Property damage was no less than $30 million.

The science behind modern weather forecasting had its impetus with the 1900 Galveston Hurricane. Amazingly, most U.S. history texts omit this calamity and relatively few have ever heard of Isaac's Storm.

Florence not our first zombie apocalypse

September 2018

Thanks to Hurricane Florence, most of us became preppers this week, stocking up on water, nonperishable food, matches, batteries, medicine and other supplies.

I'm not a hoarder, but I do keep a full pantry. I learned to do this growing up in the Midwest—where one could be marooned for days in the winter. I learned reminders living power-less through Carolina ice storms and Hugo.

Doing without lights and air conditioning is one thing; doing without water is another. No electricity means no power for our well pump. A couple of flushes and you hear that thumping echoey sound of a water line failing to deliver. When it happens, you don't want to relive the experience.

As Florence churned off Bermuda, the "stock up" urge struck again. I ventured online to see where to buy lanterns and lamp oil. This is 2018, not 1918, so the choices were slim. I considered ordering online when visions of a delivery truck swamped in flood waters urged me to try Plan B. I set out Tuesday morning in search of two must-haves: an oil lamp with a wick and oil to burn.

I like oil lamps—they offer more light than candles. Lucky for me, I nabbed Walmart's last lantern and then drove over to Michael's, where the website promised lamp oil. Lucky for me, few had discovered this fact.

Visiting a store in storm-prep mode is to invite sneers and chuckles from clerks too young to remember Hugo or the ice storm of 1996.

You should have been here yesterday, they said. We're all sold out. No more deliveries coming. The empty shelves looked like the East Bloc during the Cold War—the real zombie apocalypse. I'm sure none of those young clerks could recall the East Bloc, or September 2008 when Hurricane Ike did a number on the Colonial Pipeline, the major supplier of gas and oil to the East Coast. As local fuel supplies dwindled, the lucky ones were able to trail a gas delivery truck to a local station, which our son did during the wee hours to fill our vehicles.

Last week area residents were taking Florence seriously—too seriously. Schools and colleges were closed on Thursday, a perfectly nice late summer day, and Friday, when the first cloud bands circled overhead. By midday, treetops began a pre-hurricane dance, alternating between stone stillness and full sway.

As I write this column, wind gusts are blowing fresh out of the northeast at 15 mph. We've already filled our vehicles with gas (after waiting in line). We have taken our porch swing down, moved the furniture and plants to a safe place. Expecting to lose power, I have filled the bathtub, placed full buckets at the commodes, drawn drinking water in Themos jugs. I've also filled watering cans for indoor plants, placed outdoor flower pots against the foundation.

Hello, Florence. You aren't our first apocalypse.

GUESTS

After 56 years, Cousin Renee finally parted with her Beatles pillow.

July 2020

Ringo Starr has turned eighty. Seems only yesterday he was drumming for the Beatles. Where have the decades gone?

When the Fab Four arrived in the US, I was in fourth grade. Back then, eighty-year-olds were grandparents, born in 1884. That happy-go-lucky guy who would go on to sing lead on "Yellow Submarine" and "Octopus's Garden" could never be that old. Neither could we Baby Boomers.

Ringo's current age reinforces my disconnect with antiques stores. I recently attended an estate sale that got me in the mood to shop. I hadn't been antiquing in some time, and I must say that the inventory has become more, how shall I say, familiar?

I've enjoyed antiquing for most of my adult life. Back in the 1970s, Depression glass abounded in every shade of pastel. Victorian pieces were hot, especially golden oak. There was real carnival glass for sale, and iron toys and bisque-headed dolls. Old recordings were brittle 78s and maybe a few 45s from the 1950s.

The antiques world has done a reset. Perusing the Hickory Antiques Mall is like a visit to my parents' home during the Nixon Administration.

Depression glass and 1930s Fiestaware have given way to discontinued Corningware and that Pfalztgraff stoneware with the brown design, the one that brides adored in the 1970s.

Speaking of dishes, remember those Harvest Wheat pieces that came in boxes of Duz detergent? They're fetching collector's prices now.

A display of vintage Tupperware caught my attention. Imagine! Plastic Tupperware in bold hues of the 1960s are now sought after. Seems only yesterday my mother was invited to a home party.

Vinyl records have been a thing in recent years, scratchy sound, worn covers and all. Some antiques shops have hordes of LPs arranged alphabetically with name tabs: A for Animals, B for Beatles, C for Chubby Checker.

Back in 1965, I picked out a "Beatles VI" album for my cousin's birthday. The cover showed the Fab Four in dress shirts and ties. Perhaps it was the last time they ever dressed like businessmen. Even then, Ringo was the outlier in his black turtleneck.

Good ol' Ringo. He was always something of an odd sock, the last to join the group, the clownish, not-too-handsome drummer who occupied the back of the stage, dodging the showers of jelly beans being thrown by screaming fans. My cousin Renee would have been one of them.

These days Renee has been downsizing. Last month, she sold her Beatles throw pillow on eBay for at least 50 times what it cost back in the day. Yeah, yeah, yeah. I remember it—a white pillow with the screen-print image of the band wearing solid blue suits and red ties. Ringo appeared front and center on the pillow, all of twenty-four years old.

If Renee's treasured Beatles pillow has been auctioned, I know the world has taken a turn.

Ringo has taken his birthdays more seriously than most. Since 2008, he and his friends have been celebrating by pausing at noon—wherever they are—to wish everyone peace and love. They say if you think those pleasant thoughts when the clock strikes noon, you'll send a wave of peace and love around the planet.

This year Ringo and company will mark his birthday by giving a virtual benefit concert. It seems Ringo should be singing "Octopus's Garden" instead of becoming an octogenarian, but the peace and love part makes more sense than ever.

Bowie, books and Holcomb, Kansas

People still live in the Clutter house that Truman Capote made famous.

January 2016

British music icon David Bowie died of cancer last week at sixty-nine. Much has been said of his influence on popular culture since he burst onto the airwaves with "Space Oddity" in 1969.

Much has been made of Bowie's musical career, stage presence and bisexuality. Few knew he was a big-time reader. He regarded a perfect week one in which he read three or four books. Considering that few read more than six or so books a year, Bowie's reading puts him head and shoulders above most of us.

A recent *London Telegraph* article listed Bowie's top hundred books. Some were titles one might expect of a New Age icon: *A Clockwork Orange* by Anthony Burgess, *On the Road* by Jack Kerouac, *Strange People* by Frank Edwards, *The Divided Self* by R. D. Laing, *Between the Sheets* by Ian McEwan. Bowie read the heady stuff, literary works that make one think. He read winners of the Man Booker Prize, the Orange Prize and more, though he never went to college.

One of Bowie's favorite books was *In Cold Blood* by Truman Capote. It recounts the brutal murder of the Herbert Clutter family of Holcomb, Kansas in 1959, and ushered in the genre known as creative nonfiction.

Driving through Kansas this past September, we had the opportunity to stop in Holcomb. The afternoon we arrived, storm clouds had cast a brooding mood over the place.

Oak Avenue isn't hard to find in this town of 2,100. The familiar yellow glazed brick and frame house that Herbert Clutter built for his family sits at the end of a tree-lined lane, the same locale used by film crews to depict one of America's notorious crimes. The result was a blockbuster movie focused on the killers, Richard Hickok and Perry Smith, who were convicted and hanged.

In spite of what happened inside the Clutter house, people still live there, which I find astonishing.

The only vestige of the Clutters in Holcomb these days is a memorial to the family at a local park named for them. The larger plaque recounts their community service and good citizenship. There is no mention of their killers, or the book and movie that made all of them famous.

This surprised me too, just as I was amazed to learn that David Bowie was such a voracious reader—which goes to show how public image and private truth make for strange bed fellows.

Shedding light on pop star crushes

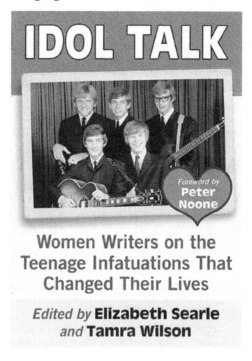

IDOL TALK

Foreword by **Peter Noone**

Women Writers on the Teenage Infatuations That Changed Their Lives

Edited by **Elizabeth Searle** and **Tamra Wilson**

The first-ever collection of essays by women writers on their teen idols.

June 2018

Yes, I know. It is a bit embarrassing to admit that any of us "mature adults" once dreamed of meeting Elvis, or dancing with Paul McCartney or breathing the same air as Bobby Sherman.

My idol was Peter Noone, Herman of Herman's Hermits, the group that gave us such ear worms as "Mrs. Brown, You've Got a Lovely Daughter," "I'm Henry the Eighth, I Am" and "I'm Into Something Good." The Hermits' bouncy, upbeat tunes had MGM Records whistling all the way to the bank. Herman and his band outsold the Beatles in 1965. All said, Herman's Hermits scored ten Top Tens, twenty Top Twenties as one of the top three bands of the British Invasion with more than eighty million records sold.

Peter was a thing for me in junior high. Then, in the fall of 1968, when I entered high school, he had the audacity to get married. I promptly gave Herman's Hermits the heave ho, though I kept their albums and posters. After all, you never know when you might need such stuff.

"When" came in 2013, the evening Herman and his new Hermits came to J. E. Broyhill Civic Center in Lenoir. After the band rocked the house, I got in line and had Peter sign several of those old albums, which he politely did as I watched his every move like a giddy thirteen-year-old.

The next day I emailed my writer friend, Elizabeth Searle, telling her that it really was possible to become a teen-ager again. She understood because we have this thing about celebrities. I had already written a book, *Dining with Robert Redford*, and she had penned the script for *Tonya & Nancy: The Rock Opera*.

Elizabeth, who lives near Boston, asked me to write a piece for her blog, "Celebrities in Disgrace," though I assured her that there was nothing disgraceful about meeting Peter other than feeling like a drooling eighth grader.

She agreed that it would be fun to co-edit an anthology about teen idols. What if we asked well-published women writers to write about their teen idol crushes? No such book had ever been published.

We drafted a proposal and found a literary agent. We contacted female writers we knew or knew of, hoping that A) they had a teen idol and B) they would be willing to admit it in an essay.

Among our contributors were best-selling authors Ann Hood and B.A. Shapiro and notable North Carolina writers including Jill McCorkle, Judy Goldman and Stephanie Powell Watts.

Learning the identity of their girlhood crushes was like opening the door in a game of "Mystery Date." We were ecstatic to nab Elvis through Goldman's poignant essay about seeing him in 1956. We reveled in learning about Watt's love for Barry Manilow. And we were overjoyed to finally land the fourth Beatle, Ringo Starr, thanks to Marianne Gingher, who's professor of creative writing at UNC-Chapel Hill.

Along the way we asked Peter Noone to write the Foreword, and he agreed.

As our final copy deadline approached in February, we were unexpectedly put in contact with Ann Moses, former editor of *Tiger Beat*, a premiere fan magazine in the 1960s and 1970s. She was eager to write copy for our book cover and we were thrilled to have her endorsement.

Our simple email exchange sparked a book published by McFarland & Company, a text that has been used in courses on women's studies and pop culture, and, of course, enjoyed by fans far and wide.

You never know what can happen when you wish upon some stars.

I saw Roy Orbison live, sort of

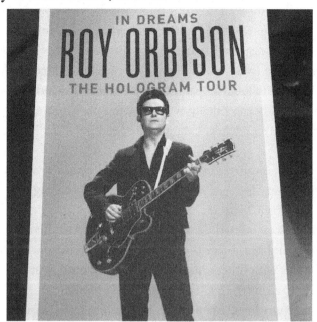

Roy Orbison's hologram made a tour stop in Greenville, SC.

November 2018

R oy Orbison may have died 30 years ago, but his hologram lives on. I saw it just two weeks ago.

In the age of fake news and other sleights of hand, the mere idea of this concert was enough to lure my friend Carol and me to Greenville, South Carolina.

As the curtain rose, sharp V-shaped beams of light shone from center stage, heralding "Roy," who scrolled up, as if from a trap door, with his Gibson guitar in hand. Hologram Roy was timed perfectly with the musicians who had us "Running Scared" for two hours through rain, dodging semitrailers on I-85.

Roy Orbison was the country-pop singer I first heard on jukeboxes in roadside cafes. His music burst onto the landscape in 1960, when I was six and not fully aware that songs on the car radio were recordings, not some guy singing at a radio station someplace. "In Dreams," "Crying" and "Only the Lonely." Rockabilly songs with orchestral backup, the kind of stuff that burns into the soundtrack of your life.

All during the concert, I kept wondering how the hologram thing worked. Roy looked alive enough, moving with the lyrics, waving to the conductor on occasion, nodding to the other musicians. Hologram Roy turned one hundred eighty degrees. Leather fringe fluttered on his sleeves.

From where I was seated in row M, I wondered how all this looked from Row A or B. He looked opaque, his coloring a little off, but he sounded great. He moved rather woodenly, which is what the actual singer did. Mick Jagger he wasn't. After a while, I came to suspend my disbelief and just enjoyed the show.

After each set, Roy poofed into animated smoke as a large screen showed documentary footage, interviews from people calling him one of the greatest singers of our lifetime.

Roy Orbison offered the whole package: original hit songs, an incredible voice and the ability to accompany himself on guitar. We associate some of his songs with other artists: "Claudette" (Everly Brothers), "Blue Bayou" (Linda Ronstadt), and "You Got It" (Bonnie Raitt).

His songwriting alone would have put him in the history books if he'd never recorded himself. But record he did, first in Norman Petty's Studio in Clovis, New Mexico, and later at RCA in Nashville—both of which I'm happy to say I've visited.

In 1963 he opened for the Beatles, as yet unknown in the US. The Orbison-Beatles tour sold out in one afternoon, and on the first night, Roy sang 14 encores before the Beatles could take the stage. That's how big he was.

Roy's last song of the hologram concert was, of course, "Pretty Woman," the 1964 hit that nudged the Beatles off Billboard's Number 1 spot, where they had hovered for most of the year.

Roy was never a teen idol. His love ballads could have qualified him, but idols are promoted differently. He was pudgy, he had a receding chin, his features more dorky than handsome. To his credit, Roy appealed to a much wider audience than fourteen-year-old girls. He wore sunglasses like Ray Charles, which made some wonder if he was visually impaired (he wasn't).

When a fellow can write and sing "Pretty Woman" to the top of the charts, who cares if he ever appeared on the cover of *Tiger Beat*?

Goodbye, yellow brick road

Elton John, larger than life, in Columbia, SC.

March 2018

Sir Elton John is retiring. Yes, the Honky Cat is calling it quits after nearly fifty years on the road, and I can't say I blame him.

I was a big Elton John fan in high school and college. I bought nearly all his albums and saw him in concert twice.

The first time was in college and the second was at the International Amphitheatre in Chicago. Both concerts were three-hour spectacles of amazing songs, showmanship and razzle dazzle. The sparkling glasses, electrified tuxedos, platform shoes, and garish costumes would startle Vegas. Indeed, Elton John could outdo Liberace. I know this because I've seen both of them in concert.

A few weeks ago, I thought of buying tickets to what may be his last North Carolina concert. The PNC Arena in Raleigh March 12, 2019. I thought about it, until I checked the ticket price $250 for the nosebleed section, $2,644 for Row 1.

I know I'm being old fashioned to raise my eyebrows for this platinum opportunity. Some pay more than $1,000 to attend a sporting event.

But those people aren't me. Even though I was a big Elton fan back in the day, I'm still a fan, more or less.

My fondness for the singer-songwriter began in high school, when I first heard "Your Song," the record that would catapult Elton to world prominence. I know exactly where I was—standing at the bathroom vanity, getting ready for school, with my transistor radio tuned to WLS. It was during the fall of 1970, a year after Woodstock. The haunting piano melody, the plaintiff voice of Elton the balladeer caught my attention. He sounded nothing like the hard-driving psychedelia that clogged the airwaves.

Cousin Gary from Los Angeles told me he had seen Elton around that time. He was playing a small venue in Southern California. Elton John looked unusual in Coke-bottle glasses, and his stage presence was such that Gary shook his head. That clown would never amount to anything.

But Elton John went on to become a musical icon. Over the years, he's had forty Top 40 albums and been knighted by Queen Elizabeth. He has received an Oscar, a Golden Globe, a Tony Award, a Disney Legends award, and the list goes on. He played the Pinball Wizard in the Hollywood version of *Tommy, the Rock Opera*.

His remake of "Candle in the Wind," re-recorded to memorialize Princess Diana in 1997, was the fastest-selling number one record in history. According to the *Guinness Book of Records*, "Candle in the Wind 1997" is the second highest selling single of all time behind Bing Crosby's "White Christmas" from 1942.

Maybe you remember Elton's live performance at Westminster Abbey that September day. He and Diana had been fast friends, raising money for AIDS and other charities. He sang the tribute flawlessly, just as he's done on his many hits: "Bennie and the Jets," "Crocodile Rock," "Sacrifice," "Philadelphia Freedom" and "I'm Still Standing," to name a few.

Born Reginald Dwight in suburban London, Elton John was a child prodigy, teaching himself to play piano by age four. Thanks to his forty-year career, he is estimated to be worth more than $450 million, due in part to his songwriting with lyricist Bernie Taupin. Most everyone knows Elton John's music. The soundtrack to *The Lion King*, alone would be enough to put him in the history books.

I'm sad that Elton John is leaving the road, but I understand. He and his spouse have two young sons. He's done Vegas for years on end. It's time to pull back.

Indeed, time is slipping away for all of us. I'm not the eighteen-year-old I was when Elton John rocked my university's arena in 1972. I don't recall what tickets cost, but I'm guessing no more than $8, a bargain even then.

Elton John turned seventy-one this past Sunday, but I figure I'll have to remember him as he was in the 1970s.

If any of you feel like shelling out hundreds of dollars for a trip to Raleigh next year, count yourself among the privileged. Seeing a true musical legend doesn't come every day, and the days of such stars are waning fast.

EDITOR'S NOTE: Elton John later announced an extended farewell tour with more affordable seats. I saw him live for the third time in March 2019 in Columbia, South Carolina.

What goes around comes around

Anne (right) and I as second graders. We corresponded for more than 25 years.

March 2016

Sometimes online trails bring unexpected blessings.

Consider the email I received earlier this month from a young woman in Virginia.

Dear Ms. Wilson,

I wanted to write and thank you for keeping the memory of my mother alive. Tomorrow will be the 19th anniversary of her death and in a nostalgic moment I decided to Google her name to see what came up and came across your blog post.

To be honest, I do not remember that phone conversation we had; I have had so many over the years with long-lost friends of my mother's that it has almost become a normal part of my life, but reading your blog post touched me. Although my mother was only there for the first six years of my life, her life has shaped mine, and the friends she had shaped her, so by extension, you have shaped me also. I know I am the woman I am today because of her influence....

My father still has the letters you sent us and they are a treasured possession for both my sister and I. So I just wanted to say thank you, it encourages me that my mother is remembered by people other than our immediate family, that she did not die to be completely forgotten.

Grab a Kleenex and I'll share the rest of the story.

In 1961, my family lived across the street from the Halliburton family in Tampa, Florida. Their seven-year-old daughter Anne and I became fast friends. When my family moved away the following summer, we promised we would write to one another. And we did for more than twenty-five years.

Every Christmas and birthday, we would exchange cards and gifts. Though 1,000 miles separated us, we had a lot in common. We were born two weeks apart. We both took piano lessons, we both majored in journalism—she in Florida, I in Missouri. We joined sororities, were interested in politics and within a year of one another, we married.

I visited Anne twice over the years, and she cut the cake at our wedding. She was a lively, polished and gifted young woman who worked on Capitol Hill. She later ran for the Virginia House of Delegates and had a bright future ahead of her. Eventually we exchanged baby announcements and kept in touch until about 1989 when her letters mysteriously stopped.

When the Internet came along, I tried to locate her without luck. What was she doing now? Where was she? Why could someone who had grown up with me all those years just disappear?

In 2014 as I approached our sixtieth birthdays, I ran an Internet search and found Anne on Ancestry.com. Her address was the same. Her husband was listed along with her daughters at the same house.

And so I wrote one more letter.

§

Two days later I received a message on our answering machine from a young woman named Megan who had some information about her mother. Anne had died of cancer when Megan was only six—a year younger than the age her mother and I were when we began our correspondence.

It so happened that I'd been asked to deliver a sermon at church three days after my birthday. This time I knew exactly what I would preach. That I should not feel bad about growing older. It's a privilege denied many. The extra time I had been given was a precious gift. I don't know why Anne had to die so young or why her daughters had to grow up without their mother. All I knew for sure is that I should not feel bad about turning sixty.

I threw a party and invited a dozen friends. And then I posted my sermon on my website blog: http://tamrawilson.com/the-day-i-preached-a-sermon I should have let Anne's family know that I'd written the sermon, but I didn't get around to it.

Instead, the Internet did it for me. Nineteen months later, Anne's daughter found my sermon text. We made each other's day.

EDITOR'S NOTE: This column morphed into an essay. "Dear Anne," that appears in Friends: Voices on the Gift of Companionship, edited by Amy Lou Jenkins and published by Jack Walker Press, 2020.

Scan this code with a Smartphone or other device to read the "The Day I Preached a Sermon" Blog.

Gliding through the year with Father Mike

March 2021

S everal weeks ago, I came upon a Facebook ad inviting me to the "Bible in a Year Podcast" with Father Mike Schmitz.

The invitation came at the end of January, that dead-of-winter time when we all need something special to keep us going, especially during a pandemic.

My own church wasn't meeting in person. During this online time of COVID-19, I didn't have a lot of places to go or people to see.

So, I pondered the offer: Free daily podcasts from a Fr. Mike, campus chaplain at University of Minnesota in Duluth, who would read, pray and discuss Scripture from Genesis to Revelation.

I signed up. Yes, me, a Presbyterian elder, following a Roman Catholic priest for a year through the Bible—not just any Bible, but the Catholic version.

Many aren't aware that the Catholic Bible includes books Protestants have never heard of, much less read: Tobit, Judith, I and II Maccabees, Wisdom of Solomon, Baruch, Sirach and additional fragments of Esther and Daniel. All were scratched from the Protestant canon centuries ago because they involved doctrines that the Reformers found problematic, such as purgatory, praying for the dead and salvation by anything other than grace alone. References to these practices were forbidden thanks to a priest by the name of Martin Luther, who had serious beefs with the Roman church.

In addition to the *verboten* books, Luther also considered Hebrews, James, Jude, and Revelation to be "disputed books." These were included in Luther's translation, but placed separately at the end in his New Testament published in 1522.

Luther's ideas on what should constitute the Bible were picked up by other reformers in the 1500s, and we all know what that led to.

I wish I could tell you what Fr. Mike has to say about Luther's edits, but we're still wading through Numbers and the Psalms. Tobit and Judith and the rest are a way off.

Until last month I had no idea that Ft. Mike was a thing. He's a prominent personality of Ascension Press of Exton, Pennsylvania, an organization with an evangelizing mission. Prior to COVID, you could find Fr. Mike appearing on panels and keynoting at conferences, unraveling thorny topics such as purgatory, same-sex marriage and the immaculate conception of Mary.

His podcasts are among the top-rated downloads of the Apple store and understandably so. If Hollywood were to cast a priest in the church of what's happening now, they'd tap this guy—a cross (no pun intended) between Father Ralph of *The Thornbirds* and Bishop Fulton J. Sheen. Fr. Mike has a friendly, common-sense presence. He explains complex ideas in easy-to-understand language.

I know I'm dating myself, but I remember when my mother purchased an assortment of Christmas cards endorsed by Bishop Sheen. This was around 1963. It was a bold step over the religious divide.

Though a lifelong Protestant, I am no stranger to Roman Catholicism. I was born in a Catholic hospital. Our next-door neighbors were Catholic. My best friend growing up was Catholic. Five out of eight college roommates were Catholic. I have Catholic relatives by marriage. Early on I learned to agree to disagree without being disagreeable.

It has taken me decades to get around to reading the Catholic Bible, but it's better late than never. The Bible in a Year Podcast has already shown me how Catholics and Protestants have more in common than we are often willing to admit.

All eyes on *Watchman*

July 2015

July 14 marked one of the biggest literary events of the year: the release of Harper Lee's other book, *Go Set a Watchman*. "Discovery" and publication of this earlier-than-*To Kill a Mockingbird* novel has spun the literary world into a dither.

Publishing is about money. Publishers exist to stay in business. That's why it's called the publishing "industry" instead of the publishing art exhibition.

So, did Harper Lee willingly allow this earlier manuscript to be published after fifty-five years? Some say the author, now eighty-nine, was duped. That's one reason *Go Set a Watchman* has so many in a snit.

Consider Atticus Finch, the hero portrayed by Gregory Peck in the film version of *Mockingbird*. He's a parent figure who helped set the gold standard for parental wisdom. But in *Watchman* we learn that Atticus has flaws. He has ties to the Ku Klux Klan. We hear the "N" word. Seeing such an unvarnished Atticus rattles us like pictures of Elvis Presley without his dyed black hair. One version is reality, the other is not, and the backlit reality is jarring.

Don't expect a beautiful baby with *Watchman*. Reading it is like sorting through dirty laundry. It's clumsy at times. Preachy. Most reviewers say this book should have never seen the light of day. I tend to agree in some respects. *Watchman* is a trial balloon that barely launches. The plot is episodic and predictable, the scenery barely outlined, the characters thinly wrought.

But these earlier renderings of Scout and Jem and Atticus Finch prompted New York editor Tay Hahoff to urge Lee to grow the childhood flashbacks in *Watchman* into the renditions we know in *Mockingbird*, a literary classic. Then Hahoff convinced J. P. Lippincott to gamble on a budding writer from Monroeville, Alabama.

It was Hahoff who saw the magic of Lee's childhood scenes in *Watchman*. It was Hahoff who guided the rewrite and propelled Lee to literary stardom. This is not to detract from the writer's talent, but puts her in historical context, just as her good fortune of arriving on the literary scene at the crux of the Civil Rights movement. Call it luck, but Lee without Hahoff would be like Orville without Wilbur Wright, FDR without Eleanor, Elvis without Colonel Parker, the Beatles without Brian Epstein.

True legends aren't lone wolves. Unfortunately, Hahoff and Lee's benefactors, Michael and Joy Brown, died not long after *Mockingbird*'s publication. With the loss of these supporters, Lee was wary about writing another book, and who could blame her? Equaling the success of *Mockingbird* would have been impossible.

Go Set a Watchman should be read from an historical point of view. It offers us a rare glimpse into the writing process. It is a powerful insight into the world of novel writing.

In the end, *Watchman* should be approached for what it is— an unedited slice of Southern culture at mid-century, brought to life through the support of a gifted editor and a publisher who took a chance on an unknown author.

We are all richer for that roll of the dice.

True confessions: Ladies of the Panty Club

*Panty Club 2 (front, from left) Connie Love and
Linda York; (back, from left) Sylvia Bajorek, Nancy Lisk and me.*

May 2017

The year was 1981 and I had just taken a job at Central Telephone Company in Hickory. Female employees gathered to celebrate birthdays over lunch—and gift panties to one another.

I know that sounds odd, but the telephone company ladies were a practical lot. Granted, a Panty Club wasn't for everyone, but few invitees turned us down. After all, receiving an entire wardrobe of new panties every year took the sting out of growing older.

Panty Club Founder Dot Scott passed away recently, and during the receiving my husband and I had the audacity to mention this obscure fact to Dot's son. He laughed. It didn't surprise him that his fun-loving Mom had earned a special place in Panty Club history. It seems that she'd been in or heard of a similar group at another workplace. Like all good ideas, this one begged to be shared.

In 1981, we Ladies of the Panty Club were less interested in burning bras than collecting an annual wardrobe of pretty undies. (The Equal Rights

Amendment would soon die its slow death from failure to be ratified in 1982.) Dot was secretary to a Centel executive, she knew all about keeping things in order. She compiled a list of birthdays of the eight of us who chose to participate, as well our size and style preferences. I remember each member: Dot of course, Betsy, Pat, Carol, Sylvia, Wanda and Sandy.

Back then we were younger and unabashed about our underwear preferences—and our sizes.

We were not the only such club in town. Icard Uniforms (near Angelo's and Woolworth's) had a hand-lettered sign near a display of fancy undies for sale: "Perfect for panty clubs."

And what better gift could a female give to another a female co-worker? For less than five dollars, one could give a welcome, usable gift in her perfect size and style.

Every birthday, we'd reserve a table at the 1859 Cafe or The Vintage House or The Pleasure is Mine for a Dutch treat lunch and revealing of panties for the birthday girl. When my friends back at Inform, Inc. heard about my Panty Club, they demanded one of their own. I'll call it Panty Club 2.

Unsuspecting onlookers stared in disbelief as this group of laughing women would ooh and aah at gifted panties in various styles and colors.

When Centel dissolved its state division office in 1984, several of us scattered. The Centel panty club was history while Panty Club 2 thrived. In fact—Nancy, Linda Mae, Connie, and Pat—friends I'd made at my first full-time job in Hickory, became my time-tested sisterhood. Though one member joined and another moved away, the core of us weathered births, deaths, divorces, remarriages, new jobs, new houses and all the rest. We became far more than a group panty swap. We enjoyed beach trips, mountain trips, baby showers, and housewarming parties. We ushered one another past the thirty-, forty-, fifty- and sixty-year milestones.

It's been years since we gifted panties, but we're still called "The Panty Club." I suppose we always will be. There's something special about a group of women who get together and get along for so many years.

A few months ago, we gathered to celebrate our eldest member's seventieth birthday, along with the "Panty Club Auxiliary"—our husbands. We swapped stories about work, retirement, in-laws and trips to see the grandchildren.

Thirty-six years and counting. Life is good.

Farewell to America's pastor

February 2018

I don't remember a time before Billy Graham.

And so, I stood with the 300 people February 24 at the Startown overpass on US 321. It was unseasonably warm, and many of us waited for nearly an hour, watching the traffic whiz by as oversized American and Christian flags flapped from the railing, waiting for North Carolina's most famous son.

A break in traffic came about 1:30 p.m. with the sound of helicopters and flashing blue lights of the highway patrol escort. The motorcade including Billy Graham's hearse passed by us as it headed south toward Charlotte.

It may sound corny, but America's Pastor was one of my heroes, a man of integrity in a world where sincerity and humbleness are difficult to find.

Like many of you, I grew up in front a TV set. On hot summer evenings Billy Graham crusades would pre-empt regular programming on one of three networks that existed at the time. I would whine to watch the other channels, but my mother, who was churchier than most, would insist that we watch "Billy."

The fuzzy black-and-white image of the TV preacher came after the preliminaries: testimonies by noted athletes or entertainers, then Cliff Barrows would direct a large choir of church people from the host community. The crowd would number in the thousands. There would be a solo by George Beverly Shea, the noted baritone, singing a hymn such as "How Great Thou Art," and finally, the amiable Barrows would introduce Dr. Graham.

Billy Graham spoke with his distinctive Carolina accent and his message was simple. Sinners should repent and accept Jesus or face the consequences. With a Bible in one hand, he arranged his sermons around current events that pointed to fulfilled prophecy and references to parables such as the workers in the vineyard. It was never too late to be saved.

Graham's major points were introduced "firstly" and "secondly" and "thirdly." It wasn't altogether hellfire, but he mentioned that idea clearly enough to get your attention. After twenty minutes of preaching, it was time for the invitation hymn, always the standard "Just as I Am" sung by that choir in the bleachers. Then Graham would say how long it would take to get up and walk to the podium to pray the sinner's prayer.

"Don't hesitate for there may never be another time for you to say yes to Christ," he would say. And people would flock to him by the hundreds.

Then, as the choir sang, Graham looked at the camera to address the TV audience. "Now is the time for you to make your decision for Christ," and he would tell you to write to him, "Billy Graham, Minneapolis, Minnesota" to receive the same literature being given to those at the crusade. That's all the address you needed. That's how famous he was.

One evening my mother wrote to Graham and all through my growing up years, his magazine, *Decision*, arrived in the mailbox, along with frequent solicitations.

Critics regard the TV evangelist as neither prophet nor theologian. Some scoff at his conservatism. Still others insist that he was shaped more by pop culture than the other way around.

Still, the man held to his faith and his message, speaking directly to more people—an estimated 215 million—in his lifetime than anyone in history.

My one and only Billy Graham crusade was his last one in Charlotte. I rode on a bus with my family and fellow church members to Ericsson Stadium in 1996. The event drew 75,000 people.

We've been to the Billy Graham Library a couple of times, and I'm intrigued by some of the mementoes on display including awards and photos and even a letter delivered to "Billy Graham, Many Apples, Minnesota."

Over the years I came to appreciate what Billy Graham stood for. His ministry withstood scrutiny and politics, war and social upheaval. Through it all, he never wavered in his mission to do God's work.

I think Billy would have been pleased with the gathering at the Startown overpass. There were onlookers of all ages and backgrounds, both black and white, license plates from North Carolina and New Jersey. Truckers pulled their rigs to the side of the highway and waited. Motorists in SUVs and sedans and pickups did the same. Some claimed parking space on the exit ramps early. Others arrived much later, and still others happened by at the last minute to pay respects to this great man.

I thought of the parable about the workers in the vineyard. Regardless of how long we waited, we all received the same reward as Billy Graham's motorcade passed from real life into history. I doubt we'll ever see the likes of him again.

President Bush, CAVU and pea soup

December 2018

Last week we bid farewell to President George H. W. Bush—"41" as he's
fondly called.

History may regard him as the best one-term president to ever serve
in the White House. He was certainly one of the best prepared. Bush was a
successful businessman, a Congressman, UN ambassador, envoy to China,
director of the CIA, chairman of the Republican National Committee, a two-
term vice president of the United States. A solid resume, for sure.

In eulogies, he was no longer a "wimp" as political foes had described
him, but the nation's Dad—Mr. Rogers posing as John Wayne. True enough.
As one of the nation's youngest Navy pilots, Bush flew fifty-eight combat
missions and narrowly escaped death when he was shot down over the Pacific
during World War II.

As president, he urged us to make America a "kinder and gentler
nation." Even in 1989, many scoffed at such an old-fashioned notion, much
less his idealistic "thousand points of light," a phrase he used to promote
volunteerism.

The President's proclivity for writing thank-you notes endeared him
to friends, family, associates and political foes. The humble act of expressing
gratitude on paper seems such a quaint custom these days, yet I'm willing to
bet when most of us see a handwritten envelope in the mail, it's the first thing
we open.

The image of Bush's note to incoming President Clinton in 1993
made the rounds on Facebook and Instagram last week. Though hurting from
a crushing defeat by Bill Clinton, Bush garnered the grace to write the future
president a note and leave it in the Oval Office.

"You will be our President when you read this note. I wish you well,
I wish your family well....Your success is now our country's success," Bush
wrote.

Over the years I've felt a connection to President Bush, not just for
his steering us through the end of the Cold War and the breakup of the
Soviet Union. Not just because I voted for him, but something more frothy: I
once saw him in person. It was during a whistle stop in 1992 at Gastonia. We
took off work and took our son, then a second grader, out of class to see the
President. What we saw was a glimpse from the train, a fleeting wave to the

crowd. A chance to say we'd seen the President.

I admired Barbara Bush's no-nonsense approach to life, her promotion of books and literacy. I loved her self-deprecating humor. She refused to dye her hair. She admitted to being a size fourteen. She said she wore her famous pearls to hide the wrinkles on her neck. She loved dogs. She was everybody's grandmother.

In 2014 we toured "41's" Library in College Park, Texas, where I spotted a wooden plaque in the gift shop. On it was carved the letters "CAVU." I knew this acronym in the book, *All the Best, My Life in Letters and Other Writings*, a collection of Bush's personal correspondence.

CAVU stands for "Ceiling and Visibility Unlimited"—Bush's motto from his days as a Navy pilot. CAVU struck a chord with me because my own father was a pilot. I grew up hearing a lot about the "ceiling" and weather being "clear as a bell" or the dreaded "pea soup."

President Bush described CAVU in his own words as "the kind of weather we Navy pilots wanted when we were to fly off our carrier in the Pacific." The notion that the ceiling is unlimited meant anything is possible with vision. One should live life to the fullest. A stark illustration came on his 90th birthday, when he amazingly parachuted from a plane. Hardly a wimp.

Bush once explained that CAVU also described his own life as it had been over time and as it was in his retirement. Life was good because he looked at the glass as half full instead of half empty.

Barriers and boundaries are all too often ones we create for ourselves. CAVU may well describe the essence of the man George H. W. Bush, and the vision he had for his own life as well as that of his children, his grandchildren and his country. For him, the sky was the limit. Bush, in fact, had attached a CAVU plaque on his home at Kennebunkport, Maine, a reminder that a can-do spirit is everything.

Appropriately, it was President Bush 41 who signed into law the Americans with Disabilities Act, prohibiting discrimination based on disability.

The CAVU plaque I bought in Texas has hung in my home office for more than four years. So far no one has ever asked what it means. If someone does, I'll have to tell them about President Bush and my Dad being pilots and how having a vision of where you're going can help you avoid the pea soup.

FIND YOUR PLACE

You know…where the such-and-such used to be

June 2019

Forty years ago, Tym and I moved to Catawba County.

We had both grown up in in rural Illinois, a land platted in a grid. Directions were given by the compass. Go a mile north, turn left and go three miles west.

But in this booming place with a gentler climate, we learned that locals navigate by where things used to be.

Directions were given from the "old mall" (Catawba, which was still operating) and the "new mall" (Valley Hills, in the middle of nowhere.) Valley Hills sat in no-man's land between Hickory and Newton. The only other thing out that way was Po Folks Restaurant on the corner where later, Sagebrush and Fire Bonz used to be, before the building caught fire, literally. Today it's where Five Guys is, not far from where Krispy Kreme used to be before it moved to Startown Road, down a piece from the big intersection near the furniture mart where the Mull's motel, restaurant and drive-in theatre complex used to be.

After forty years, we've learned how to give local directions.

Recently we drove through southwest Hickory and reminisced about what used to be along Highway 64-70. Yes, we still call it that, though the "64" was dropped years ago.

Amazingly, the former Kroger building is still there next to Roses. Back in the day, if you drove toward Hildebran, you'd find Kathryn's Cheese House, which seemed to be half way to Morganton. Back then there were massage parlors and adult bookstores around town—not tons of them, but enough to make us wonder if the Bible Belt was a mirage.

In 1979 there were three Belk stores: the old mall, new mall and an empty shell of a place downtown that met disaster before we arrived. I think it burned, but it was before our time.

But oh, that new store! At Belk Valley Hills you could actually shop, have your purchases giftwrapped and eat lunch without leaving the store. Kathryn's ran the eating establishment for a time. As newlyweds, we spent a lot of time in the Belk's Budget Shop on the lower level.

For the budget-conscious, there was also Kmart and Sky City next to the A&P in the strip mall. That mall included Village Inn—the place for pizza.

Walmart wouldn't arrive until well into the 1980s, building the store where Hamrick's is now. It also housed Media Play at one time.

Two of our first restaurants still exist. One is Max's Mexican Eatery that stands alone near where Mom & Pop's restaurant stood on real estate now occupied by the Randy Marion Sav-A-Lot dealership. On up the highway was Western Steer steakhouse and a Chinese restaurant called Fang's.

The first breakfast we ever ate in Catawba County was at McDonald's across from where Everett Chevrolet Buick used to be and Quality Cleaners that has cold storage for woolens and furs—which should have told us something about the local insect population.

Behind McDonald's was a textile mill, Joan Fabrics. On hot summer nights, when the doors were open, you could see people inside, running looms under florescent lights on second shift.

When we came to town in June 1979—before we rented an apartment—we stayed at Howard Johnson's, where the Walmart Neighborhood Market is located on Highway 70. I remember reading a copy of what I thought was the main local newspaper, the *Hickory News*. It was jam-packed with society news, which felt as if we'd stepped back to say, 1949.

It took us a bit of looking to find Hickory's downtown—up Fourth Street between the Chamber of Commerce and Hickory Motor Lodge. It seemed more than strange for the downtown to be so hard to find. Maybe the town hadn't gotten used to the fact that 64-70 had become Hickory's front porch with an extension called Interstate 40.

Hickory and Catawba County were experiencing a lot of growth and change, which made the navigation by vanished landmarks such a fool's errand. All the "used to be" references meant two things. 1. The place had grown and changed a lot before we got here, and 2. There was a difference between in-the-know locals and befuddled newcomers.

We came to live here on a trial basis, and the fact that we stayed four decades says something about the friendly nature of Catawba County.

Recently, I called up All Glass to have my windshield repaired. The place had moved, Tym said, so I called ahead to verify where the business was. They were behind the McDonald's on 70, the lady said. My mental map honed in.

Are you where Joan Fabrics used to be? I asked.

Why yes, the lady said.

I may not be a local, but I'm no longer a newcomer.

Maiden, Newton on another map

April 2019

No question. I'm a sucker when it comes to history—especially family history.

Recently while perusing the maps and migration section of Ancestry DNA, I checked out County Dorset, the area in southwestern England where some of my distant ancestors originated. That's what my DNA test claims, and my paper trail confirms it.

Dorchester, England, and nearby Weymouth were where my fishermen—Thomas Gardiner, John Woodbury, John Balch and Thomas Griggs—lived before they set sail for the New World in 1624. The group landed near what is now Gloucester, Massachusetts, a place that's still known for fishing.

My imagination paints a picture of these brave men with beards and tall black hats, knee britches and large buckles on their shoes, loading up their nets in search of cod to dry and ship back to the Mother Country.

Cod was, in fact, a staple for Europeans who ate fish on Fridays and a host of holy days—so much so, that the supply of fish in European waters dwindled considerably by the early 1600s. Enter these Dorset fisherman who saw an outstanding business opportunity, and off they went to "Cape Cod."

Recently, I went web surfing along the English coast. If you've never done this, open Google Maps and pretend you're a bird.

My flyover covered the shores of County Dorset. Incredibly, within five short miles of Dorchester and Weymouth, England is a place called "Maiden Newton." I blinked. I live between Maiden and Newton, North Carolina! What are the odds?

The two Maiden/Newtons are 3,900 miles apart, as the crow flies, as if a crow could fly across the Atlantic.

I've never visited County Dorset, England, much less Maiden Newton population 1,100, but I saw on Google Maps that there's an ancient, terraced area nearby called "Maiden Castle" that looks intriguing. The so-called castle is actually one of the most complex "hillforts" in Britain, dating some 6,000 years ago.

Maiden Newton and its environs figured into the writings of Thomas Hardy, who wrote *Far from the Madding Crowd, Tess of the D'Urbervilles,* and *Jude the Obscure.*

The web tells me that Maiden Newton has a Norman-era church which would have been five hundred years old when my people were tramping around the area. No doubt some of them saw this church building; maybe they even attended services there.

All of this British history sounds impressively old, and then I think of our own "Maiden Newton." Native Americans—ancestors of the Catawba and Cherokee—inhabited Catawba County as much as 10,000 years ago. Spanish explorer Juan Pardo and his group camped in what is now Catawba County, in 1567. Some claim that one of their camp sites may have been between Maiden and Newton.

Pardo and his band are credited with establishing the first European settlement within the interior of North America. That site was called Ft. San Juan, located next door to the Indian town of Joara in what is now Burke County. If you haven't visited the Joara site, do yourself a favor and check the website at https://exploringjoara.org

Exploring Joara drives home the fact that we live in an ancient land inhabited eons before European settlers arrived.

History is relative, depending on whose relatives we're considering.

Scan this code with your Smartphone or other device to visit the Joara site.

The curious tale of Isaac Wise

January 2018

Recently, my book club discussed *A History of Catawba County* published by local reporter Charles Preslar in 1954. The volume relayed the county's story including the legend of a local patriot, Isaac Wise.

The Wises are said to have lived at the head of the South Fork River. On a modern map, that's near the intersection of Highway 10 and 321 in Mountain View.

Preslar writes, "In the 1770s and 80s, Tryon, Lincoln and Burke were conceded to have been 'hot-beds' of Toryism. A study of pension applications reveals that each year from 1776 to 1782, there were 'routes' from a few days to three weeks into these counties to put down uprisings and to disperse Tory groups."

Three years before Preslar's book was released, the Catawba County Historical Association had marked the young hero's grave. The site later became Haas Cemetery southeast of Newton.

As the story goes, Isaac Wise, age seventeen, was hanged in 1776 for spying against the British crown. He was captured by Tories near the home of Simon Haas who lived near what is now Prison Camp Road. Isaac was hanged on the spot. Haas later removed the body for burial nearby. His wife, Susanna, furnished her best linen sheet for a shroud.

Three years later, Simon Haas died of an apparent heart attack while stopping for a drink on Smyre Creek. He was laid to rest next to Wise. It was fitting since Haas had served the patriot cause in the North Carolina militia.

For generations after the war, Preslar noted, Catawbans were intent on "forgetting the war's misery, and there was little interest in stirring up old bitterness, as the area was evenly split Whig and Tory."

Wise's story was passed down by word of mouth. Details were lost, and facts were likely distorted.

Preslar's account had Wise fleeing the South Fork community for Salisbury, when he was caught by a band of Tories at the Haas property. It was believed the Wises had once lived in Salisbury, though some others claimed the family originated in Bertie County on the Carolina coast.

What is certain is that Wise met with vigilante justice. In order to hang the teen-ager, the Tories needed rope, and a man named Martin Shuford was dispatched on horse to find it. The horse stumbled and threw the rider, who fell on a tree root face down and broke his nose. Shuford ever after became known as "Crooked Nose." He died from wounds in the Battle of Ramsour's Mill in 1780.

We know as much or more about the man looking for rope to hang Isaac Wise than we know about Wise himself.

Was Isaac Wise a patriot?

Historian Gary Freeze posed the question in his book *The Catawbans Volume I.* Wise could have been a patriot hanged by Tories or "could he have been a petty criminal executed for his misdemeanor," Freeze writes.

Who is correct? There appears to be no documentation for Wise, save his tombstone erected one hundred seventy-five years after his death.

If Wise was indeed a spy as the legend claims, who or what had he seen? What secret had he told?

That's the problem with legends. Details are obscured by time. Facts turn fuzzy.

Wise was not a common name among local settlers, save for Daniel Wise, who was presumably Isaac's father. Daniel is said to have fled Eastern North Carolina with his family because of his Tory sympathies.

The name "Isaac" carries extra meaning for our legend, too. Think of Abraham in Genesis, who was asked to sacrifice his son Isaac. In Isaac Wise's case, any intervention by God apparently fell on deaf ears, though we do not know if his father was even present.

History proves that at the time of Isaac Wise's death, Western North Carolina was embroiled in the rebellion. Emotions ran high. The Battle of Quaker Meadows took place in July 1776 near Morganton. The engagement was part of a campaign against the Cherokee who had allied with the British to harass settlers.

We modern Americans like to think of our colonial counterparts living idyllic lives until the American Revolution came along to stir things up. In reality there had been several colonial conflicts prior to the 1770s, the French and Indian War of 1754-1763 being just one example.

Likewise, the notion that most colonists marched with George Washington is a fallacy. History tells us that what is now Catawba County was deeply divided, as were much of the thirteen colonies. Families switched allegiance at will to protect their lives, their livelihoods and property. And who could blame them?

American patriots, often little more than ragtag bands of determined freedom fighters, won independence from Great Britain by a hair and a prayer.

Isaac Wise is remembered because he was on the winning side and died a martyr.

As my book club discussed, western Catawba County was largely settled by Germans who, for the most part, had little interest in stirring King George's pot. Many had sworn allegiance to the monarchy upon their arrival in the new land. Some had fled the wretched Seven Years War in the 1750s and 60s. Becoming involved in more bloodshed wasn't their cup of tea.

True, I have oversimplified a complex chapter of history. The problem I have with Isaac Wise's story is that it's not complex enough. So many loose ends make us fill in our own blanks because we want to know the rest of the story.

The legend continues because Isaac was a tragic hero who "wisely" chose the winning side. His story stirs our hearts.

My ancestor rode the orphan train

A former orphan train rider, Sarah McGuirk later married a Union Army veteran.

May 2015

A while back my friend Luana, was discussing bestselling novel, *Orphan Train* by Christina Baker Kline. I shared the fact that my great-grandmother was an orphan train rider back before the Civil War.

And then Luana said, "I think that story would make a great program."

I agreed and went to work. I contacted the Columbia University Rare Book and Manuscript Library in New York, and I collected images of documents and a few photographs that have been handed down in the family. The end result was "Sarah McGuirk, Orphan Train Rider," a program I present as a Road Scholar for the North Carolina Humanities Council.

Every time I give my "Sarah" talk, I'm amazed at how many have never heard of orphan trains though the mass resettlement program has been the subject of documentaries, books and TV programs for years.

Rev. Charles Loring Brace, a Presbyterian pastor, founded the orphan train movement in 1853 when he saw the appalling condition of some 30,000 children roaming the streets of Manhattan, ill-clothed, ill-fed and ill-sheltered. Brace founded what became known as the Children's Aid Society that worked with the New York Juvenile Asylum and other orphanages to place children with rural families across America.

The "orphans" weren't necessarily parentless. In some cases, the children had one or both parents living, but family circumstances made it impossible for the parents to care for the children.

One of the "street urchins" Brace helped was my great-grandmother Sarah, who was living in the Asylum (orphanage) on 176th Street by July of 1858. I know this from copies of original documents found at Columbia University.

By September of 1860, her train left New York bound for Piatt County, Illinois—about one hundred fifty miles south of Chicago. There she was taken in by a local judge and farmer, John Hughes and worked in his household that included an ailing wife and young children.

Documents from Columbia show that Sarah and the thirty-five orphans traveling with her were accompanied by "Mr. Allen," an agent based in New York. The placements in this particular case do not appear to have been random as is often depicted in orphan train books and films. Rather, Sarah's train was headed for a specific place where farmers were prosperous and therefore better able to take in orphans. It is quite possible that Judge Hughes had been contacted by the Children's Aid Society well before the train arrived.

Nor were the children simply dropped off with strangers never to be heard from again. Sarah's file noted that the placing agency back in New York corresponded regularly with her foster family, ensuring that she was doing well.

By 1869, Sarah was married to Alexander McKinley, a Union Army veteran who lived on a nearby farm. The couple had six children including my grandfather, William. And when Sarah died in childbirth, Hughes' daughter Belle married Alexander and took his surviving children to raise. Thus, the Hughes family did my Sarah a tremendous service, twice.

In all, an estimated 250,000 children were placed with families in small towns and farms from 1853 until 1929. I feel fortunate that Sarah was one of the lucky ones to have been rescued from an overcrowded, disease-ridden city and placed on a Midwestern farm where she was able to not only survive, but thrive.

Slave narrative links friend's family to mine

February 2021

When my friend J. T. said he'd found a North Carolina slave narrative involving his family, I had to know more.

In the 1930s, a former slave named Parker Pool recalled Yankee soldiers coming through Johnston County back in 1865. Pool, J.T. explained, worked his ancestor's farm in the Smithfield area.

Pool's account was part of the Federal Writers' Project, a collection of narratives compiled by the Works Progress Administration. The WPA employed people to interview former slaves and preserve their stories about life before emancipation. In all, some 2,300 first-person accounts were collected.

Parker Pool worked land near J.T.'s Pool family in Johnston County. After the Battle of Bentonville in March 1865, Union troops including the Ohio infantry marched to Goldsboro, then northward to Raleigh.

The WPA transcripts were written in the vernacular. Quoting Pool, "I think I seed enough Yankees come through dare to whup anything on God's earth. De Yankees camped three miles from our plantation at Mrs. Widow Sarah Saunders across White Oak Creek on de Averasboro Road…"

"De Yankees played songs o' walkin' de streets of Baltimore an' walkin' in Maryland. De really played it. Dey slaughtered cows and sometimes only et de liver. I went to de camp atter day lef' an' it wuz de awfulest stink I ever smelt in my life. Day lef' dem cows part o' 'em lying whur ey were in de camp. Dey killed geese an' chickens an' skinned 'em. Sometimes dey skinned de hind quarters uv a cow, cut 'em off an' lef' de res'."

He continued, "When dey tole me I wuz free I didn't notice it, I stayed on and worked jest lak I had been doin', right on wid missus and master. I stayed dere a year atter de surrender."

"I dunno what ter think o' Abraham Lincoln. Dey said he wuz all right. I guess he wuz a man God loved, er all right man."

When I read the account of Union soldiers raiding the countryside, I realized a slice of my own family story.

My grandmother's uncle was Lt. John E. Lane of the 17th Ohio Infantry Regiment. He had grown up near Lancaster, Ohio, hometown of General William T. Sherman, and served the entirety of the war. According to records from the National Archives, Lane saw the Siege of Corinth and the battles of Perryville and Stones River. He was part of engagements at Missionary Ridge, Kennesaw Mountain, Chickamauga, Resaca and Atlanta. Dare I say it? He was part of Sherman's infamous March to the Sea.

By March 1865, Lane's company arrived in North Carolina to engage in the Battle of Bentonville on the 19th. It was the last major stand of the Confederacy.

I studied battle maps of Johnston County. The army split—some headed for Goldsboro, others to Raleigh. The shortest route to Raleigh would have been along the Averasboro Road.

Butchering livestock and destroying property wasn't new to Union troops, who—battle-hardened, hungry and anxious to teach the Rebels a lesson—did what they saw necessary to achieve surrender. I don't like to think my relative cruelly participated in wasting livestock, especially when food was scarce for civilians. I don't want to consider the horrors that John Lane saw in battle any more than J. T. wants to consider his family owning slaves. But truth is truth, and it often isn't pretty.

Some of the Yankees that Parker Pool saw that day could have been men from John Lane's unit—maybe even the lieutenant himself. Lt. Lane would have been a striking figure. Records show he was six feet tall with light skin, blue eyes, and auburn hair. Think Prince Harry as a Union officer.

Until now, I had not considered that my relative could have passed by J.T.'s ancestor's property, how our families may have intersected one day at the end of the war.

Lane and his company were in Raleigh by April 14. Shortly thereafter they would have received word of the death of their Commander in Chief, Abraham Lincoln, which occurred on the 15th.

By May 24, the regiment was in Washington City as it was known then, to participate in the Grand Review of the Armies. I imagine the long blue lines of troops marching through the capital, past the reviewing stand of President Andrew Johnson.

John Lane was mustered out that July in Louisville, Kentucky. He had traveled the full circle in four years—from Ohio south through Kentucky, Tennessee, Georgia, the Carolinas, Virginia and D.C. He had served throughout the entire war without injury, which was a feat in itself.

That fall he married his sweetheart, Ellen Crist in Ohio, then settled in Shelby County, Illinois, where he was superintendent of the county poor farm. The couple raised five children.

Uncle John Lane was a larger-than-life figure to my grandmother, in part, because she never knew him. He died in 1893, two years before she was born. He had survived four years of the bloodiest war in American history. Then one day he was walking the tracks near his home and was struck and killed by a train.

Incredibly, his wife Ellen died thirty-six years later, struck by a train while crossing the very same tracks, which proves again, how truth can be shockingly unbelievable.

Tym at Balch House, a property linked to the Salem witch trials.

July 2018

R ecently I visited a house built by my ninth-great grandfather, Benjamin Balch.

The Balch House, located in coastal Beverly, Massachusetts, dates to 1679, and is one of the oldest wooden houses in North America.

I discovered the amazing site last summer while poking around on Ancestry to find documentation linking me to this old Massachusetts family.

Benjamin Balch, wife Sarah and eleven children lived in a frame house on Cabot Street in Beverly, which is across the river from Salem, the famed "witch capital" of New England. Benjamin was the son of John Balch, a fisherman from Dorchester, England, who came to the new world in search of opportunity: fishing for cod, drying it on racks and exporting it as "stock fish" to Mother England. In search of more tillable land, the Dorchester Company eventually founded what is now Salem—well before it had any witches to hunt.

Visiting this house was a privilege. Not only is the wooden structure extremely rare, but it's open to the public. Entering the front door, I tried to envision those who had lived here—men in their tall black hats, wide white collars and buckled shoes; women in coif caps, aprons, and long full skirts.

I tried to soak up the 17th century atmosphere—imagine what it would have been like to live within those plastered walls, sleep beneath those pegged beams and tread those same wide-planked floors.

Floor planks in the Balch House dwarf my feet. The trees were felled as early as 1660.

These ancestors would have depended on British ships for tea, linens and hardware—even the diamond-shaped glass for the windows. A display of archaeological findings included bits of china, pottery and a shoe buckle, items left by the Balch family, Puritans who contributed to my DNA.

The house remained in the Balch family into the 20th century.

In an upstairs bedroom, our guide told us a startling story about one of my distant uncles. In 1690, the Balches' nineteen-year-old son David became gravely ill and reported visions of a "confederacy of witches"—a group of local women—whispering at the foot of his sickbed. He named two of them: Sarah Wildes and Dorcas Hoar, the latter reputed to be a fortune teller in nearby Salem.

This "spectral evidence" was used against both women when they were accused of witchcraft two years after David's death. Wildes was hanged July 19, 1692. Hoar, though condemned to death, was reprieved after Gov. William Phips put an end to the witch trials after his own wife was accused.

In all, twenty people and two dogs were put to death for being involved in "witchcraft" during the eighteen-month terror. The human victims were later exonerated, though it was of little comfort to the accused, their families and friends.

Investigating further, I found that Deacon Peter Woodbury, another of my colonial uncles, was dragged from his quarters and caned during the witch hunt frenzy. He was then in his fifties and a respected member of the community.

I don't know why Peter was caned, but mob violence is never pretty.

Greed, gossip, ignorance and old grudges figured into the Salem hysteria. As accusations mounted, paranoia and fear gripped Salem and much of New England. How did the Balch family deal with the knowledge that their dying son's hallucinations had contributed to a young woman's execution?

I shudder to imagine.

EDIBLES

If this isn't a food desert, it sure feels gritty

March 2018

Dare I say it? Newton is a food desert. It's been that way since Harris-Teeter left town.

A "food desert" is a trendy label meant to shame corporations for pulling out of less-than profitable locations. It's defined as an area, typically with low-income residents, that has limited access to affordable and nutritious food. As long as we have Walmart Neighborhood Market, we're not technically a food desert, but the lack of an exciting grocery store makes things feel gritty.

Recently, I got into a Facebook discussion about the dearth of a "good" grocery store in Newton. I'll throw Conover in there too, while I'm at it. It's been years since we had an upscale grocery in town. Or even a medium-upscale store.

There was a time when Newton had both a Lowe's (the present location of People's Bank corporate headquarters) and a Harris-Teeter (present location of Walmart). Both had a full-service delicatessen along with a seafood department and bakery, floral shop, and well, you know what I'm talking about.

Nine times out of ten, the products featured in Sunday coupon sections were available at these stores. They had great BOGO (buy one, get one) offers and even buy two get three offers. It was fun to shop there.

Further back in time, Newton residents could easily walk to a supermarket—the A&P on North Ashe, for one. Small grocery shops existed in residential neighborhoods years before that.

Lowe's left by the early 1990s. Harris-Teeter exited in 2007. Yes, it has been more than ten years in this deserted place of ours. Ten years of bouncing around between Walmart and Food Lion and driving those extra miles to Aldi. Life feels a little more fragmented, a little less certain.

A neighborhood grocery store is more than a place to stock up. It's home port where you know the floor plan. It's a gathering spot, a place to greet neighbors, be recognized by friendly store associates. It feels like home.

With the dearth of grocery stores here, I think of a Charlotte trip as a place to stop at Whole Foods. A Pinehurst stay is a place to bring a cooler and stock up at their brand-new Harris-Teeter stores (two of them). A trip through Winston-Salem evokes a thought—is there anything I need at Trader Joe's or Whole Foods?

I carry it a step further on vacation. Whether in the US or abroad, I make time to peruse a grocery store because it's so telling about a culture. It's amazing to see what people consider palatable. I still covet the excellent selections at the Tesco Superstore in Gloucester, England, and the rather bizarre assortment of stock fish and overpriced Easter eggs at Bonus in Reykjavik, Iceland. I marveled at chunks of local salt for sale at Harmon's in Salt Lake City.

And then there's Wegman's, the New York-based grocery wonderland that has cropped up in Virginia and Maryland. Think Disney as a grocer with themed cafes.

If I were on vacation in Newton, I would be sorely disappointed. We don't have an amazing grocery to visit. Not even a funky little mom-and-pop store.

Stocking up on provisions may be a genetic memory of when my ancestors trekked across the Atlantic and then by horse and wagon into the prairie grass of the Midwest. Going to the store was a big deal. I spent my first seven years in an Illinois farming village with cattle grazing across the road. Shopping for food involved a short walk to Lockart's General Store with a tiny post office in the back, barrels of salt herring by the counter, and a Sunbeam bread box out front. The owners called you by name and custom sliced your bologna, wrapping it in white butcher paper.

Lockart's carried bolts of yard goods, notions, overalls, nuts and bolts, coloring books, writing tablets with movie stars on the cover, aspirin, canning supplies, penny candy, a cooler with an underwater corral of soda bottles, and a freezer with Dixie Cup ice cream treats. All these necessities were housed in a storefront reminiscent of thousands of small town main streets.

Growing up back then didn't feel like life in a food desert because I didn't know that places like Harris-Teeter and Wegman's existed, but now that I do, I can never be satisfied with good enough.

How we're helping hungry kids

June 2021

Since January, I've been a volunteer with the Catawba County backpack program, one of several affiliated with The Corner Table.

It's not difficult on my part. I show up at the building off Tate Boulevard on a weekday morning or a Sunday afternoon and spend an hour or so filling plastic bags that are stacked in large pallet boxes to be picked up by other volunteers who take them to various schools.

It's part of the long-standing effort to fight hunger in all three school systems. Food is sent home weekly with students to provide meals for weekends. The mission of the program is to eliminate hunger as a barrier to a good education.

Nationwide, 22 million school children receive free or reduced-price meals through the school lunch program and breakfast programs. But while these nutrition programs feed kids on weekdays, there's a gap on weekends when many of these children go home to bare cupboards and depleted refrigerators.

The backpack food, all donated or purchased with donated funds, includes an assortment of nonperishables for kids to eat between Friday and Monday.

On one of the days I packed last month, the bags included a box of flavored crackers, two containers of Cheerios, a package of muffin mix, a can of ravioli, a can of chicken, small bag of rice, and small pack of Oreos. Not a delicatessen, but welcome nutrition, nonetheless.

The mix varies according to what's available. Sometimes the bags include dry pasta and tomato sauce, pudding cups, gummies, corn or green beans. Other days, we may be packing fruit cups, Pop Tarts, tuna and peanut butter. The focus is on kid-friendly foods that are easy to prepare.

Recipients can pick up their food each Friday during the school year and place them discreetly inside their backpack. Recipients do not have to answer questions or qualify.

Often, teachers and guidance counselors recommend students in need. Or the students recommend themselves. Over the summer months, the backpack program continues with food bags at library branches across the county. Bags of free nonperishables are placed near the checkout desks.

The program operates on an honor system much like a tiny library or a blessing box set up at a church. If your child truly needs help with food, the packed bags are free for the taking.

Amanda Freeland, who coordinates the program, says school cafeterias will be open to help feed hungry kids. The idea is to address children who live in "food deserts," places where there is very limited or no access to nutritious, fresh food that is affordable. Food deserts generally exist in rural areas, and Catawba County has plenty of those.

Backpack volunteers range from school children to young adults to retirees. They are male and female from all backgrounds and ethnicities, just like the food recipients.

Some volunteer as individuals who simply want to help out. Others are fulfilling community service requirements for graduation or are doing service as part of a civic club or church group. Volunteers pack the food bags, help stock shelves, sort donations and stack and help load cars with food bags. Some volunteers are one-timers; others volunteer most every day the facility is open. To volunteer, you simply fill out a form on-line and show up at the appointed time. Packing sessions generally last an hour or so.

One particular day this spring, I filled bags with a lady who said volunteering gives her an opportunity to pray for a child who will receive a particular bag. A caring gesture, for sure.

The county's backpack program began in response to the Great Recession in 2008-2009 and has been serving local children ever since. Freeland began working for the program then and has seen it expand from school to school. This year, the Backpack program has served more than 1,500 children at forty-five sites. That's an average of thirty-three students per school who would otherwise not have enough to eat on weekends.

The Backpack program is one of several programs of The Corner Table, a nonprofit that seeks to provide meals with compassion, respect and dignity to those affected by hunger in our community. The Corner Table also manages the soup kitchen and bag lunches for soup kitchen guests to tide them over on weekends. They're all programs that these guests—some of them homeless—regard as a lifesaver.

The Corner Table programs operate through thick and thin. In spite of the restrictions and challenges of COVID, the soup kitchen served nearly 32,000 people with take-out meals while providing backpack food for forty-nine out of fifty-two weeks. Truly remarkable.

The Corner Table could not exist without community funding. A major force in the effort is the Baker's Dozen Women's Society, a group of local women tapped to raise money to help provide meals for the hungry.

I'm proud to be part of the 2021 Baker's Dozen this year. We're a group who enjoys getting together to share ideas and friendship while supporting one of our community's most rewarding causes.

More information is available on The Corner Table website, http://www.thecornertable.org/ Click on the "Fundraising and networking societies" to see who is involved this year. So far, we've raised nearly $30,000, with six more months to go!

Please use a Smartphone or other device to scan the code above to visit The Corner Table website.

Memories of Savannahs and Savannah

March 2019

Having been a Girl Scout as a child, and later, an assistant troop leader and employee of the local council, the "green" month of March still reminds me of my scouting days.

Girl Scout Week honors founder Juliette Low's birthday, and as any good Girl Scout knows, Miss Low was born March 12, 1912, at the family home on Oglethorpe Avenue in Savannah, Georgia.

Back in the 1960s, cookies were sold door-to-door. My troop leaders placed a bulk order of the cookies and distributed the cardboard cartons to each girl. I was assigned three that first year, one of each kind available: Thin Mints, Scot-Teas (shortbreads) and Savannahs, the oatmeal- and peanut-butter patties that have been renamed Do-Si-Dos. I have no idea why they're Do-Si-Dos; Savannahs seemed a perfectly good name to me.

There were no recipes featuring Girl Scout cookies, no suggestions to freeze them for later. Cookies were a treat of the moment, appearing like crocus and jonquils after a cold, blustery winter—in March and April, when the weather was nice enough to allow us to sell door-to-door, unaccompanied by adults.

In 1963, cookies sold for 45 cents a box. Selling multiple boxes was encouraged, and the figures enhanced my multiplication skills: 2 x 45 cents = 90 cents. That number fact has been forever stamped on my brain. If I'd been a better cookie seller, I might have also memorized 3 x 45 cents = $1.35 and 4 x 45 cents = $1.80, high finance in my third-grade world.

Adults weren't very involved in cookie sales other than to distribute the boxes and goad the girls to turn in their money. Woe to the scout who wasn't bold enough to sell at least one carton of twelve. Proceeds helped fund summer camp for members. There were no order blanks, just boxes of cookies needing a home. Cookie sales were considered a learning experience for girls to learn self-confidence, salesmanship and arithmetic.

I wasn't the best cookie seller, but I liked Girl Scouting. That's why I went on to serve, however briefly, as an adult. Was there anything more fun than a troop wiener roast or earning badges? I don't remember how many I earned as a junior scout, maybe eight or ten. Having a colorful sash on my green uniform was a source of pride and accomplishment.

When I worked for the Catawba Valley Area Girl Scout Council in 1992, I had the opportunity to visit Juliette Low's home with my family. At the time our young son, then a Cub Scout, was into hermit crabs in a big way. While taking the tour, the guide, a fussy older man, offered historical facts about each room and then asked for questions. Our son raised his hand.

"And what's your question, young man?"

"Do you have any hermit crabs?" our son asked.

The group tittered as the guide explained that no, he didn't have any and frankly, he'd never been asked that question before.

We walked to the next room, and again, after giving his spiel, the guide asked if anyone had a question.

Our son again raised his hand. "Do you know where I can get hermit crabs?"

Everyone chuckled. The guide suggested Tybee Island.

We didn't bring any hermit crabs home on that trip. It was winter, and the critters were out of season, but if we had, I suppose one crab would have cost maybe $1.35, or 3 x 45 cents, less than half the price of a box of Girl Scout cookies today.

Catawba's sweet potato snacks

May 2016

I've lived in Catawba County for decades, but I'm still learning things about local culture.

Take sweet potatoes.

They're not my favorite food, a sure sign I'm not a Catawba County native. If I were, I would already know that sweet potatoes are a snack food.

I learned this nugget of wisdom at the Catawba Book Club. The group is studying Gary Freeze's *The Catawbans Volume I*. Recently we discussed local foodways and before I knew it, we were talking sweet potatoes.

Once upon a time, orange-colored tubers were a huge deal around here. In the early 1900s, local farmers produced more sweet potatoes than most any county in North Carolina. A large sweet potato house existed near Catawba, and locals rented space to store their sweet potatoes for later consumption. That is, if a family didn't have a root cellar already.

I have never been privy to a kitchen that keeps cooked sweet potatoes on hand for snacking, but I don't doubt that they exist. Eating a sweet potato—raw or cooked—had never occurred to me until I sat in on this book club and heard the locals talk.

Our discussion leader, Richard Eller, pointed out the agricultural roots of our county in more ways than sweet potatoes. Catawba was once a cotton growing place. Commercial cotton gins operated in Newton, Startown, Terrell and elsewhere. In fact, cotton farming explains the sweet potatoes. What one crop robbed from the soil (cotton), the other replenished (sweet potatoes).

I'm always fascinated with foodways that involve readily available ingredients. Every culture has its version of take-away foods, which makes me wonder how I've missed all the hints about living in what was once a sweet potato capital. It makes me wonder what else I've missed. It helps to commune with the true locals, to have them explain how things were and how they are— explore why folks see the world in a particular way.

The curiosity seeker in me likes to connect some dots that have faded from public view and to grasp them and enrich my life before they slip away for good, such as sweet potato fields and sweet potato houses and those curious orangey snacks on the kitchen table.

Cookies to cure the lonelies

December 2017

Earlier this year, I crossed paths with Bruce, a family friend at my niece's wedding. I hadn't seen him in years.

"You were a good kid," he said.

"I was?" I meant I hoped I was good, but I had no idea what he was talking about.

He quickly explained.

The year was 1971. Apparently, I'd sent a large box of homemade cookies to his boot camp in Louisiana. I believe he was stationed at Camp Beauregard, the place where National Guardsmen trained during the Vietnam Era.

It was a scary time, and I imagined what it would be like to be in such a hot place, hundreds of miles from home, next door to recruits who would most certainly be shipped to Southeast Asia—a place with a lot of sad endings. By then we were used to body counts on the *Nightly News*. 1971 alone saw 2,414 casualties.

Surely these cookies were a hit if they are still being talked about 45 years later.

"You and your Mom really outdid yourselves," Bruce said. Clearly they had cured the lonelies for a while.

In truth, my Mom probably had little to do with the project. The only cookies she served came in a cellophane bag from the supermarket. I was out to prove that my home-baked variety was better than store-bought.

I'm sure I gave Bruce a blank look, for I had no memory of the cookie incident at all. Not one flicker. Maybe it's because I made cookies a lot that year. I was taking Home Economics.

My best guess is that the cookies were snicker doodles. I borrowed the recipe from my friend Ginny. Her mom was the sort who baked homemade cookies a lot, and I liked their cinnamon flavor. I still have the handwritten recipe in my recipe box, a souvenir from the days when baking homemade cookies was a fresh adventure. The recipe appears in my neat teen-aged script, before a lot of note taking and reporter's scribble took their toll.

The neat script is as foreign to my current penmanship or lack thereof than my ability to make and send cookies, though I admitted to Bruce that I have sent similar care packages to other soldiers, including a co-worker who served in Desert Storm. The day he returned from deployment, he made a bee line to thank me.

A box of cookies is no big deal, or so I thought.

Knowing my mother, she would have huffed and puffed about packing Bruce's properly in a tin to keep them fresh and unbroken on their long ride to the Bayou State. We would have taken the package to the post office, had it weighed, paid maybe $3 or so to ship. Mom, the practical type, would have groused that the postage alone was more than cookies you could buy at the store.

But it was the thought that counts, and the memory of cookies from home stays with a soldier a long time…forty-five years in this case.

The late great Maya Angelou once said, "I've learned that people will forget what you said. People will forget what you did. But people will never forget how you made them feel."

GINNY'S SNICKER DOODLES

1 cup soft shortening
1 ½ cups sugar
2 eggs

Sift together: 2 ½ cups all-purpose flour
2 teaspoons cream of tartar
1 teaspoon baking soda
¼ teaspoon salt

Roll into small balls. Roll balls in 2 tablespoons sugar and 2 teaspoons cinnamon
Set the balls on an ungreased cookie sheet. Bake at 400 degrees for 8-10 minutes.
Take out before they brown.

Makes 2 ½ to 5 dozen.

The lure of the food beauty pageant

Food beauty pageants lure me to the county fair.

September 2015

There was a 489-pound pumpkin at the Catawba County Fairgrounds this year. A gourd as big as a rain barrel.

There it sat, like a manatee in plant form, next to prize barley and canned goods and needlecraft projects in the exhibit hall.

The blue ribbon didn't reveal the winner's name, but it was one honey of a fruit.

Most attend the county fair to see the farm animals or the cotton candy or the Tilt-a-Whirl. I go to see the canned goods and home exhibits, and I wasn't disappointed. This pumpkin was a humdinger. At 1½ pounds per pie, the gargantuan fruit could fill 325 pie shells, and at eight pieces each, that's enough to serve every resident of Claremont and Sherrills Ford with pie left over.

There's something about the sight of home-grown foods preserved in a glass jar that piques my interest. I think of them as glass jewels— emerald gherkins, garnet-colored beets, golden spiced peaches, ruby-colored salsa, pearl onions. Science meets art. Everything that can be preserved is there on the shelf—salsas, jams, beans, pickles, even slices of livermush.

In a land of plenty with a supermarket in every town, it's odd to be intrigued by home canned goods. Why would anyone go to the trouble to can quart of green beans when you can buy a family-sized can for $2.59?

Maybe it's appreciation for all the hard work it takes to walk that tightrope between science and practicality. I've done some canning myself, and I know how hard it is to pick and prepare perishable foods, much less pack them prettily.

Home canners choose to enter a steamy kitchen on a hot July evening to process seven quarts of green beans that might take three hours, not considering the time it takes to pick, wash and string the beans in the first place.

There's the warm-up of the canner, the pressure-building phase, placing the petcock on the steam valve, watching the gauge hover at eleven pounds of pressure for twenty-five minutes. Then comes the cooling-down phase, removal of the jars from the canner. You can get a scald if you're not careful.

In case you missed the local canned goods exposition, the state fair in Raleigh is in October. Judges take the science as seriously as the product. At the state fair, color and appearance take the lion's share of points. The rest of the credit goes to liquid, pack, appropriate size and something called "jar fill"—that is, the product is at the level of standard recommendations for the glass container used.

I have never garnered the nerve to enter the food beauty pageant, but I admire those who do. It's putting one's best efforts forward to see how they measure up.

Visit a home canning display and think of the effort that goes into it. Think of the bragging rights for the blue-ribbon winners. You'll be happy to silently cheer them on, along with monstrous produce such as the big pumpkin.

Recipe file full of food gems, history

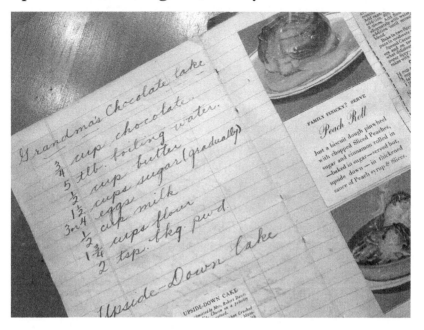

In the lean year of 1936, Dad's Christmas gift to his Mom was this handwritten cookbook.

December 2019

A while back I found myself rifling through my accordion file of recipes to find directions for Autumn Fruit Salad. It's in my bag of tricks for crowd-pleasers... a dish that's really a dessert disguised as salad.

As I rifled through all the clippings and handwritten notes, I decided to thin the file, which is a daunting task considering years of collected recipes. You recognize a friend's handwriting from, say, the 1990s and have no idea what that dish looked or tasted like. That's why I write a date on recipes, so at least I know I've tried them.

But if I haven't replicated a dish in say, twenty or thirty years, maybe it's time to throw it away. After this most recent purge, the bellows of the accordion file are less strained.

I did keep a recipe labeled Robert Redford's Green Olive Salad. I cannot imagine throwing away anything labeled "Robert Redford." He's one of my favorite actors. I published a story collection titled *Dining with Robert Redford*.

As a matter of fact, I still have a newspaper clipping from 1983 for a dessert called "Next Best Thing to Robert Redford." This exercise in culinary sin featured chocolate pudding, Cool Whip, cream cheese and a crumbled pecan crust. I remember making it for my Sunday School class.

During my recent recipe purge, I tossed the duplicate for a delicious bean salad based on balsamic vinegar and finely chopped onion. Two friends named Sylvia gave me that same recipe.

I have a collection of dishes I call "funeral food," for want of a better term. No matter who you take them to, you're guaranteed empty dishes to take home. The "menu" features chicken casserole with almonds and water chestnuts (trust me, it's good), zucchini squares and that elusive pineapple-apple salad/dessert—crowd pleasers, to be sure. Serve those dishes with a side of fresh peas, and you have a meal fit for a king.

I borrowed this menu from Mrs. Dellinger of Cherryville who hosted a ladies' tour of her log cabins several years ago. I'm glad that she was generous enough to share; several of us would have lost sleep trying to figure out the ingredients.

Among my recipe stash were instructions from a family heirloom: a notebook my Dad had given his mother for Christmas in 1936. The family lived on a wheat farm in Western Canada. In my Dad's adolescent handwriting were copies from their mother's file box or recipe drawer. Dad had gone to the trouble to paste cutouts from newspapers and magazines to dress the thing up. Among the recipes he chose dated from the 1920s: Coolidge Butter Scotch and Flapper Pie, Goldilocks Potatoes and Dandelion Wine.

My Grandma McElroy took the recipe book seriously, as she added many more recipes in her own script. "Brunswick Sunday Supper" features cubes of chuck steak, chopped, onions, peppers, tomato sauce, stewed tomatoes, salt, pepper and "2 tablespoons lard." The newspaper clipping includes the silhouette of a tumbling skier—indicating that dinner guests will go head over heels for the supper or, more likely, you should serve it in cold weather.

I imagine Grandma serving this dish for her farmer husband and six kids on a cold night in Alberta. It's filling and fairly inexpensive, which made it a perfect choice for that time and place.

The dessert section of the recipe book gives a nod to Canadian winters. My Dad wrote: "Get snow (clean) sprinkle 1 t spoon sugar over. Poor a little cream & stir. Then put snow in the quart. Put back in snow or ref. for about ½ hour. Then bring out & shake well for 8 minutes. Serves 2." It's accompanied by this PS: "Instead of snow & sugar and cream, use ice cream."

"Grandma's Chocolate Cake," makes me wonder which grandmother this came from. If it was my grandmother's grandmother, it was either Matilda Hart or Matilda Lane. I'll call it "Grandma Matilda's" and leave it at that.

The same aunt who gave me the recipe book also bequeathed me a glass cake stand once owned by my great-grandmother Lane. I initiated the stand a few years ago using "Grandma Matilda's" recipe. I imagined that I was visiting her farmhouse in 1895. Pity it wasn't a recipe for Lane Cake, that Southern delight that riffs on pecans, coconut and booze.

A loose recipe in my grandmother's handwriting is labeled "Illinois Corn Salad," a salute to her native state—one of those vinegar-based mixtures meant for canning.

Oh yes, and something called "Bean Salad," a Midwestern side dish found on most buffet spreads and potluck suppers across the Midwest. It involves kidney beans, chopped egg and a raw-egg dressing made with butter. I use mayo these days. Whenever I've served this to North Carolinians, most think it's gross and refuse to eat it, which means more leftovers for those of us who know what's worth eating.

Kidney bean salad, as my grandmother would have made it.

Thanksgiving: That middle-child holiday

November 2019

Poor Thanksgiving! Like a middle child, it languishes between two legendary partiers: Halloween and Christmas. Thanksgiving can scarcely compete.

American history teaches us that in 1621 the Plymouth Colonists and Wampanoag Indians shared the first Thanksgiving feast together to celebrate the harvest. Well, actually it was a three-day celebration.

Don't tell that to the docents at Berkeley Plantation in Virginia. Folks there say the First Thanksgiving took place along the James River after a band of British settlers arrived on December 4, 1619. That thirteen-month jump on things gave Virginia claim to the First Thanksgiving. So much for those upstart Pilgrims! But the fact that settlers of both colonies—and the eleven others—celebrated Thanksgiving at various times reflects on the religious heritage of our founders.

Being grateful for God's blessings is in America's DNA.

In 1789 George Washington issued the first Thanksgiving proclamation, calling upon Americans to express thanks for the joyful conclusion to the country's war of independence and the successful ratification of the U.S. Constitution. His successors John Adams and James Madison also designated days of thanks.

But leave it up to a woman to push for a true national holiday. Sarah Josepha Hale, author of the nursery rhyme "Mary Had a Little Lamb," worked for more than thirty-six years, writing editorials and contacting officials to give Thanksgiving its rightful place on the national calendar.

North Carolina's General Assembly agreed to a joint resolution to declare Thanksgiving a statewide holiday in 1849. A year before, Gov. William Graham had declared, Thanksgiving to be "a season for kind, social sentiment—for the forgiveness of injuries—for acts of good neighborhood and especially for the charitable remembrance of the Poor."

It was President Abraham Lincoln, who proclaimed the last Thursday in November to be the national day to observe Thanksgiving. In 1863, it was observed on November 26, a mere week after Lincoln delivered his famous Gettysburg Address, a speech to help dedicate the cemetery to the fallen.

Thanksgiving was celebrated on the last Thursday in November until 1939 when President Franklin D. Roosevelt moved the holiday up a week in an attempt to spur retail sales during the Great Depression. The change was met with so much opposition that two years later the president reluctantly signed a bill making Thanksgiving the fourth Thursday in November.

When I was growing up in the 1950s and 60s, Thanksgiving was a true shut-down holiday. Weeks before the event, my mother and my Aunt O planned the menu for our combined families: roast turkey, oyster dressing, slaw, and green bean casserole made with French-fried onions and cream of mushroom soup. The cranberry sauce (homemade, never out of a can) was served in a glass bowl.

After the meal, we drew names for our family Christmas gift exchange, with the first shopping being that weekend. The feast was always served as the mid-day meal after Macy's Thanksgiving Day Parade ended and the bowl games began. No one considered dining out for Thanksgiving; restaurants were closed.

No one considered shopping, either. Thanksgiving was the next thing to a high holy day, and still is, to those who resist the temptation to squeeze the observance into an hour or two—the dining part. Retail and sports claim the rest.

Still, there are some who consider Thanksgiving as something other than a shotgun start to the Christmas spending binge. Those faithful souls who attend Thanksgiving Eve services. Like 17th-century settlers, some actually pause to thank the Almighty, though they grab few headlines.

OTHER COURSES

The curse of cursive

October 2016

When I was seven, we moved from Tampa, Florida, to Illinois. Before I left, I exchanged addresses with my friend Anne who lived across the street. We had both just finished second grade so we had a lot in common.

Our letter-writing lasted for the next twenty-five years. The first letters were written in printed block letters, and eventually, cursive script learned in third grade. When I saw Anne's envelope arrive in the mailbox I knew immediately who it was from with its well-rounded letters. In the early grades, penmanship was graded in school.

We never thought of not writing in cursive. Had I used block letters, Anne would have written back, "What's wrong with you, Tammy?"

Heaven knows every eight-year-old wants to be grown up. The reason I didn't call Anne on the phone in 1965 was because a long-distance call back then was too expensive. Our parents weren't about to allow us to make long-distance calls to the tune of $5—at least $30 in today's money.

Today young people marvel at the quaint thought of receiving a handwritten letter, writing back and waiting days or weeks for a reply.

Times have certainly changed. The only documents handwritten these days are thank you notes and shopping lists. Everyone emails, posts, instant messages or snap chats. If something is really important, we make a phone call.

Don't ask anyone under twenty to read a handwritten letter in cursive. Cursive writing instruction went out years ago, and that fact upsets some adults. Not knowing cursive, they say, is the worst possible consequence for a free society.

Without being able to read historic documents, future generations are condemned to repeat history—never mind that ignorance of history has existed for eons. Lack of cursive is a sad commentary on education, others say. Teachers are being lazy. They're doing our children a disservice.

I see great value in being able to conduct historic research, but how many of us do that? When was the last time any of us wrote a letter in cursive, much less a two or three pager?

When was the last time we wrote a shopping list to ourselves and couldn't read our own handwriting?

Are books published in cursive script?

No way. Cursive by nature is difficult to read, given the wide variances in letter formation, neatness and so on. There is a reason why publishers use block letters as opposed to French script or even italics.

Let's face it. Hand writing went out the window when the personal computer arrived with its cousins the laptop, iPad and Smartphone. It's quicker and more legible to text or type a message than to write it.

Insisting that children learn cursive is something like traditionalists who demanded that Greek and Latin remain part of the core curriculum. Scholars may lament the loss of these classics, but few students take such classes.

Fewer and fewer jobs require cursive. Little Emma and Nathan aren't likely to become history scholars or researchers. Economics propels most of the real world. If it doesn't make money, it will be abandoned.

Yes, Alabama just passed a law mandating cursive instruction in their schools. How else, they say, can anyone sign their name on a check?

The problem is that Millennials don't have checks; Generation Z that follows probably won't know what a check is.

When the cursive arguments subside, the market will rule. It always has. If you're following the money, don't bet on cursive.

Type-In? No thanks

There's a new trend out there for hipsters: the type-in.

As the story goes, typewriter enthusiasts are holding gatherings in bars and restaurants to type to their heart's content.

Yes, it's true. Twenty years after most typewriters were swapped for word processors, old-school typewriting is making a comeback.

Even actor Tom Hanks and musician John Mayer are releasing a typewriter documentary.

A Type-In is an organized event that can include typing speed contests, distribution of stationery, letter-writing sessions and a typewriter swap.

I place this phenomenon in the same category as people who think that vinyl LPs are cool. Nostalgia is one thing, but there's a point where I don't get it, and for me, Type-Ins clearly occupy that point.

The only Type-In I ever attended was more than forty years ago. We called them typing classes in high school and Reporting I in college.

My Personal Typing class was offered on manual Smith Coronas in the typing lab of our high school. No fancy electric models. Those were reserved for the advanced students.

But I learned the keyboard configuration which makes no sense at all when you get down to it. The "QWERTY" keyboard, developed for the worlds' first typewriters back in 1868, was developed by Christopher Scholes, using advice from telegraph operators to translate Morse Code, which shows how one thing leads to another.

Regardless of its origin, the QWERTY system served me well. I went on to enter the Missouri Journalism School one year ahead of the Woodward & Bernstein tsunami. That was 1975, when *All the President's Men* inspired droves of students to become hot-shot reporters.

I took Reporting I using a manual typewriter in what had been the living room and dining room of a crumbling bungalow near campus. The place was packed with students because it was a required course. We clattered away, completing assignments, literally cutting and pasting sheets of paper together to create stories in one continuous feed.

151

At the time I thought it was rather antiquated for a revered journalism school to use such old-fashioned equipment, but we got the job done.

I never quite had enough strength in my little fingers to press the "a," quote marks, and comma keys hard enough.

Typing was slow and my brain worked fast. At the end of each line, we had to swing the arm to reposition the platen, the roll that held the sheet of paper. Hopefully I wouldn't run out of paper before I ran out of ideas.

Fledgling reporters were encouraged to report just the facts, not to editorialize and entertain.

Now typing enthusiasts are actually haunting thrift stores in search of these old manual machines, which is masochistic in my view. I know young people like to try old-school things, maybe type away while fancying themselves as Hemingway or Kerouac or Faulkner.

Actually a few famous authors still compose at typewriters: David McCullough, Joyce Carol Oates, Danielle Steele and Amy Tan all claim to use typewriters rather than word processors, but they're the exceptions.

To me, the idea of hard-pressed keystrokes and eraser wheels with the little whisker brushes seems as much fun as wrestling undeveloped film and toxic chemicals in a darkroom, which I also did as a cub reporter right out of college. I'm grateful for digital equipment, to be frank.

I sound a lot like my mother. She couldn't understand why anyone would want to use a sewing machine when you could buy ready-made in town. Likewise, she couldn't imagine anyone wanting to use a pressure canner. What one generation throws out, the next finds enchanting.

Maybe Type-Ins are a positive response to the over-automated life we lead. They say it's more special to send someone a typewritten note on a piece of paper than to send an email that can be quickly deleted.

I get that. So why not take things a step further and handwrite a note and hand-address the envelope?

Oh yeah. Young people don't know cursive, and if their handwriting is anything like mine, they wouldn't be able to read it anyhow.

Going plaid in a solid gray world

Our old love seat makes way for its plaid replacement.

November 2017

If you have any doubts about what color is "in" these days, it's gray. Light gray and dark. Ash, platinum, silver, nickel, charcoal, slate with some beige, with some white and black thrown in.

This stark reality was reinforced when my husband Tym and I went furniture shopping recently.

I don't know what's more stressful—trying to agree on furniture you'll use for years or picking out a car—which are largely silver, white and black these days as well.

Regardless of how the country is divided politically and socially, everyone has shifted to neutral when it comes to interior decoration. Maybe that's because they want to be soothed rather than confronted by bold colors.

Except us. We are insisting on a pair of red-and-green plaid love seats and a coordinating wingback recliner. Almost nothing has wings anymore, but we kept browsing the rows of easy chairs and mocked-up living rooms, hoping.

We soon discovered that Fall 2017 isn't the time for plaid upholstery. The trend now is "urban chic" or "post-industrial rustic," or whatever they call hip interiors these days. We were looking for something to blend with our red and green cabinetry…something homey instead of homely. This is a room we truly live in, a cozy space with a fireplace and blanket chest coffee table, a scuffed antique dough box, a spool end table and other collected stuff.

We scanned showroom after showroom, wandering through a sea of muted neutrals and splotches of ashen whites and misty smoke tones with the occasional animal print or bold black accents.

All this left me as cold as hoarfrost.

"Where are the bright colors?" I asked one salesperson.

She shrugged. "Not here, that's for sure."

We hadn't shopped for furniture in nearly ten years, so what we were looking for was yesterday's news. When we last decorated, we dared to include tomahawk red, grazing field green and a funky turquoise called "haint blue," as it's known on the Gullah coast. All three wall colors were tempered with paint resembling wet sand.

Being surrounded by Neutralville is discombobulating. We could keep looking for brighter colors and argue about what to do about living room furniture, or we could "settle," as many do, for what's in style.

And then, we spotted "our" chair, a wingback recliner in muted gold brocade. It was marked way down, obviously a holdover from the days when it was stylish to be traditional. It had our name all over it.

By now, we were aware that we would have to order the plaid loveseats. We compared the chair with some fabric swatch—a rare plaid in red, gold and green—and voila!

No furniture manufacturer will mass produce plaid upholstery in an un-plaid world, but we have what we want: furniture that sits comfortably and blends with our red-and-green cabinets and warm oak floors.

I know what you're thinking—red and green—they must be Christmas fanatics.

In fact we prefer vintage colors that were popular back in the last century, before industrial was chic or gray settled into every nook and cranny.

It's true, red and green are fashion's no-nos, but bowing to fashion dictates isn't the quickest path to contentment. Colors and fabrics and accessories in the home makes it just that: a home.

Meanwhile, we look forward to Christmas, when the loveseats arrive in all their plaid glory to keep Mr. Wingback company.

Breaking up was hard to do

January 2020

My landline is history. After thirty-two years of answering my "464" telephone number, I cut the cord a couple of weeks ago. Or at least I think I did.

The breakup began in September when, as a new widow, I called AT&T to put the telephone account in my name.

Let's just say things didn't go well. I was on the phone with them four and a half hours. In October I decided to switch to Spectrum—a process that took six weeks.

In the midst of all this, my cordless phone and answering machine stopped working. In spite of a new battery, the dead electronics languished, taking up an entire corner of my kitchen counter.

I thought of Marie Kondo, the anti-clutter queen who admonishes us to throw out things that don't spark joy. Clearly the phone and answering machine were not making me joyful. The plastic case of answering machine had yellowed with age, and the robotic man who asked callers to "Please leave a message" had gone silent. Instructions for reprogramming the equipment were long gone.

That's how it is with life. One day everything is perking along as it has been until it stops without warning. I quit trying to make calls on the old phone though the extension in the bedroom kept ringing with callers urging me to extend my vehicle warranty, to take a brief survey, to switch my credit card balance, to donate blood to the Red Cross.

Spectrum assured me that the landline would eventually be disconnected, though as of last week, the landline was still on life support, and I was stupidly answering junk calls.

I needed a clean break from the telemarketers asking for "Tomorrrah Wilson" or wishing to speak with "The Main Decision Maker in the House."

Why was I paying for a landline that annoyed me?

It was a Marie Kondo kind of question.

If I could break up with Ma Bell, there was surely enough moxie in me to sever the landline. In a rash of ill temper, I called Spectrum to end my landline service. I disconnected the bedroom extension.

Still, the loss bothered me. My family had used that "464" number since we acquired a Newton address. The year was 1987 and our son was eighteen months old. I thought of all the calls that had been carried over that number: lighthearted conversations with relatives who are now deceased, news about new jobs, new babies, new spouses—bits of life that will never come again.

Back in 1987, we were still part of the 704 area code, until Charlotte outgrew itself and most of Catawba County was reassigned to 828. Not too long ago we could tell where a caller was by the area code. Today that's no longer true. Telephone numbers follow people around like ghosts from the past, proclaiming that they once lived in New York or Seattle.

I cradled the black cordless receiver in my hands. Would today be the last day to talk over that phone? No, the last call had been taken weeks ago—before the battery faded and the new one failed to hold a charge.

Back in the 1980s, I never considered that the landline would totally disappear. We were wired to every other phone in the world. How could that possibly change?

Then I bought a cellphone. And against my better judgment, I began divulging my cell number to acquaintances, my dental office and my church. Then credit card companies wanted it and so did my bank, and before I knew it, I became less and less of a 464 person. And now I am no longer one at all.

When mail was gold

September 2018

Every few years I find myself hunched over a keyboard, transcribing handwritten script for posterity.

Call me a sucker for history or a glutton for punishment. Over the years I've transcribed a friend's Civil War letters, and done the same for thirty-four years of my mother's diaries. I've also copied out my father's travel journal from Out West in 1939 and the writing of my grandmother who made a "motor tour" of the East Coast that very same year.

This summer, I transcribed the last of a four-year set of journals composed during the Great Depression. Opal, my mother's sister, kept a diary from 1930-1933. I'd put off 1932 because the handwriting was impossible to read without a magnifying glass. Finally, though, I set a deadline and tackled the chore. No, torture would be closer to the truth.

The tedium of deciphering cramped handwriting isn't for the faint of heart. But besides that, writing the daily comings and goings of most anyone's life is…well…boring.

My Aunt Opal squeezed her golden thoughts into a space one inch by two inches, so deciphering the entries was service beyond the call of duty. How she wrote such small script is beyond me. The nib of her fountain pen must have been the size of a hypodermic needle.

Opal's life as a college freshman at Eastern Illinois State Teachers College gave me a glimpse of college life during the Great Depression. Every single day she recorded when she got up, when she went to bed, what classes she attended, who she'd seen and what she'd done. And virtually every day there was a mention of mail. "Got letter today from…" or "Got card today from…" "Wrote letter to …" or the dreaded "No mail."

It seems so quaint, the idea that people wrote their thoughts on paper, and mailed them to childhood friends and family and sweethearts. In Opal's case, the mail was regularly dispatched twice a day.

I could identify with her anticipation of mail. I remember getting cards and letters in college. It was a thrill to go by the mail boxes and find treasure waiting for me: a letter from a friend, a postcard from Mom, a party invitation. It was such a bummer to have no mail to open. In the 1970s, letters were still handwritten. It took at least a day or two—or more—for those precious messages to make their way through the postal system.

For Opal in the 1930s, mass media didn't come into play until one of the girls acquired a portable radio. Soon those in her rooming house were "radioing," listening to live football games and music and newscasts. On November 8, 1932, Opal listened to the election returns that sent Franklin D. Roosevelt to the White House. She and her roommate listened until midnight.

A month later, Opal listened to the Notre Dame-California football game live on December 10. She could enjoy her favorites, Guy Lombardo and Wayne King.

Opal, I learned, rarely called home, which would have been long distance. Neither did students in my day. The tradition in the 1970s, at least, was to make those calls Sunday evening, when rates dropped, though all too often the caller competed for a limited number of lines. I remember the telephone company recording "We're sorry. All circuits are busy now. Please try your call again later. Good bye."

For better or worse, technology has all but eliminated the handwritten letter or the notion of exorbitant long-distance charges. We'd rather text anyway.

So, when was the last time I received a handwritten letter with a stamp on it? Not counting Christmas cards or postcards, I do know who sent it: Rev. Fred Thompson of Newton, sharing his caring thoughts, as he always does. The handwritten envelope grabbed my attention at once, for in these days of Instagram and Snapchat, an actual letter is the gold standard more than ever.

CD players going the way of the stereo console

September 2019

For those of you who haven't bought a new vehicle lately, I have news for you: There are no CD players.

I learned this ugly truth last fall after purchasing a new Equinox and transferring my paraphernalia to the new vehicle. Sadly, there was no need to move my CD collection because Chevrolet discontinued CD players a while ago. Other automakers have done the same.

How dare they! Nobody asked me if I wanted a CD player. It was not an option, which makes the loss all the more stinging. It had been four years since we'd bought a vehicle. The transition had happened while we weren't looking. It was gone, cold turkey without a goodbye.

There I was, driving around with buyer's remorse, lamenting my new CD playerless life, wondering why artists still sell CDs to fans at concerts.

I know the thing these days is to upload music onto "devices." But that's not as simple as popping a CD into the dashboard player. I grew up with a phonograph in the living room that played 78s, 33 1/3 LPs and 45 single records in mono. Then came the console for stereophonic sound. In the 1960s, these must-have music players were standard in most dens.

Since I began driving in 1970, I've been doing the music shuffle from AM to FM radio, 8-tracks to cassettes and CDs. And satellite radio. I understand that technology changes, but how are music fans to enjoy our prized CD collections on the road?

My husband suggested I look for a portable CD player that would plug into the speaker system of the Equinox, but to my amazement, there aren't any good options available. Woe be to us music lovers who still want CDs in our driving life.

So what of audiobooks? Don't people usually listen to those while driving?

I suppose there are ways to upload books onto a "device" and take them in the car to use with ear buds, but I don't want to deal with all that. Companies are still manufacturing books on CD and the library still has scads of them available for checkout, presumably to people who drive older vehicles.

The technology to disconnect prompted me to stop by my mobile phone carrier and ask how can I replace my missing CD player.

A helpful young employee introduced me to Spotify (a monthly subscription) and how I can download albums and such on my cellphone and link that to my auto's speaker system. The catch here is "subscription." I may pick some favorite songs or albums, but I never get done paying for them.

I did try Spotify on a long drive last spring and learned that the setup would allow me to talk hands-free on the phone, listen to email messages and the like, which creates far more distractions than my CD player ever could.

The future shock of it all—how the world suddenly dropped CD players—brings to mind that novelty of car record players in the early 1960s. They existed because auto manufacturers assumed drivers might want to skip the static on AM radio and listen to their own records.

The key was "option." Drivers had a choice. The auto record player didn't take hold until the 8-track era a few years later, eventually replaced by cassettes that were often found with their clumps of audiotape spaghetti discarded along the side of the road.

Vinyl records went the way of the stereo console in the 1980s, only to reappear twenty-five years later. For some odd reason, young people are nostalgic for the scratchy sound of a record player needle on vinyl. In fact, record stores have cropped up in Hickory, Lenoir, Valdese and elsewhere.

I suppose I could wait and see if CD players return to new vehicles. I know what goes around comes around, but I'm not too hopeful.

Where have all the sewers gone?

April 2018

I can't remember a time when I didn't know how to sew. By age five, my mother had put a needle and thread in my hand and showed me how to stitch fabric.

One of my fondest memories was going to the fabric department of Jon's Department Store in my small Midwestern hometown. I chose material for my own doll clothes. My mother told me not to go hog wild. Cotton fabric was as much as forty-nine cents a yard. Money didn't grow on trees.

I have scraps of those fabrics still: a dainty ballerina print, a delicate yellow and pink calico, a bold Hawaiian orange (Hawaii had just become a state.)

My sewing machine came later—a Sears Kenmore model for my eleventh birthday. From that point on, my wardrobe was populated by sewing projects. Creating something useful from nothing seemed way more exciting than watching summer reruns. A kindly neighbor lady taught me the basics of using a pattern and adjusting it to fit. I took Home Ec in high school, though schoolmates made fun of me. Home Ec wasn't cool.

I sewed costumes for the school play, my high school graduation dress, my flower girl's dress. Years later, I made maternity outfits, our son's baby clothes, stuffed animals, cloth dolls for our nieces, gift aprons, Halloween costumes, chair pads, curtains for our new house. In one stitching frenzy, I sewed mattress ticking for a roll-away cot.

When we moved to Catawba County in 1979, home sewing was still something women did. There were several places to buy yard goods: Clyde's Fabrics along the railroad tracks in Hickory, Kmart (in the old W. T. Grant building on US 70 West), Piece Goods (near that same Kmart) and the legendary Mary Jo's Cloth Store, before it caught fire and moved from Dallas to Gastonia.

Over time, my interest in sewing ebbed and flowed. I wasn't particularly into sewing again until my granddaughter was born nineteen months ago. Then the stark reality hit me. Home sewers have left the building.

Thanks to NAFTA, most all fabrics are imported, and the quality has suffered. Mary Jo herself warned me about this several years ago. She helped me find fabric for a dress I was making to wear to a Hawaiian-themed wedding. "That's the last of the lot. There won't be any more of this made in America."

She was right.

Sadly, her landmark store has shifted from a haven for quilters and home sewers to an outlet for upholstery and drapery fabrics and bridal supplies. Sewing has become a four-letter word: W-O-R-K; it's something people hire other people to do—professional upholsterers and seamstresses. Few high school students will ever spend half a semester learning to sew like I did. Their kindly neighbor lady is shopping the bargains at Belk, not cutting out fabric to sew dresses.

Fabric store entrepreneur Mary Jo Cloninger passed away in 2017. Back in 1951, she started with a $500 loan and a few scraps of cloth and realized the American dream, spinning her idea into a world-famous destination for fabric and sewing that drew customers from across the Southeast.

I remember seeing busloads of quilters and home sewers disembarking at Mary Jo's, the lodestone of sewing nirvana. Bolts of cotton cloth and cotton blends by the hundreds were labeled with hand-lettered signs: animals, astronomy, automotive, baby, cartoons, Christmas, Disney, floral, fruits and vegetables, sports, Civil War, religious. It was inspiring to take in all the colors and designs.

What we didn't see back in 1979 was the coming dearth of not only fabric making, but fabric buying. While many of you weren't watching, hometown fabric stores died away as yardage prices skyrocketed to $9.99. So much for saving money with the old Kenmore.

If you want to buy yard goods in Catawba County these days, you have three choices: Joann Fabrics and Crafts, Hobby Lobby (national chains), Walmart (another national chain), or fabric.com.

Local fabric stores have passed to the scrapheap of Remember When, save at least one exception. Last fall, on our trip west, we happened upon the Bakersville Pioneer Village in Webster County, Missouri. I was dubious until I stepped into the seed store filled with what appeared to be every heirloom seed known to man.

And then, Eureka! There is a back room were shelves of calico in more colors than a crayon box. Instantly I became a five-year-old again, hem-hawing about fabric. I eventually settled on a yellow floral and a blue cowgirl print that will become outfits for my granddaughter, all at the bargain price of $4.99/yard. It was a good day.

Notes from an impatient patient

May 2018

I know there's nothing so boring as an "organ recital" about ill health, but here goes.

Sciatica came calling on April 29 when I bent over to get dressed. I felt a pop in my lower back.

Within four days, I had taken my first ambulance ride to the Emergency Room. where I had my first CAT scan, and received my first steroid injection and dose of morphine. I'd also had an x-ray and two IV drips and met my health insurance deductible for the entire year.

I'm sure there are ailments more painful than sciatica, but I don't want to find out what they are.

The intake nurse at the emergency room asked me to rate my pain from one to ten.

"How about eleven?" I panted.

"Have you ever had thoughts of harming yourself?"

Not until today, I wanted to say. The sciatic pain felt like a knife in my hip. No, make that two knives.

Five days into this torment, I'd had enough. I was frustrated at maneuvering a walker around furniture and doorways. Between sciatic attacks, I planned trips through the house. One foray upstairs was like a trip to town, crawling up sixteen steps with a list in my pocket to remind me what needed to be picked up or "done" before I returned to home base.

Pretty soon the word got out. Well-meaning folks called and dropped by. Some brought food, offered to do chores, shop for groceries and so on. I was grateful for all that, but at the same time, I'm the impatient, independent sort who has a hard time accepting help. I watched weeds grow by the foot while the dust and cobwebs accumulated in every corner. I reluctantly hired a cleaning service.

Four weeks into this ordeal, I'm happy to report that the pain has diminished. I'm thankful for concerned friends and family, and a spouse who put up with my grumbling and pushed the wheelchair through Walmart one day with me holding a gallon of milk, a bunch of bananas and other odds and ends that needed buying. I caught the eye of other disabled shoppers, most of them in electrified carts, gingerly maneuvering past me, the weenie in the loaner wheelchair, juggling merchandise like an amateur.

Sciatica made my world shrink and my awareness grow. Until then, I'd never given much thought to the slope of sidewalks, maneuvering around aisle displays, reaching merchandise on top shelves or using a credit card terminal positioned several inches above my head.

I had never considered how it is to use a motorized cart. (Once you're done with it, how does it get back inside the store?) I hadn't thought about the inconvenience of getting in and out of a wheelchair in the rain or how clumsy it is to cook a meal while sitting down.

Sciatica has brought several things to my life, among them a wake-up call that this "old-person's ailment" is part of my here and now. And like a lot of things that pop up in life, it's not something we want; it's something we get.

What a difference 19 years make

September 2020

Nineteen years ago, my husband and I were flying to a family reunion. It was Friday, September 14—three days after the 9-11 attacks—and airports were just reopening.

Security was extra tight. Two officers at Charlotte Douglas International Airport checked our car trunk and asked several questions when we arrived at 6 a.m. Once inside the terminal, we waited in line for two hours, missed our scheduled flight and were rebooked for midday.

We ate sandwiches provided by the Red Cross that had set up a temporary canteen. We attended a prayer service at noon outside the terminal.

Attitude about life had changed on a dime. When all aircraft were grounded on September 11, hotels filled with stranded passengers. To meet emergency demand, some kindhearted residents opened their homes to strangers. On what had been one of the most horrific weeks in American history, it appeared that we were becoming a kinder, gentler nation.

Our plane to St. Louis was no more than a quarter full. We sat two hours at the gate until a plainclothes man with a briefcase came aboard and took a seat in the last row. We assumed he was a sky marshal, a new air safety requirement.

When we arrived in St. Louis that afternoon, the terminal was all but empty. The car rental agent said we were his only customers that day.

No doubt a lot of people thought we were crazy to fly at all, but everyone was on high alert. We were in fact safer that Friday than we would have been a few days earlier.

Of course, most of us know exactly where we were on 9-11. We know what we were doing the moment we learned that two planes had hit the World Trade Center.

For me, September 11, 2001, began as a warm, clear day at Weymouth Center in Southern Pines—literally next door to Ft. Bragg. I was on a writing residency with two friends, and the day before, I'd purchased a book about the great San Francisco earthquake of 1906. I remember reading it before I went to sleep on September 10, imagining the conflagration that engulfed one of America's largest cities and killed some 3,000 people.

The San Francisco tragedy was still weighing on my mind that next morning when one of my friends knocked on my door to alert me that two airliners had struck the Twin Towers in New York.

Realizing that the U.S. was under attack, we knew we should leave Southern Pines. Ft. Bragg and all US military installations were on high alert. My friends and I hurriedly packed and hustled on home, listening to real-time radio coverage of the attack on the Pentagon and the downing of United Flight 93 near Shanksville, Pennsylvania.

America changed overnight as we came together to celebrate the pride and resolve of our nation.

Flags and yellow ribbons popped up everywhere. The display of patriotism in the weeks and months after 9-11 had us rallying around our flag and our new president, George W. Bush who, incredibly, enjoyed an 80 percent approval rating less than a year after the contentious election of 2000.

Volunteers stepped up to help with recovery efforts. Generous citizens collected supplies for first responders and others in need. Churches held prayer vigils. Blood donors lined up. Citizens filled tractor trailers with supplies bound for New York. Young people enlisted in the military.

The nation underwent a metamorphosis like none anyone had seen since Pearl Harbor. Certainly no one in my generation had witnessed anything like it.

But the patriotic fever has subsided.

We are in a different political climate. Mention 9-11 these days and you may hear a debate about the wrong-headed aspects of the Patriot Act. You might get a tirade against Bush 43 and his infamous weapons of mass destruction. You might hear a rant about prejudice against Muslims or claims that the attacks were a conspiracy between the Bush and bin Laden families.

One thing we can agree on: The War on Terror has been costly. More than 4,400 American lives have been lost so far in the Afghanistan and Iraq wars combined, exceeding the toll from 9-11, which was 2,977.

America is a far different place than it was nineteen years ago.

Mob cancels Civil War monument

June 2020

Spray painting and destroying monuments has been a thing these days, instigated by rage over the death of George Floyd.

We've heard about the beheading, burning and drowning of a Christopher Columbus statue in Richmond, the furor over the Abraham Lincoln Emancipation statue in Boston, where a resident has initiated a petition to demand its removal because the slave figure on the monument appears subservient to Lincoln.

Meanwhile, in San Francisco, a statue of Ulysses S. Grant was toppled by protesters although Grant led forces to defeat the Confederacy and as President, clamped down on the Ku Klux Klan during the era of Reconstruction.

Ironies abound these days.

Earlier this month, protesters defaced the memorial to the Massachusetts 54th on Boston Commons. This one shook me. It's considered one of the nation's greatest pieces of public art to come out of the Civil War.

The disrespect reminded me of when vandals struck a country graveyard when I was a child. I remember my mother's distress upon driving out to the cemetery in Shelby County, Illinois, where four generations of our family were buried. Vandals had toppled most all of the tombstones. Investigations showed rope marks and tire tracks. The old marble stones had toppled easily, torn from their bases, and of course some broke into pieces. Stone ornaments on top of my great-great grandparents were snapped off and shattered. Small marble slabs marking their grandchildren's graves weren't immune to the vandals' rage. They lay face-down on the grass, like victims of a massacre.

My mother paced about as she surveyed the destruction, covering her mouth, moaning and crying. I had never seen her so outraged. Who could desecrate a cemetery? What kind of sick mind would do such a thing?

My ancestors were farmers who had come West by covered wagon to till the soil and raise a family. These were our people. Their monuments were damaged, their graves disrespected. This business was personal.

The sheriff investigated, but no one was ever arrested. Township taxpayers had to cover the cost of repairing dozens of grave markers though the stones were never fully restored. Once broken, weathered old marble can't be made new again, just as I cannot un-see what I saw in that country cemetery more than fifty years ago.

A similar outrage washed over me when I saw photos of graffiti marring the memorial for the 54th Infantry Regiment in Boston. I've seen it on visits to Boston, a bronze relief depicting Black recruits led by Col. Robert Gould Shaw on horseback.

You may remember Shaw. He and his unit were portrayed in *Glory*, the 1989 film starring Matthew Broderick, Denzel Washington and Morgan Freeman. I remember seeing it at the Carolina Theatre. The movie was an inspiring portrayal of an overlooked chapter in American history.

After President Lincoln signed the Emancipation Proclamation in 1863, a thousand men signed up for the Union Army. Had any of them been captured in the South, they would have been enslaved or murdered, but the cause of freedom was so important to them, they signed up anyway.

The 54th Massachusetts would prove instrumental in the attack on Ft. Wagner near Charleston, South Carolina. Thirty of the men were killed in action on July 18, 1863—just two weeks after Gettysburg. William Carney, an African-American sergeant with the 54th, is considered the first Black recipient of the Congressional Medal of Honor for his actions that day in recovering and returning the unit's U.S. Flag to Union lines.

Those Black lives should matter.

The bronze portion of the Shaw memorial was created by famed sculptor Augustus Saint-Gaudens and has stood on Boston Commons since 1897. Saint-Gaudens worked fourteen years to complete the bas-relief bronze using African-American models to show the soldiers as human beings, not caricatures. That gesture alone was a big deal in the days of Jim Crow.

Obscene graffiti now covers a plywood covering erected to protect the monument until it is restored.

I have no idea what George Floyd's death has to do with the 54th Massachusetts or the Saint-Gaudens monument. I don't know why the memory of one of America's first African-American infantry units should be cheapened with spray-painted vulgarities.

It's what happens when the mob rules.

Vietnam series revisits national heartache

September 2017

The Vietnam War: A Film by Ken Burns and Lynn Novick has kept many of us mesmerized since the first installment aired on September 17. The PBS series, directed by two legendary documentarists, is well-researched, well edited and thought-provoking.

But I began watching with trepidation, unsure that I wanted to engage the Vietnam War again. Only a couple of weeks ago, my John Hoyle DAR Chapter conducted a ceremony honoring Vietnam veterans when the Vietnam Traveling Memorial Wall came to Conover. I attended out of a sense of duty.

The Vietnam documentary has been another matter. Ten nights of footage and narration about this lost war is a lot to absorb.

Then someone commented, "You're probably too young to remember much about Vietnam," and I bristled.

I was nine when President Lyndon Johnson widened America's commitment to prop up the faltering government of South Vietnam. Newsreels and body counts played in the background of my formative years, a migraine that never eased, a haunting specter of draft notices for relatives, neighbors, friends, brothers of classmates. The numbers kept growing to the point we were numbed.

I remember sitting on the living room floor playing with dolls when I first heard the word "Vietnam" on the news. The TV screen showed a map of this odd-sounding place—a curled, irregular shape clinging to Southeast Asia like a giant leech.

It was the first war that America lost, so those who served in that conflict—though as bravely as in any other war—never received the thanks or the respect accorded other veterans. America lost 58,220 soldiers, and another 304,000 were wounded. The war's cost was even greater considering invisible scars left on family members and the nation's psyche. Up until then, America seemed so invincible.

When the curtain fell in 1975, I was a junior in college, and I welcomed the news, though I did not savor the photo of a Huey picking up desperate evacuees from a rooftop in Saigon. The "unwinnable war" as Secretary of Defense Robert McNamara secretly admitted in 1964, was truly that. This humiliating scene was the reward for more than eleven years in a quagmire half a world away.

I grew up in a family that never supported the war, an extremely unpopular stance in the mid-60s. Dinner conversation sometimes focused on the military draft. We had relatives in Canada, my Dad would point out. It didn't take me long to figure that if I'd been a male with a low draft number, it would have been easy to pay them a visit and forget to come home.

My parents were neither hippies nor street protestors, but deep down they had more in common with the angry mob than the flag wavers.

By 1972 my would-be draft-dodger self wore a POW bracelet, a metal circlet on my right wrist. Engraved on it was "Capt. Lawrence Helber, USMC," a random name sent to me by Voices in Vital America, the nonprofit that sold the nickel bracelets to build awareness of POWs and MIAs. I hated the war, but I didn't hate fellow Americans who had been caught up in it.

Young men born in my year, 1954, were among the last to be assigned draft numbers, though the draft was abolished early in 1973. President Gerald Ford signed conditional amnesty for draft dodgers and deserters in 1974. President Jimmy Carter extended it to a full pardon in 1977.

Every war must have its youngest casualty. He was Dan Bullock of New York, age fifteen when he was killed in 1969. He lied about his age to enlist. If he had attended my high school, we could have been sophomores together.

I cannot think of Vietnam without thinking of Billie, my brother's best friend in sixth grade. Billie spent most days around our house, went on family vacations with us, and at the time I thought of him as an extra brother.

In college he roomed with Jim, my best friend's brother. As I recall, both of them majored in agriculture at Southern Illinois University. Upon graduation, both were drafted into the Army. Billie went to Vietnam. Jim remained at Ft. Campbell, Kentucky, serving as a medic. Never was the randomness of fate more clear to me.

In December 1970, Billie died in Bien Hoa Province. He was barely twenty-three.

Visiting the Vietnam Traveling War Memorial in Conover this month, I found Billie's name on Panel 6W, line 110—one soldier among a sea of casualties in a war that Americans are still trying to reconcile. I stood silently, wondering how his family coped with such a loss.

The PBS documentary only confirms what my parents said in 1964, that the President was lying and that we had no business in Vietnam. But knowing that they were right doesn't ease the sorrow.

Had I been a male born on my birthday, my number would have been 226. I would have never been drafted, so I would not have moved in with my aunt and uncle in Canada.

VIVA, the POW bracelet office, closed its doors in 1976. By then the public was tired of hearing about Vietnam and cared less about the POW/MIA issue. Capt. Helber went missing in action on Jan. 24, 1966. He is memorialized on the Wall. I still have the bracelet.

Although the official US casualty count is 58,200, veterans continue to suffer premature deaths from exposure to Agent Orange, post-traumatic stress disorder and other causes.

I hope the PBS series gives renewed perspective to this lost war, not just for those who saw combat, but for those of us who watched in real time and for those who didn't. Hopefully, we Americans will learn the lessons this horrible history teaches, but learning from history isn't something we do well.

HOLIDAY FARE

Why I love Valentine's Day

My Valentine half birthday cake with 6 ½ candles.

February 2019

Being born on August 14 means Valentine's Day is my half-way mark. Suffering through the winter doldrums, the bright spark of candy and cupcakes were a welcome relief as a child.

The year I was four and a half, Mom threw a cupcake party for me and the neighbor girl to celebrate my half birthday— any excuse to brighten a snowy February day. I don't remember how long the half-birthday gig lasted. At least another year or two, because a photo exists of me seated at the kitchen table holding a heart-shaped candy box with a plastic doll on the lid. My age, six and a half, is noted in the family photo album.

In those days, candy boxes were done up right with lace ruffles, ribbon and silk flowers stapled to the lid. Who cared if the candy was terrible? The fancy box made up for it.

At school, there were heart-shaped window decorations and maybe, if the teacher went all-out, a tissue honeycomb heart perched on a corner of her desk, or another one suspended from the ceiling.

Valentine's Day was an excuse for a class party, thanks to Room Mothers. These homemakers signed up to bring goodies to their child's class for holidays—Halloween, Christmas, Valentine's Day, Easter. Room Mothers came in pairs. One brought the treats—always homemade—and another provided candy and napkins. The party came after lunch, during "milk time."

Occasionally a rebel Room Mother dared to skip the school milk and bring waxed cups and red Kool-Aid. She was a lady after my heart.

I wanted to be a Room Mother when I grew up. I was particularly charmed by the creative ladies who put special favors on top of the cupcakes—adorned party picks, though today such frivolity would be considered a lawsuit waiting to happen.

Around 1992 I was my son's Room Mother at Startown School. My long-held dream had come true. And then I learned that school policy had changed. "Room Parents" could no longer bring homemade goodies. Store-bought treats took some of the fun out of the class party. A pre-packaged Little Debbie cake was no match for a home-baked cupcake with a huge dollop of strawberry icing.

Whenever Valentine's Day rolls around, I still think about vanilla cupcakes with strawberry icing, sprinkled with red hots. And pastel "conversation" hearts with stamped sentiments such as "be mine" or "luv you."

Valentine's Day was more than eats. Days before the big classroom party, we spent Art Time creating crepe-paper covered shoeboxes or hanging large construction paper envelopes to collect cards from the whole class. Heart cut-outs, doilies. Is there anything that holds more promise than the sight of a school Valentine box stuffed with hand-signed cards?

Long about fifth grade, I took things to another level when I spotted a Hallmark Make-It-Yourself Valentine kit at the drug store. As a budding crafter, I begged my mother to buy it, and she reluctantly did. In early February, I went to work on the kitchen table cutting out the cards, assembling heart-shaped doilies, glitter, and stickers and pink feathers and red plastic jewels onto the cards. Elmer's glue was my best friend as I tried to make these special greetings for all thirty classmates.

After the first half dozen or so, the neat stuff was already used and the rest of the glue-able do-dads were growing scarce. So, there I was, trying to beat the clock being "creative" and having less and less fun with every hand-decorated card. By the time #30 rolled around, I was wishing I'd never heard of the Hallmark Valentine kit.

We all know the Valentine etiquette: never leave anyone in the class out, including the teacher. Especially the teacher.

Valentine receptacles were decorated shoe boxes until someone came up with the clever idea of making oversized envelopes from red and white construction paper. The top flap was to display your name and the whole affair hung on the front of school desks to be filled with penny Valentines, or five-cent ones, or ten-cent ones, depending on your vintage.

I'm still a sucker for tissue honeycomb hearts and candy boxes and "Victorian" fold-out cards. The fussier the better.

War casualties are more than numbers

June 2019

On May 26, I joined a small crowd at the Memorial Day ceremony in Eastview Cemetery in Newton to honor American service men and women for their sacrifice in the line of duty. There was a wreath-laying ceremony, speeches by veterans, a mayor's proclamation, a gun salute and "Taps."

Among us were veterans' groups and re-enactors in wool Confederate uniforms. And there were members of the Daughters of the American Revolution, the United Daughters of the Confederacy and Order of Confederate Rose. This event honored all war casualties.

Over Memorial Day weekend, the *Hickory Daily Record* published a list of Catawba County's war dead since the Mexican-American War. (Catawba County wasn't founded until 1843.) Among the lost were local family names from Abee to Zerden—two pages of lists, the most being from the Civil War and World War II.

I counted them all. Catawba County lost 178 of its sons in World War II—a staggering number, but a fraction of the 565 lost during the Civil War. Historical context makes that figure even more shocking.

To lose 565 men today would represent less than 1% of our population of 158,000. Those 178 men lost represented less than 1 percent of the county's population at that time.

But the 1860s was a whole other matter. At the start of the Civil War, Catawba County had only 10,729 residents, according to the U.S. Census Bureau. The war claimed five percent of our county's population. To put that in perspective, it would be like losing 7,900 county residents today.

The Civil War was a very big deal.

Historians estimate that America lost 750,000 soldiers, both Union and Confederate. The three-day battle at Gettysburg alone saw nearly as many casualties as the United States lost during the entire Vietnam War. Such carnage is unimaginable.

As historian James McPherson once said, "The Civil War created 200,000 widows and half a million or more fatherless children. It left large parts of the South a smoking ruin and destroyed more than half of Southern wealth."

The War Between the States still haunts us, and rightly so. The enormous cost of that war alone should make us pause to ask serious questions about the current state of division and incivility in this country. We ignore history at our own peril.

Thank heaven for fireworks fails

June 2016

Fireworks call my name. Maybe it's the colors or the sounds or the unexpected. There you are, seated on a blanket under the stars on a midsummer evening, waiting for the sky to light up and noises to rattle your bones, delivering unexpected thrills—even when you're expecting them. On July 4th, you're a kid again.

The names alone are enough to excite: Frisky Starburst, Paparazzi, Calling All Cars, Night Life, Tropical Fantasy, Desert Blitz, Apocalypse Now.

Among my favorites are Magic Crystals, those colorful little pyramids that spin and buzz, then blast off like a toy space shuttle. They soar to tree height and higher.

Once while driving home from Tennessee after July 4th, roadside vendors lured me in with half-off merchandise. A fire sale, in other words.

I spotted the tractor trailer "store" as the North Carolina state line loomed ahead. It was either buy now or say goodbye till next year.

I turned in. The trailer was chocked full of unexploded merchandise—from rockets and M-80s to Crowing Roosters and curling Black Snakes that make charcoal ribbons on the sidewalk.

The men minding the store—I'll call them Dumb and Dumber—pointed out that everything was half off including my prized Magic Crystals. I could hardly contain my excitement. I paused for five seconds before I decided that two boxes were going home with me.

When I left the trailer, something caught my eye—a bonfire blazing not fifteen feet away. Dumb and Dumber were disposing of empty cardboard boxes. If just one spark ventured too close....

I hurried to my car, threw it into gear and spun out of the parking lot faster than a Magic Crystal could clear the rooftop.

Thinking back, I should have warned those men about starting a fire so close to the tinder box. The news coverage would have gone statewide if not national.

But I was too panicked to think twice. Sometimes it's every man and woman for themselves.

It's Halloween in Cleaverville

Introducing my youngest California cousins to trick-or-treating.

October 2017

Halloween used to be a kids' holiday. There were school carnivals with cake walks, and several evenings of trick or treating.

Back then, kids traveled after dark with older ones in charge. They stopped at houses where they knew the people who would play along, trying to guess which costumed character was who. It was the days of *Leave It to Beaver*. Neighbors were engaged with one another. Adults knew most kids by name.

Clever mothers tried to out-do one another, creating costumes for *Wizard of Oz* characters, robots, giant pieces of candy, ghosts, witches and princesses. One girl in my school dressed as a pack of Lucky Strikes. No one became upset or preachy. It was all in good fun.

Halloween parties at school or church or scout troops involved bobbing for apples and playing ring toss.

Then, as adults discovered Halloween in the 1970s and 1980s, the holiday descended into creepiness with graphic yard displays, risqué costumes and adults-only parties. Claims of tainted treats prompted hospitals to offer free x-rays of candy. Parents refused to let their children trick-or-treat without supervision.

Two years ago, Cousin Gary from Los Angeles came to visit in late October. His kids, aged five and six had never gone trick or treating. I suggested the Trunk or Treat at First Presbyterian in Newton, then check out the candy scene in the surrounding neighborhood.

The hour we spent at the church and later on Sixth and Seventh Streets was like a step back in time. Most houses had jack-o-lanterns and porches lit, some of the residents dressed up to hand out the treats and the kids squealed with delight.

"We can't do this at home," Gary told us. And it's true, most urban places are too dangerous to consider allowing kids to trick or treat door to door. Even though my cousin lives a half hour from Main Street, USA in Disneyland that's billed as "The Happiest Place on Earth."

It's not that residents of Newton are an easy mark for out-of-towners or that they are obligated to gift candy to the whole town. Or maybe I am saying that. The good people of Newton are creating a precious memory for tomorrow's adults, which is no small thing.

Those golden-lit streets the last evening of October are a gift that is all too rare these days. In the end, it's not about the candy; it's about a welcome mat for all who wish to participate whether we live here or not. Newton isn't a utopian Cleaverville, but compared to most places, it comes pretty close.

That Halloween night I realized how lucky I am to live in such a friendly town where residents leave the lights on to welcome neighbors for this timeless ritual of childhood. I was proud to show my West Coast relatives how good life can be in our corner of the world.

Gary's kids were so impressed that they begged to come back to Newton. You can bet Tuesday evening, we'll be back at the Presbyterian Church trunk or treat and walking up the block with hundreds of other little people, enjoying time with friends and family in our homegrown version of the happiest place on earth.

Time for the Thanksgiving swap

November 2017

Every Thanksgiving, my husband Tym and I share the holiday meal with friends Charlie and Nancy Lisk of Vale. Thursday will mark the thirty-second time we've shared the turkey.

This year is our turn to host. Picking the menu is never hard; we're all traditionalists when it comes to Thanksgiving dinner. It'll be roast turkey, dressing, mashed potatoes, cranberry sauce, green beans, slaw and dessert. I think Nancy is making an apple something or other, and I'm thinking about a sweet potato cake I saw online, which shows how recipe sharing has changed since the mid-80s.

Unlike others who take shortcuts, we have never considered going to a restaurant or ordering from a deli.

But we usually shake things up with at least one side dish. One year it was Brussels sprouts, another year a Weight Watchers stir fry.

Our swap began when the Lisks invited us to their house for Thanksgiving. The year was 1986, and none of us had family close by. At the time there were four adults and two toddlers around the table and their Irish setter beneath it.

Life was complicated in its own way, and packing up our son's gear, we absently drove off with the leftovers on top of our car. We assume some lucky scavenger enjoyed our turkey leg along the highway.

More than a few times we've invited a "mystery guest" to the meal. This has included friends without family around, family in town for the holiday. Last year the mystery guest was a mutual friend from Charlotte. These days, we consider our former toddlers as "guests," since they're both in their thirties now.

We like the idea of extra guests, and over the years we've entertained a pair of newlyweds, the neighbor boys, a divorcee, a family in the process of moving, a nanny from Australia and my relatives from out of state.

One big advantage of host-swapping is that you only have to clean your house for Thanksgiving every other year.

In 1997, we postponed for illness. In 2002, I received the call right after dinner that my mother had died in Illinois. Three days later, Nancy's mother passed away in New Jersey. Thanksgiving isn't always joyous, but neither is life.

Our kids have grown up without memories of a "family" Thanksgiving, including the bickering that can accompany such gatherings. As they say, you can pick your friends, not your family.

On Thanksgiving 2015 we were back to the original four adults (still married to the same spouses) and Nancy's youngest daughter. This year it will be her oldest. Our former toddler, meanwhile, is 2,500 miles away, with a toddler of his own. Yes, the more things change the more than stay the same. Our son is carrying on the tradition in California this year, inviting friends over for turkey dinner.

Through thirty-two years of change we've enjoyed three constants: roast turkey, cranberries and stuffing—comfort food for misshapen lives.

When what you thought was there, isn't

June 2017

Nostalgia is a tricky business. Sometimes what you long for can never be recaptured.

That ugly truth came crashing down on me a few weeks ago when Cousin Renee called. "It's not there," she said. It, I knew, was her metal dollhouse, a three-story one last seen in the 1950s. It resembled the Anderson home on *Father Knows Best*.

I know this sounds shallow, but I've coveted that toy since my parents gave it to my cousin back in1957. I was three; she was six, and I remember her big "surprise."

That Christmas Eve I learned the meaning of deep-seated envy. How could my parents—my parents—give her such a deluxe house when my sibling and I had only a common two-story?

Back then metal dollhouses were classic colonials with lithographed shake shingles and cross-hatched windows. The interior featured painted curtains, pictures and rugs, but those prefabricated accessories bothered me, even as a kid, because they restricted how rooms could be arranged. Even as a child I was vexed by placing furniture in front of shelves painted on the wall.

Vintage two-story models are sold on eBay now, but that special three-story model eludes me. A picture is all I want, just one more walk through the funhouse of childhood.

"It's not there, Cuz," Renee said. The disappointment in my voice took me back to the years of wanting to just see the house. "It's up in the attic," my aunt said, which meant there was a chance you might see it in your lifetime, maybe not.

My aunt was a keeper. Very little was thrown out or given away. She rarely went through anything though; she didn't want to stir up dust or memories. Over the years I would ask Aunt O about the dollhouse.

"Up in the attic" meant it was still there, though no one dared to place a ladder to scramble into the dusty garret—not in subzero winters or broiling summers. No one had been up there in decades, so the attic kept its secrets undisturbed.

When Aunt O passed in 2013, Cousin Renee was charged with the task of sorting through the contents of her mother's house, and it has taken a while. Recently she hired a man to clean the attic. He filled the double garage full of stuff, cousin reported, even her first bike with training wheels, but no dollhouse.

Have him look again, I wanted to say. I've been wondering about that dollhouse for more than fifty years. How dare it be gone!

In my mind's eye, the dollhouse is a mansion, well-appointed with plastic molded furniture in deep brown and bright yellow and blue, and the plastic doll family to occupy the space. It takes up the entire kitchen table. It has features our dollhouse did not—maybe shutters that open and close, cabinets with hinged doors, flower boxes, staircases, a front door that doesn't pinch your fingers when you open it. It probably has tiny pans on the stove, a dog and a cat, maybe a tan Desoto like my aunt and uncle used to drive. If that had been my dollhouse, it would have been the centerpiece of my life. I would have named the pets and the family—Jim, Margaret, Beey, Bud, and Kathy.

In the museum of my mind, the dollhouse sits on the kitchen table, though the last confirmed sighting was in their basement, a musty, dank cellar. My brother remembered it as being rusty and cobwebby.

When the family moved to town, I want to think that the dollhouse made the move, loaded onto the neighbor's truck and hoisted to the new attic. I want to think it's still hiding there, if a three-foot dollhouse can indeed hide in a narrow garret.

But it's not there.

Hallmarks of Christmas card giving and receiving

December 2017

As I begin this column, I have just finished updating my Christmas card log. Yes, I still send paper Christmas cards and I track the sent and received business in an actual book. It's a small phone directory, actually, which is another disappearing part of our culture. Writing mailing addresses—the house number, street, town, state and zip code—seems so quaint.

I figure each card costs at least $1.10, a relative bargain considering the cost of greeting cards plus forty-nine cents in postage, not counting cards sent overseas.

Every day this time of year, we receive a clutch of cards from distant friends and acquaintances. Other than the glitter cards, I don't find this custom particularly annoying, and I'm something of an expert, having begun my Christmas card routine when I was a college student. I wrote notes to friends and relatives while studying for my final exams. Letters weren't typed back in the 1970s. A typed letter was just too stiff and businesslike for Christmas.

I remember my mother—a compulsive card-sender and note taker—sniffing about impersonal mimeographed letters written in the third person. "Who do they think they are?" she'd mutter.

Who they were, I knew, were busy people (mostly women) who were organized and efficient. Or women who knew that their own handwriting was hopelessly illegible.

My mother, meanwhile, hand wrote each letter in fountain pen—later with a ballpoint. Her chiseled writing style was distinctive, but hard to read. She'd enclose them in a Hallmark card—Gibson or American brands weren't quite up to snuff. If we were going to correspond with these people once a year, she reasoned, we should send the very best.

As I entered adulthood, I knew that I was my mother's daughter. I would send cards, but I wouldn't wait to send them until Christmas Eve, which my mother sometimes did. Handwritten letters were a slow go.

For years after Tym and I married, we sent (rather, I sent), more than one hundred cards each Christmas.

The years since have taken their toll. Our list has shrunk to about sixty-five, as recipients weed themselves out. Some people die, of course.

Others fade away and don't leave a forwarding address. Or if they do, the forwarding period has expired and the person hasn't bothered to tell us where they are, nor will they ever. They're easy cross-outs.

Yes, I enclose typed, photocopied letters (sorry Mom) though I've noticed most no longer write letters. That may be because so many of us keep in touch through social media. Or maybe because people are just too busy or lazy to bother.

The remainders are surprising. We still exchange cards with an artist I met in Vermont twenty years ago. Haven't seen her since. We still exchange cards with a writer I met in West Virginia in 2002. Haven't seen her since either.

There are former neighbors in Florida, A first cousin in Alberta who I haven't seen since I was ten. Maybe someday we'll meet up. I also exchange cards and letters with a third cousin in Wisconsin who was very kind to send me some rare family photos.

I still get a card from my best friend in grade school.

We exchange cards with former co-workers who moved away twenty years ago, my Dad's former secretary, family friends, a slew of college friends from Missouri whose last names begin with "S."

Our poor card directory has experienced some changes in the four short years I've used it. Arrows point to new addresses, some of them in nursing homes or retirement villages. Sticky notes cover up the addresses that have changed twice already, or are simply crossed out forever with the notation, "died in 2016" or "died in 2017" to give them a simple epitaph.

Every year we add recipients. Recent ones include our son's in-laws in New York, my co-editor in Massachusetts, my niece who got married and moved to Albuquerque, a writer I met in graduate school who now teaches in Iowa.

We have mailed cards this year to fifteen states and four foreign countries: England, Australia, the Philippines and Canada. These and the rest of our cards were addressed, signed and sealed by December 1.

My mother would be shocked at my efficiency, but not as much as knowing it costs $1.15 to mail a card abroad. That's as much as she would have spent for an entire box of Hallmark cards in the 1960s.

For sentimental reasons, I've kept our holiday card registers as a mosaic of our life. It's a record that we've cared enough to send a once-a-year correspondence. I don't have the heart to throw them away, these dead-letter address books with their cross-outs tracking some people's moves in and out of houses, marriages and life.

Keep those cards and letters coming (and going)

December 2015

If you're a traditionalist, you know early December is card season. If you have several out-of-towners on your list, you're preparing a holiday letter too.

By cards, I'm not talking emailed Jib Jabs or eCards by Jaquie Lawson. I mean old-fashioned stamp-it and mail-it cards. Determining who to receive your holiday greetings isn't rocket science, but if you're sending more than a few letters to people in your own zip code, you probably aren't getting out enough.

Christmas letters are an institution. The trick is to keep the letter informative and not too boastful while covering the bases. The "bases" consist of job, family, change of address, pets and trips. If you're retired, you mention more trips and volunteer work/hobbies.

I've written a Christmas letter each year since we moved here thirty-six years ago, a nice, tidy record of our life in North Carolina. I want to think that most friends and family enjoy reading our annual update, but creating it takes some care.

Some of the most effective messages are short and sweet. One gentleman we've known for decades is getting up in years. His holiday message came last week: "Just here. Eighty-seven years old. Got your card. Happy Xmas." Even "Christmas" is abbreviated.

I pondered this cryptic message and determined that it works. It's informative and not braggy. He's told us he's alive, not much has changed and he acknowledged we're still alive too, followed with a cheerful greeting. When I'm eighty-seven, I hope I can manage as much.

I know from reading letters and transcribing more than a few (including thirty-four years of my mother's diaries) that we lead lives of quiet desperation. In other words, we're boring.

If you're new to the Christmas letter game, you may need some pointers from One Who Knows, so here goes:

1. Keep it short. Those letters that ramble on front and back in eight-point type are too rambly. Brevity is the soul of wit and restraint the heart of valor.

2. Print the letter on legible paper—not too dark, not too light, not too much frou frou in the margins. Use a legible font. Please, no cute script or Olde

English type that's hard to read. This isn't Olde England.

3. Dial back the braggy stuff. It's great that Sonny just made Phi Beta Kappa and Sissy was awarded a full-ride to Carolina, but we probably don't need their grade point average. And it's great that your Celebrity Cruise isn't called "celebrity" for nothing, but we don't need to know how many times you dined with the Captain and/or Tennille. (If you don't know who Tennille is, you've probably never written a Christmas letter.)

4. Acknowledge that the receiver exists. Toast their good health, happiness and prosperity, Say you look forward to seeing them or hearing from them, even if you don't.

5. Avoid the "organ recital"—those letters that list every cold, bout with the flu, flare-ups of bursitis and psoriasis. Certainly you will want to give an update on serious illness, accident or major surgery, but brevity rules.

6. Announce your new spouse. We were mystified by a friend who signed his card "Rick and Chris." We weren't sure if "Chris" was a domestic partner, an adopted child or a pet. For this reason, I only include our dogs' "signature" for those who know that Jolene and Mr. Furr are canines.

7. Avoid politics.

8. Don't tell us about your new vehicle(s).

9. Pare the list. Once a "tradition" begins, it's hard to stop, even if the recipients are still alive. Try anyway.

10. Include a return address. This is essential if you ever want to hear from us again. If you're in a witness protection program, a post office box will do.

All that grit is probably glitter

You know the familiar crunch when you pick up the mail in December. Holiday cards are full of more than good cheer. That's evident when the glitter drifts out when you open the envelopes.

I find few things more annoying than glitter, unless "It's Christmas Time All over the World" a song recorded by Sammy Davis, Jr. with a children's chorus. That song got stuck in my head a few years ago. It took weeks to get rid of the ear worm.

I know that I shouldn't rain on others' holiday songs or cards, but I can't help it when the stuff floats into every crevice—computer keyboards, carpet, the dog. I appreciate the effort it takes to buy cards, address them and attach stamps. It's the glitter I can do without.

I also know how difficult it is to find Christmas and New Year's cards that are glitterless. I went on a hunt this year for such cards and found that no easier than finding greetings that are not printed in China.

Glitter's evil cousin, Mylar confetti, moved in to stay several years ago—about the time people were sprinkling the stuff into envelopes for party invitations and holiday greetings. Some carried it a step further, decorating dining tables with tiny silhouettes of bells and stars and wreaths.

Makeup companies chimed in, adding glitter to eye shadow. Why anyone would want glitter near their eyes is beyond me, though I'll admit I've caved to glittery nail polish; however, I give myself a pass because the glitter in polish stays put.

Bona fide glitter has been the bane of mothers for years. When I was growing up, my mother fussed at me every Christmas. "Don't get that stuff all over everything," which of course, I did.

Let's face it: glitter is the crowning glory of children's art projects. Who among us hasn't decorated paper angels with glittery wings and halos? You had to use mucilage glue to get the glitter on evenly. Maybe you remember those glass bottles with the pink rubber tops.

In the late 1950s, my preschool self was enchanted with glitter that came in three colors: silver, gold and multicolored. If glitter could have been a Christmas tree back then, it would have been one of those aluminum models with round glass ornaments and a color wheel floodlight.

Yes, glitter is festive and cheerful—a natural for holiday décor and gift wrap. And cards, I suppose, though many of us consider glitter to be as charming as cracker crumbs in the bed or sand on the floor.

Glitter—that seemed to pervade my life as a kid in the 1950s and 1960s—has been around for generations. In Victorian times, it was made of ground glass. Today's product is finely ground plastic that raises environmental issues because it winds up in the oceans.

I've tried to figure out why glitter comes and goes out of fashion, and I think it may have to do with fairy dust. That is, the need to "sugarcoat" troublesome times. Take the Cold War, for example. When I was busy decorating pictures of angels with gold glitter, the news was full of missile silos and bomb shelters and pictures of Nikita Khrushchev pounding a table with his shoe. Back then, we would borrow all the fairy dust we could get.

Maybe the reason glitter has such appeal today is because the world needs sparkle so desperately.

Last summer, I attended a weeklong conference at Hollins University in Virginia. It's an all-female school that celebrates graduation in a big way. All around campus—in mid-June—were green and gold sparkles in the cracks of sidewalks—remnants of intentional glitter spills from weeks ago, which brings me to one afterthought: glitter doesn't go away. Ever.

Static electricity makes the stuff cling to every surface known to humankind. Like the glitter my mother warned me, "Don't get that all over everything."

Glitter is forever.

My Patti Playpal Christmas

With Patty Playpal, before she lost her leg.

December 2015

Recently I came across a black-and-white snapshot of my five-year-old self and Patti Playpal, the life-sized doll Santa left under our Christmas tree.

In the picture I'm standing at the back door in my navy blue coat and hat, the thirty-five-inch doll standing beside me in my outgrown red coat and hat. It's early January. Patti has become my new best friend, the little sister I'd asked for and would never receive.

Patti Playpal, the brainchild of Ideal Toy Company, began a trend of life-sized dolls that wore size three clothing. My Patti came in a red gingham dress, white pinafore, white anklets and black patent leather shoes. Her straight auburn hair wasn't exactly my color, but close enough to be considered family.

1959 was one of the last Christmases I fully believed in Santa Claus—reindeer on the roof, big sack and all. Somehow Santa had squeezed this large doll down our chimney without getting her sooty. I quickly renamed her "Susan," the name I would have given a baby sister.

Patti Susan went with me everywhere. One day she accompanied me to kindergarten to astonish my classmates for show and tell.

Another day I insisted on taking her to my mother's hair appointment. The beauty shop was located in a converted Victorian home. I was assigned to sit in what had been the front parlor and play quietly while my mother had her weekly hairdo.

The process took eons.

One particular afternoon I twisted Patti's leg a little too far. It detached from its socket. I panicked. My mother would have a fit thinking I'd broken my prized doll.

I wound up leaving the body on the sofa and carried the leg into the dining room-turned-beauty shop where my mother sat in a swivel chair with a drape over her shoulders, her head covered in bobby pins. Another lady was having her hair trimmed while a third customer sat under a roaring dryer hood. When the women saw me carrying the large doll leg, they gasped.

Fortunately, the leg was easily reattached by the hair dryer lady, and all was well with the world.

My mother the Keeper of Everything, insisted on keeping Patti's original box, and I, my mother's daughter, still have the doll in her original dress, in that very box.

I unearthed the Patti Playpal the other day. She doesn't look bad for fifty six. Her arms need to be re-strung, her hair could use attention, but for a few minutes this weekend, I was the little girl racing to the Christmas tree to meet the next-best thing to a baby sister.

Why we have this angel and that cat on our tree

The toy cat from Dad's funeral arrangement.

December 2017

For the past 18 years, our Christmas trees have had two ornaments with extra special meaning: a stuffed cat and the angel topper. They honor my parents.

Mom and Dad suffered dementia in their last years. At that stage in life, it's next to impossible to know what to gift a person other than lotion and bed socks. My mother already had a cherished stuffed cat that she named "Jake." I had run out of gift ideas when I came upon a bisque angel with an ivory taffeta gown. She was part of a display in a gift shop. The year was 1996.

My mother's room in her extended care unit needed sprucing up, which the angel did nicely. I don't remember if she said much about the angel, but I'm sure she quickly forgot who had given it to her.

Dad followed into the wilderness of dementia less than two years later. He had been a lifelong cat lover, and here's where the real story begins.

Unusual news travels fast. As I checked out of the local motel the day after Dad's funeral in 1999, the desk clerk asked, "Is it true that your dad was buried with his cat?"

Yes. Less than an hour before Dad's funeral was to begin, my Cousin Gary discovered that Kee Too, my Dad's favorite cat, had died during the night. Gary called my brother, who called the undertaker and yes, there was time to bury the cat with my Dad. So the kitty was brought to the funeral home and was placed inside the casket, beside my father's feet.

My parents had always liked cats. By the time I left for college, they began to collect strays. Dad befriended two tortoise-shell cats, Jim Olson and Mrs. Olson, another named Louie Who Who, and years later, Kee Kee, a cat that commanded a $500 reward when he went missing one winter. Dad's newspaper ad for the missing tabby drew attention from local reporters and eventually the Associated Press that put the story on the wire: "Illinois Man Willing to Pay $500 for Lost Cat."

After weeks and months of false sightings and calls from charlatans trying to claim the reward for any old feline, the real Kee Kee was returned by a boy my father knew. The cat had somehow wandered a few miles to a farmhouse down a busy, snowy highway. Dad paid the promised reward.

I gave this angel to Mom in the nursing home.

After Kee Kee passed, another tabby, "Kee Too" came along to fill the void. As Dad slipped into failing health, Kee Too continued to live at Dad's place of business, staying inside every night except the night before my father's funeral.

When my mother passed in 2002, we followed suit and placed Jake inside her casket. And so, like ancient Egyptians, my parents were laid to rest with cats who had blessed in their coming in and their going out.

Sometimes you remember what *wasn't*

December 2018

I still remember the toy telephone that Santa Claus brought the neighbor kids.

I know. Christmas isn't supposed to be about envy. I should be grateful for the gifts I did receive, but longing is a powerfully fickle thing. You think you want a certain gift until you realize what you really want is what some other kid got.

So maybe I was a spoiled child who didn't deserve gifts with so many starving kids in China, but who among us hasn't envied someone else's gift?

The coveted toy telephone was a country wall model made of tin, with a crank on the right side of the box to signal the operator. I knew such phones; my aunt and uncle had one in their farmhouse. It jangled in spurts all day long— two shorts and a long or three shorts or a long and two shorts— the Morse code signaling who had a call on the party line.

Christmas is all about nostalgia. Many of us try to re-create the I-*still-believe-in-Santa* holiday we knew when we were five or six. This takes me back to our tinsel-covered tree with opaque colored lights. David Seville and the Chipmunks perform "The Christmas Song" on the phonograph where a plastic Santa guides his sleigh through a swatch of cotton batting.

The other night, I messaged Jill, one of the neighbor kids who received the toy phone. She's now a Facebook friend. I thought sure she would remember the phone, but she doesn't, which is a pity. It was one of the first "talking" toys with a recorded voice mechanism that played when you cranked the phone. My brother and I remember the script, all these years later. "Howdy partner. This is Central. What number do you want? I'll ring it for you. Rrrr Rrrr."

The fact that the "operator" said the same thing over and over didn't bother us. The more we heard it, the more we wanted to hear it again. The neighbors' toy phone was great, made all the better because my brother and I didn't have one.

I've looked up the vintage toy on eBay. It was called a Ranch Phone made by Gong Bell Manufacturing Company of Connecticut. The box was illustrated with lithographed cowboys and cowgirls, a stagecoach, a roped steer—perfect for kids who watched *Fury, Zorro,* and *The Roy Rogers Show.*

Over time, my brother and I have discussed the Ranch Phone, not knowing its proper name, but remembering how neat it was.

Eventually I learned to forgive Santa for the Ranch Phone oversight.

Years later, I landed a job at Central Telephone Company in Hickory. And the starving children in China grew up to build manufacturing plants so that most every toy Santa brings to American children these days comes from Shanghai or Beijing or Hangzhou.

Ranch Phones can still be purchased on eBay. I haven't sprung for one yet, but the idea that I can still buy one is a comforting thought.

Every Christmas tree tells a story

A survivor of the Christmas ornament massacre.

December 2016

There's a rule in our house. No Christmas tree before Thanksgiving, preferably not before December 1.

Ours went up on December 6 this year. There was nothing magic about the date; both of us were home and it seemed like a good idea. Unlike years past, we opted for the fake tree we bought three years ago. No muss or fuss about finding a tree to fit the space; all that was decided at a Christmas store in 2013. We adore the smell of Fraser fir, but once you've invested in an artificial, you must justify the expense.

Decorating the tree is my bailiwick because I'm the one who wants to put the tree up in the first place. There was a time when I would solicit help to string actual glass bubble lights on a real tree. That time has faded in favor of simple—and boring—white minis that take a fraction of the time to put in place. That's before adding the garland.

I'm eclectic when it comes to ornaments, though this year I'll admit I leaned toward colored glass and away from Hallmark commemoratives except for one dated 1979.

A relative bought us a nice "Our First Christmas Together" Hallmark ornament back in the day when "together" meant newlywed. A friend bought us a spare which came in handy a few years later. At some time in the early 1980s my husband and I were deconstructing the tree. On New Year's Day most likely. Fragile ornaments were piled everyplace and for some careless reason, we thought it was OK to place several of them in a toy wagon on top of the television set.

The wagon crashed to the floor. The sight of our prized ornaments dying before our eyes was horrible. Among them was the fancier, more beautiful version of "Our First Christmas Together," that succumbed to the ornament massacre.

Over the years, we've gone through ornament phases—braided straw, crocheted snowflakes, needlepoint, Hallmark collectibles, small stuffed toys and porcelain figures inspired by Beatrix Potter. When my mother passed, I inherited some elderly ornaments, including a plastic cottage cheese carton lid with a glued illustration of Rudolph cut from a Christmas card. I made that one as a child.

This year's tree will have samples from our personal history. There will be some small red glass balls that were the only ornaments we had in 1962, when my family was living in a rented house. There are two angels I made in Scouts that have foil wings and glass bell skirts. There is the red wooden stocking with "Merry Christmas Mom and Dad" that our son made for us in 1988. And there is a Harrod's red-coated guard bought from London by a friend in 1997. There is a cuckoo clock ornament bought in Germany. A bisque lobster platter is a nod to my alma mater in Maine.

All of these and others go on our tree along with a "Ten Years Together" ornament that my Mother bought us before Alzheimer's made her forget who we were. A small stuffed cat has rested in the branches of every Christmas tree since 1999. The cat was rescued from one of the bouquets sent to my Dad's funeral that year. Dad had a thing about cats.

We think a Christmas tree should be personal, not contrived by color or style or subject. This year we'll give a nod to the tinseled trees of childhood, proudly wearing a coat of foil icicles. I offer no apologies for my mishmash tree because it tells many stories.

This year is our first as grandparents. I took a bold step by calling our son to see if he might be interested in part of our horde of ornaments. Baby Violet might like to grow up with vintage stuff on her tree.

Yes, he said, they would like some old ornaments, so this weekend I'll search boxes of the extras, picking some to ship to California—pieces of our past to share with the future.

SALMAGUNDI

I found a stray cat; then this happened

September 2016

Angels are preached about on Sunday, I know, but what I encountered this past Wednesday renews my faith in them.

This story begins at the Newton Walmart parking lot. I had stopped by for a few groceries and as I walked to the entrance, I heard a wailing sound—a cat in distress. I looked over along the edge of the lot. A black kitten was crouched near a small bush.

Maybe she'll be gone when I return to my car. Maybe she's just in my imagination, I told myself.

Not fifteen minutes later, I emerged from the store. She was still wailing beside the bush—a meow every five seconds. Obviously, the cat had strayed from home. More likely she was dumped by her owner. One thing was certain: she wouldn't survive long in a busy parking lot.

I had no business taking on a cat. I wanted to ignore her pitiful calls. I wanted someone else to "do something." Instead, I walked over there to see what I could do.

It was a hot afternoon and the cat was black. No wonder she was panting when I approached her. She was half grown, alone, scared. Thin, no doubt hungry and thirsty. She didn't appear hurt. She purred mightily. I picked her up.

Then the impossible happened. A maroon-colored car drove up, and a young man with glasses stuck his head out of the driver's window. "I love cats," he said, his arms outstretched.

"I can't keep her," I said. "It's a nice kitty, but we have dogs and we're going out of town."

"Well," he smiled. "My wife might kill me for bringing another animal home. If we can't keep it, I'll take it to the Humane Society."

And so I handed the kitty to the young man. He smiled. And then the Good Samaritan drove away.

It reminded me of a time fifteen years ago, on the way to work when I came upon a little poodle that had been hit along Settlemyre Bridge Road. The dog was alive and bleeding.

I stopped, got out of my car, dodged drivers who horned at me to get out of their way. I scooped up the dog. He didn't snap or try to bite, which was a small miracle. Then, as I turned toward my car, wondering what I was going to do next, a car pulled to the side of the road. A woman got out and said "I'll take the dog. I'm on the way to the emergency vet clinic in Hickory."

Within seconds, she was on her way. I didn't get her name or her license plate number. I was too stunned. I remember walking into work that morning with blood on my forearms, tears in my eyes for what I'd just seen—something more than a coincidence.

What are the odds that a lady will happen by on her way to the emergency vet clinic? What are the odds a young man will stop in his tracks and take a stray kitten off your hands?

Both instances occurred seconds after I had picked up a distressed animal. Willing hands came to my rescue.

Was it sheer luck or something more? All I know is that both times my simple action was seen by someone else, who then stopped to help.

What we do matters. Others are watching.

Laurel & Hardy moments live on

May 2019

There's humor in the unexpected.

One morning, I opened the refrigerator and the door came off. Bottles of jam, salad dressings, drinks and condiments crashed to the floor.

My bare foot was within inches of being crushed. Luckily, none of the glass broke and my husband was home to help lift the door back to its hinges, hoping that we could keep it closed until it was fixed. That would take a while. It was Easter weekend, of course. A repairman wouldn't be available until Monday.

In the meantime, we had guests coming on Sunday. I hastily made a list of what to take out of the refrigerator that I might need for the next two days that would hopefully fit into the small refrigerator in the garage.

I did the food switcheroo and we then taped the big refrigerator door shut so that no one would forget and open the door again.

Even the repairman later told us that it's rare for the lower hinge to come loose, but it does happen.

I thought of the time when I was home alone in our first house in Mountain View. I was standing in the kitchen when a loud noise and rumble made me think we were having an earthquake. An entire section of our kitchen cabinets came loose from the ceiling. Canned goods were tumbling out the doors and one end of the unit was dangling precariously over the counter.

I quickly called the next-door neighbor to come help. We gingerly emptied everything from the cabinet and propped up one end with pieces of firewood until we could get a handyman to re-mount the cabinet.

The episode taught me to never store heavy canned goods in an overhead cabinet and to be sure all future cabinets were mounted with heavy-duty lag screws.

Mishaps have happened over the years. One evening, after having friends over for dinner, we lingered over dessert with candles burning.

When we finally got up to carry things into the kitchen, my friend glanced through the door and asked, "Do you have a fireplace in your dining room?"

Our candles had burned low enough to ignite their Lucite holders. Flames were scorching the table cloth and our new table. Lucky for us, the incident is nothing more than a story and a reminder to never leave candles unattended. And don't use acrylic candle holders. They're flammable.

But this doesn't top the infamous Laurel and Hardy day in 1985. One afternoon, my husband was on a ladder painting the guttering out back when a friend I'll call Terry came to visit. While my husband was chatting with Terry, the ladder came down in the bushes, paint can and all. It's a wonder he didn't wind up in the emergency room.

Recovering from that mishap, the two of them somehow decided it would be great fun to light one of our old cherry bombs to see if it was still "good." They lit the fuse. The cherry bomb worked all right. After the loud boom, a spark landed in a patch of dead grass. Thankfully, the garden hose was long enough to extinguish the blaze before the back lot went up in smoke.

Later that afternoon, Terry wound up helping a couple of church men mount a window air conditioner for a shut-in. Someone lost his grip, the unit slipped from the window opening and crashed to the ground.

Fortunately, no one was injured which is what makes humor so humorous. It's that thin line between comedy and tragedy that allows things to turn out all right.

About that dated data...

December 2015

Until last week, a plastic box languished in the bottom of my drawer. The box was the size of a bread loaf containing slices of plastic—computer diskettes from the 1990s—my backup system before flash drives and Carbonite. The computer that could read such disks was junked three years ago.

I tossed the floppies out in a fit of New Year's resolutions to clean up and clean out. The information on the diskettes is now gone forever because the machinery to read it isn't available.

It reminded me of a project I did ten years ago. My friend Texie Doolittle and I were asked to transcribe family letters owned by the late Helen Pulliam of Newton. It took us eighteen months off and on to meticulously decipher every jot and tittle. The documents were written in various forms of legibility but working together, we deciphered the story of a family caught up in the American Civil War.

Over those tedious months we learned to identify the writer by the language and shape of the letters, the cadence of their words, the date and location of the writing. We came to know the writers and empathize with their struggles. The letters took us there through original documents.

The letters were later made available to archives in various states, along with a typed script of the contents in case CDs are no longer readable. I know this will happen. CDs will go the way of 78 rpm records, reel-to-reel audiotape, cassettes, floppy disks and diskettes.

I think of today's students who are not learning cursive handwriting. It's too old fashioned and cumbersome for the digital age, educators say.

The inability to read cursive means today's students cannot read original documents before the typewriter and handwritten history. They cannot read grandpa's letters or grandma's recipes, or share the kind of experience Texie and I had, discovering an intimate slice of history written by those who lived it.

Not being able to read old documents forces those who come after to trust earlier translations. It stifles one's ability to research, ponder and interpret. And the implications for an informed, free society are staggering.

Another day, another song

August 2015

My brain is a morning jukebox, thanks to XM radio. As a Sirius subscriber, I listen to more music now that I'm paying for it. It's commercial-free, which means I'm hearing more songs per hour.

So, I wake up each morning with a different song in my head. No, not an earworm, but strains from a once-hit record that I've heard in the past day or two or three.

I took note of what I "heard" recently.: "Every Day with You Girl" by the Classics Four, "Bowling Green" by the Everly Brothers, "My Back Pages" by the Byrds, "Worst That Could Happen" by the Brooklyn Bridge, and the list goes on. By 9 a.m. the music fades off "my mental turntable as the rest of the day kicks in.

The remembered music has been happening for a while now, and it's seldom instrumental. I can hear all of the lyrics that I couldn't sing if my life depended on it.

My mind is doing a double take of songs I've heard in the recent few days and for some reason it will fixate on certain melodies. Usually, a song I haven't heard in a long while.

Music affects us more than we imagine. What is it about my mind that selects a certain song to play back to me?

Almost always I can identify where I heard the tune—either on the radio, in a store, on You Tube…something in the very recent past. This probably has to do with the dream cycle. We go back in time through the night and make our way back to current events by the time we awake. Only these songs of mine can recur even if I get up in the middle of the night.

Thankfully these tunes aren't the earworm that tormented me for weeks during the holiday season of 2013. I could not identify the title or the singer, though I described the song to a music major who worked with me to figure out who sang the blasted song and what the name of it was.

The mystery was solved eighteen months later when XM played the aggravating song, "It's Christmas Time All Over the World" by Sammy Davis Jr. Thank you XM, for letting me know what to never listen to again.

But my mental morning jukebox has become so predictable, I joke with my husband, "What'll it be tomorrow?" The next morning, he mentioned Engelbert Humperdinck.

Two hours later, Humperdinck's "Release Me" comes on the radio, which says something about the power of suggestion.

Summertime is . . .

Pick the hottest day of summer to can green beans.

July 2019

Ah summer! There's something about this overheated time of year that makes us shift gears and relish the season.

For me, summer is:

1. Fresh-squeezed lemonade.

2. Snacks in a picnic cooler.

3. Reading a paperback novel under a beach umbrella.

4. The aroma of coconut oil.

5. Carnival rides and cotton candy.

6. Pulling a cold drink bottle from the vending machine in a neighborhood grocery store with a wooden floor. You know it's wooden because you're barefoot and the storekeeper lets you in anyway because the storekeeper knows your folks and nobody cares about shoes anyhow because it's summertime.

7. Kool-Aid and sugar cookies at Bible School.

8. Picking up treats from the outside window at the Dairy Queen. You can still do this in Hickory, I'm happy to say.

9. The smell of baked vinyl in a vehicle.

10. Water balloon fights and lawn sprinklers.

11. The hum of a window air conditioner.

12. Drapes pulled to keep out the heat.

13. Cutting dress fabric on the kitchen table. Too hot to do anything outside; time to sew.

14. Seersucker, straw hats and white shoes before Labor Day.

15. The snap of a screen door.

16. Smoke from a backyard grill.

17. Watching the gauge of a pressure canner.

18. Packing woodsy stuff for camp.

19. The scent of timothy hay on a drive through the country.

20. The buzz of cicadas at sunset and the silent twinkle of lightning bugs after dark.

21. The clatter of katydids. Record this noise and play it to someone from outside the South; they'll think you live in the Twilight Zone.

22. A drive-in theatre lit up at night, especially the neon sign by the highway. (Kings Mountain, Shelby and Albemarle still have such theaters.)

23. Lying flat on the ground to spot satellites and falling stars.

24. The distant rumble from the speedway.

25. Inviting friends over to shoot off Bottle Rockets, Spinners and Roman Candles.

26. Remembering the July 4 when the whole bag of fireworks ignited at once. (Everyone dove for cover. It was an early night.)

Life in the Sea Captain's House

The real Sea Captain's restaurant in Myrtle Beach.

May 2020

While walking the dogs recently, I spotted an SUV out by the mailbox. I stopped and asked the driver if she needed help.

"No," she said. "We're studying architecture."

The lady, perhaps a homeschool parent, was driving her teen-ager around the neighborhood to study various home styles. Until then, I hadn't considered my street as an art project.

I pointed to my home. "It's a Maine coast cottage."

"It does have that flavor," the woman said. "Do you like living there?"

I told her I did, but I didn't tell her how we agonized over details such as the color of the roof. Who notices roofs unless you're shopping for one?

"The steep pitch is for shedding snow in New England," I told her.

Obviously, we're not in New England and don't have much snow, but I think she got my meaning.

As I continued on my dog walk, the SUV stopped at other houses: a Williamsburg colonial, a split level with half-timbered Tudor features, a mid-century contemporary, a Georgian-inspired two-story—a wide variety of American home styles.

In truth, our house wasn't patterned after anyplace in New England. The real inspiration was the Sea Captain's House restaurant in Myrtle Beach,

Our home, dressed up like the Sea Captain's House.

South Carolina. Maybe you've seen that house-turned-restaurant along Ocean Boulevard. Maybe you've enjoyed meals there. Over time, this Grand Strand landmark has been threatened by development—high-rise hotels and parking lots. Somehow the owners have kept the bulldozer at bay, which is amazing, considering how Myrtle Beach has abandoned any semblance of its history.

My husband and I had dined at the Sea Captain's House over the years. Before we finalized our plans to build in 2007, we visited the popular restaurant to soak in the details. We admired the gray shakes, the shed dormers, the knotty pine paneling. I asked the manager if I could photograph the interior and exterior, and she agreed.

The Sea Captain's House was built as a beach cottage in the 1930s by the Taylor family of High Point. It was turned into a guest house in 1940 and a restaurant right before Hurricane Hazel barreled up the coast in 1954. The structure is classic, homey and obviously durable—qualities my husband and I admired.

In creating our own "beach" cottage, we came to invent a fictional sea captain who "lived" in the house. What would he choose? Certainly a ship weathervane and jelly jar light fixtures. And why not a ship-in-a-bottle on the mantle? Sea glass in a jar?

Anything that didn't fit the nautical theme was cargo from the sea captain's many voyages, we told ourselves. Our "captain" was quite a shopper, but also an unpretentious fellow. He'd lived in our house for years, as our story went, so naturally such an "old" place would have a scuff or two on the floors, chew marks on the woodwork (thanks to the dogs), and scratches on the doors (dogs again). The sea captain liked the lived-in look.

Shortly after we moved in, a visitor asked, "Just how old is this place, anyway?"

It was the ultimate compliment.

In 2017 the Sea Captain's House of Myrtle Beach invited Instagram followers to submit a favorite story about the restaurant.

"Your restaurant inspired our house," I told them. I went on to explain how we'd patterned our house after theirs. I skipped the part about the "sea captain" being a fictional character we'd invented to settle arguments about how to decorate. That sounded too kooky.

But whatever I told them worked. The restaurant posted my anecdote with pictures.

Itchy palms, bottle trees and haint blue

July 2021

I grew up with a superstitious mom muttering sayings about what caused luck to go one way or the other.

Dropped my dish rag, somebody's coming

Nose itches, somebody's coming.

Ears burn, somebody is talking about you.

Itchy palms meant money was on the way. Bubbles in a coffee cup meant the same thing.

A cricket in the house meant good luck. Apparently fake crickets work. My cousin gave me a brass cricket to place on the hearth.

Spilled salt brings bad luck. So does opening an umbrella in the house. And heaven forbid, don't break a mirror. That means seven years of bad luck.

Mom insisted that if she was preparing to leave the house and had to go back inside to fetch something, she would sit down before leaving and use the same door she came in.

A ring around the moon meant bad weather was coming.

The worst omen of all was a bird in the house. That was a sure sign of death. Caged birds didn't count—her mother kept canaries years ago. Rather, wild birds were the ones to watch out for, even if they were only trying to get inside. So, if a sparrow hit the window, we were doomed.

Birds also called up rain. Rain crows, they were called. I'm not sure what this bird looked like, but my mother could tell its song.

Cows lying down in a pasture meant rain.

No leftovers after a meal were a sign of dry weather.

Weather predictions were important in farm country.

After moving to North Carolina many years ago, I added more lore to the list.

The often-quoted good luck charms for New Year's Day—ham hocks, collard greens, cornbread and black-eyed peas.

Hearing thunder in winter means snow within seven days. Fogs in August predict measurable snows during the coming winter. Folks keep track of the fogs with beans or buttons in a jar.

Bottles in a tree capture bad spirits before they get in the house. It's a custom of the Gullah people from Coastal Carolinas and Georgia. I'm one of those Janey-come-latelys who has a bottle tree at the edge of the yard. As the legend goes, blue bottles capture bad spirits and keep them from haunting the property.

Which brings me to Haint Blue. "Haint," a Southern pronunciation of "haunt," also originated with African Americans of the Low Country. Explore Beaufort or Charleston or Savannah, you'll notice older homes with blue shutters, doors, trim and porch ceilings painted various shades of robin's egg blue.

Enslaved people brought with them belief in evil, angry spirits who could not (or would not) leave the physical world. Painting the porch ceiling or shutters of a house a pale blue color would keep the spirits away. Once the evil ones saw blue above and around them, they'd be tricked into thinking they had encountered moving water, which, of course, evil spirits cannot cross.

Haint Blue has been traced to the indigo trade that employed many enslaved people in colonial times. Indigo was, in fact, a cash crop grown on land deemed unsuitable for tobacco and rice production. South Carolina produced the dye almost exclusively for the British market. Things were humming until the Revolutionary War. But once we were no longer part of the British Empire, the market dried up.

With such colorful history, I remembered the virtues of Haint Blue when we built our home in 2008. Our builder had never heard of Haint Blue before and was intrigued by my claim that painting a porch ceiling could be the difference between a happy house and one plagued by bad juju.

Our chosen shade of Haint Blue was Sherwin Williams' "Ocean Grove." Bright, bold and noticeable, it would deflect any and all haints.

For good measure, Ocean Grove was applied to a deacon's bench near the garage door and a rocking chair on the porch. Since then, I've added Haint Blue accents throughout the house: a painted basket, framed art, cushions, table cloths, flower pots and more.

These days Haint Blue porch ceilings have been popularized by designers and homeowners who wish to capture a traditional Southern look. Haint Blue samples are all over Pinterest and the Gullah tradition has been featured in *US News*, *Today*, *Southern Living* and elsewhere. Some retailers such as Home Depot have offered Haint Blue paint palates.

I'm sure Mom would approve.

Overdue book grabs national attention

April 2021

Have you heard about the woman who kept a library book for sixty-three years?

I read this bizarre story, thanks to email from Candace, a friend who saw it in *The New York Times*. The recent article told of seventy-four-year-old Betty Diamond who kept an overdue library book in her possession—carrying it with her wherever she moved—for more than six decades.

I rank this story up there with notes in a bottle that cross the world's oceans, and Christmas cards from World War II that have just been delivered by the U.S. Postal Service. Such stories are irresistible.

The book fine was two cents a day in 1957, when Diamond was a ten-year-old library patron in Queens, New York. At that rate, she would have owed $459 as of 2021. But at a certain point, fines stop and the library assumes the book is lost and charges a replacement fee.

Diamond opted to make a $500 donation to the Queens Public Library Foundation in lieu of replacing the book, *Ol' Paul, the Mighty Logger, a Paul Bunyan Tale* by Glen Rounds. A published playwright, she now lives in Madison, Wisconsin, where she manages a local theatre.

My years working at Catawba County Library System informed me about overdue library materials. Customers liked to take advantage of the amnesty weeks offered in early December. Those with late fees have been able to return materials with fees waived, no questions asked—provided they donate some nonperishable food for local food banks.

It's a pay-it-forward Christmas gift of sorts, and a lot of residents have found this more appealing than making the walk of shame with overdue materials in tow, paying hefty fines.

Not that library staff would shame them; rather, we shame ourselves in such circumstances. Who among us hasn't discovered a missing book or CD slipped beneath a car seat or behind the nightstand? Who hasn't felt a pang of dread having to return these items late?

Most people want to make things right. There's something about the sanctity of books—especially library books—borrowed from the hallowed shelves of the public library, that makes lost materials especially grievous. We learn this rule as children and most of us never forget it.

Diamond's late book doesn't hold the all-time record for lateness. According to *Guinness World Records*, that honor belongs to Robert Walpole of England, who borrowed a book from the Sidney Sussex College in 1668. The book was returned 288 years later. No fine was collected, presumably, because Walpole was long dead.

Catawba County borrowers most often forget to return materials about witchcraft and weird stuff—aliens, ghosts, monsters, crop circles, Easter Island monoliths and the like.

I contacted Lynne, my former boss, to confirm that I was remembering this correctly. She added a few more categories—test books for college entrance exams, and how to learn Spanish and English for non-native speakers. Oh, and Big Foot. Anything about him—or it—is difficult to keep on the shelves.

Betty Diamond's waylaid book was about a man with big feet, not Big Foot. The most puzzling thing to me was why she would willingly allow a compounding library debt to follow her for most of her life.

She borrowed that book during the Eisenhower Administration. Back then books were checked out with cards tucked in paper pockets glued inside the back of each book. When dates were stamped on the card, the patron was required to sign his or her name on the card. All this sounds medieval, I know, but there was something serious about signing your name on the line—like a solemn oath—to return the borrowed item.

Searching a book in the library collection was done with actual cards kept in small wooden drawers of a cabinet at the library.

Remarkably, Blowing Rock Community Library still maintains a manual card catalog—the feature abandoned by Catawba County and most other area libraries in the 1990s.

The Blowing Rock library website boasts their nostalgic aspects. The building, erected in 1949, houses old-time charm a plenty: warm wood paneling, iron chandeliers, stone fireplace and rotary telephone. And, sure enough, the library maintains its multi-drawer manual card catalog. Like the one that would have been used in Queens back in 1957.

I'm still trying to put myself in Diamond's place, and I can't imagine keeping such forbidden fruit as a grossly overdue library book. Most us would have taken care of that business at the get-go. At the very least, we would have snuck up to the book drop under the cover of darkness, dropped the loot and sped away.

I would have done that within five years; ten at the outset. No way I would have carted an overdue book from my parents' home to college, to my first apartment to my second apartment, and house to house for 63 years.

That's why Betty Diamond's story is so intriguing.

MYSTERY MEALS

Pennies from heaven

April 2015

I don't know what it is about pennies, but this past month they've made some unusual appearances.

On a recent trip to Washington, D.C., I discovered a shiny new penny lying near the sink in a public restroom. It struck me as odd as I never see coins in such places, much less brand-new ones. At the time, I had not noticed seeing a 2015 penny before. It was April 8 and the year was barely a quarter spent.

The next day, while getting breakfast at a downtown bakery, I spotted an empty seat near the window and made my way over to it. Right where I was going to sit was another bright shiny 2015 penny. It glowed back at me as if to say, "I dare you to notice me."

I would have dismissed the twin appearances as happenstance until the following day when I was purchasing an item and received my change—a penny. It wasn't brand-spanking new this time, but semi-shiny all the same.

Three new pennies in a row.

The day after I returned home, I stopped by the grocery store in the rain, opened the car door and spotted a shiny copper disc on the wet pavement. Apparently, this penny had been bright and shiny before it was run over.

Some would say the pennies were a figment of the imagination, a mere coincidence, silly good luck.

During the time I was seeing all those pennies, I had just drafted a memoir sequence involving a pet burro I had when I was a young child. Her name was Penny, but I don't think a long-gone animal caused the shiny coins to appear.

Author Debra Marquart wrote an essay about a similar phenomenon in the back of her marvelous memoir, *The Horizontal World: Growing Up Wild in the Middle of Nowhere.* The book won the PEN/USA Creative Nonfiction award and for good reason. Debra, one of North Dakota's gifts to the book world, is a fabulous writer.

In the memoir Debra shared her thoughts on her father's death and how shortly after he passed, dimes began to appear. First, they were found around his easy chair, then in unexpected, unrelated places including the seat in front of her on a double-decker bus in London, England. She saw these as gifts from her father, visitations if you will.

Spiritual people call such phenomena "Godwinks." They believe that such coincidences are nudges from heaven, "attagirls" and "attaboys" from God Himself. This idea was the focus of *When God Winks* by Squire Rushnell, an ABC-TV executive who published the book in 2002.

I don't know what these pennies mean. The writer in me says their appearance was more than chance. The collector in me said to save them, and so they sit at my computer desk as reminders that I am in a connected world that begs me to ponder everyday things I can't explain, such as the song I heard Sunday morning when I turned on the radio: Billie Holiday's "Pennies from Heaven."

Truth can be stranger than truth

April 2017

The other day a friend shared a remarkable coincidence. It seems that a friend of hers had sold a condo in California. The buyer, it turned out, was a half-brother of the seller, who never knew this sibling existed.

How is it possible that a person moves some 2,500 miles and sells property to an unknown relative?

It happens.

I could have told her about my Aunt Marion who shared my joy of family history. About ten years ago, we were working on our Lane ancestors of Colonial Maryland when Marion decided to take a trip to Los Angeles to visit her daughter.

While she was away, I went online and found a man named Fred—a distant cousin—who had done extensive research on our Lanes. I emailed him, and he assured me he would be back in touch when he returned from Australia where he was visiting his daughter.

When Marion returned home, she phoned to tell me, "I met this nice man on my flight from LA," she said. "He sat next to me, but I didn't talk to him until we got off the plane and he realized that I needed a wheelchair." As he pushed Marion down the concourse, they struck up a conversation.

"The man asked me if I was from Maryland and I said, not originally, but my colonial ancestors were," she said.

It turned out that he was the same Fred I'd "met" online a week earlier.

What are the odds? Quite remote, I would think, except these things seem to happen when they involve family ties.

I once met a lady poet at Sewanee Writers Conference in Tennessee. I told her I remembered a poetry reading she gave at the Bread Loaf conference in Vermont five years earlier.

She was startled. How could I remember her poem so distinctly?

"Because it was about Dale Earnhardt, and folks where I come from take Earnhardt very seriously," I said.

"Not so much in Maryland," she said.

I asked her where she lived in Maryland.

"Oh you've never heard of it. A small place near Baltimore."

"Try me," I said.

"OK. I'm from Bel Air—Kingsville actually. My husband is an Episcopal priest there."

"Is the church small and on a corner with steep banks, at a busy intersection, and an old graveyard around it? I think there's a flashing light at the corner."

"Yes, that's right," she said.

"Does your husband wear a beard and wire-rimmed glasses?"

Her eyes bugged out. "Why yes he does!"

"I've met him," I told her.

Her husband had actually shown me and a friend around the graveyard the previous summer. The Kingsville church built in 1817 had replaced an earlier one where my Lane Family had worshiped during the 1740s.

The poet didn't talk to me much after that. She said she didn't do much family research, but I think the truth was she thought I was witchy.

Phantom odors: Spirits or coincidence?

October 2020

Have you ever awakened to the smell of breakfast cooking when nobody is in the kitchen? Or the mysterious scent of a cologne or tobacco smoke when no one else is around?

Phantom odors are a familiar component of the paranormal world. Skeptics, on the other hand, reason that such experiences are explainable coincidences, but these puzzling odors seem linked to a former resident and his or her stroll through life.

I don't claim to have psychic ability, but an experience back in 2006 had me wondering. That spring, family friend Ed, a was in failing health at a local nursing home. One day I took him a small bouquet of roses. Since Ed was legally blind, he couldn't read a card or note, but the floral scent was something he would enjoy.

Not long afterwards, Ed passed away.

A week after his funeral, I remember smelling roses in our living room. The scent probably lasted no more than a minute, but it was so strong, I checked to see if maybe we had a Glade Plugin attached to an electrical outlet. Of course we didn't, but I wish we had; then I could have easily explained the phantom scent.

Instead, I thought of Ed's roses, and figured he had visited me in spirit.

Throughout the ages, unexplained smells from reported experiences have included bread baking, tobacco (cigarettes, cigars and pipe), former fire damage, perfume, deodorant, hair spray, the occasional smell of sewer gas or rotted meat.

To the psychic's line of reasoning, a building can literally absorb these past odors and replay them in short bursts at random times.

Does this make any sense? No, but neither do the phantom smells.

Over the years, I've heard people claim they've smelled odors associated with a long-departed soul, and who am I to say they haven't?

One such instance involved Historic Rosedale, a two-hundred-year-old plantation house in Charlotte. Some reports of spirit activity at the house involve an enslaved woman known as "Cherry." She served as nursemaid for the children of Harriett Davidson Caldwell, the plantation owner's wife, who fell ill and died in 1845. As the story goes, Cherry would sneak smokes of rabbit tobacco, much to the chagrin of Mrs. Caldwell's husband.

The Rosedale website extols Cherry as a much beloved figure in Caldwell family history. "Cherry loved to smoke her pipe but Dr. David Caldwell forbade smoking in the house. Cherry smoked in the girls' bedroom late at night, taking care to hold her pipe when it wasn't in her mouth so that the smoke was carried up the chimney."

A few years ago, a strong smoke odor prompted the staff of Rosedale to call the fire department. When the unit arrived, the rabbit tobacco smell was still apparent to the executive director of Rosedale—a personal friend of mine—and one of the firefighters who happened to be African American.

In this case, the phantom odor lingered for the better part of an hour, though the source was never determined.

How was it that the smoke wasn't detectable to everyone in the house? Was it the power of suggestion or something more mysterious?

Smoke also figures into a story involving my Cousin Renee of Champaign, Illinois. On June 22, 2007, Renee and her husband were awakened by smoke. They raced outside to see their next-door neighbor screaming in front of her burning house on Brett Court.

Renee and other neighbors ran to the woman's door to pound and yell, trying to rouse family members trapped inside. Their efforts were in vain. The neighbor's husband, two children and a family pet perished in the fire.

The horror haunted everyone there that night. Grief counselors were called in. Firefighters who responded to the blaze visited with the neighborhood children to talk about their fears in an effort to help them heal.

Within a few months, the charred house was demolished and a new one built on the empty lot.

A year later, on June 22, the smell of smoke returned to Brett Court. There was no fire, but Renee, her family and some of their neighbors agreed that they had smelled smoke that day. The odor was especially puzzling since a burning wood stove or smoldering leaves are unusual in late June.

The phantom odor in 2008 would have been amazing enough, except that the "smoke" returned to Brett Court on the anniversary of the fire for the next ten years.

When that creepy feeling comes calling

October 2018

One of my first ventures into creepiness was years ago at the Andersonville National Historic Site in Georgia. We stopped for maybe an hour, but an hour was long enough. There's something about a place where thousands have died in a short period that has residual energy. I didn't see or hear anything odd at Andersonville, but I did feel an oppressive sense of foreboding.

Years later, my family stopped in Gettysburg for the full battlefield tour—the museum, the campfire storytelling, hiring a park ranger to drive our car and give a narration. After spending a day in and around Little Round Top, Seminary Ridge and assorted other battle sites, my husband and I agreed that the place was creepy. We felt an overwhelming sadness. We wondered how it must be to live in the shadow of such epic grief. Some 51,000 human casualties in three days turned the sleepy Pennsylvania town into a slaughterhouse. Most every home and church became a hospital or a morgue, so I can only assume that the ghosts were working on us.

That same kind of creepiness gripped two hiker friends on the Appalachian Trail recently. A friend I'll call Kitty and her husband were hiking in Madison County near the Tennessee border when they came upon Shelton Laurel. Venturing along the creek, the two suddenly felt a profound sense of gloom. Though neither was aware of the Shelton Laurel story, both sensed that something horrific had happened there.

Later, they read about the execution of thirteen starving Union sympathizers in 1863, seven months before Gettysburg. A Confederate regiment tortured and shot both men and boys after a dispute sparked by stolen salt, of all things. The incident was the inspiration for the Ron Rash novel and movie, *The World Made Straight*.

Kitty is still walking the trail off and on, but when it's time for her to hike the segment leading past the graves of those massacred at Shelton Laurel, she won't go alone.

Speaking of that Civil War episode reminds me of another encounter with residual energy. In 2009 my husband and I took the John Wilkes Booth Escape Route Tour, a historic twelve-hour excursion from Ford's Theatre in Washington to the site of the Garrett Farm near Port Royal, Virginia, where Booth was killed by a federal officer.

The Escape Route tour included a stop at the Surratt House Museum in Clinton, Maryland, the home of convicted Lincoln conspirators Mary Surratt and son John.

The day we visited was unusually warm for early May. As I stood in the dining room as I listened to our tour guide, I felt an extremely cold presence in front of me— as if a refrigerator door had been left open. No one else seemed to notice a dip in temperature. I told myself it was only my imagination.

A short time later, we walked upstairs to see the attic where the conspirators had hidden a rifle. Our guide mentioned that the attic might be too warm for some of us.

Not me. As soon as I stepped into the attic, the unfinished space felt as cool as a meat locker.

I have no explanation for the cold spots in the Surratt House Museum, except to say Mary Surratt's spirit is apparently restless.

Historians question her guilt. Many regard her trial and execution as a travesty of American justice. That may explain why she still visits some of her visitors.

Haunting season is back

October 2019

Who's had a ghostly experience?

I asked that question recently while speaking to a local church group. Some bravely raised their hands, including myself.

Most every culture shares some concept of the spirit world. Most attribute the experiences to people who have passed on and are somehow able to re-appear to the living. While many consider such apparitions to be figments of the imagination, as many as 45% of Americans believe in ghosts, according to a recent Huffington Post/YouGov poll.

A survey by Realtor.com suggests about 30% are open to living in a haunted house while 42% said they wouldn't consider it. I assume the latter group is among the 45% who believe in ghosts.

Ghosts are apparitions, haunts, phantoms, specters, spooks, reputed to be the soul of a dead person or animal that can appear to the living. Too bad the surveys didn't ask the ghost deniers if they would be willing to spend the night in a cemetery.

I've had some eerie encounters over the years. Haven't we all? Those pops and cracks of the house settling, unexplained cold spots, orbs, sounds that resemble voices, that feeling of being watched when you're alone.

As a college student, I lived one semester in a 240-year-old townhouse. Laundry was done in the basement—usually alone and at night. On more than one occasion, I remember making a quick exit, because I always felt someone was watching me. Long after the semester ended, I learned that the house was indeed haunted.

Over time, I've come to accept that there are some things we cannot explain.

Take Historic Rosedale, for example. It's a 200-old plantation house in North Charlotte that's reputed to be inhabited by ghosts. Several years ago, I was invited to an after-hours tour by the executive director, who's an old friend. While visiting the attic space that had once been used as a classroom, three of us felt an electrical current tingle up and down our backs, much like electric pulses from a TENS system.

If that's not freaky enough, consider the kitchen herbs. Rosedale's original kitchen was an open-hearth affair in the basement. To re-create the historic atmosphere, curators have hung sprigs of dried herbs from the rafters.

On that after-hours tour and every visit since, the herbs have independently swayed, twirled and quivered as they hang suspended from overhead beams. Some turn in opposite directions at the same time. You can't make this stuff up.

Rosedale's ghosts are no secret, by the way. The site hosts haunted history tours and paranormal investigations. More info: https://historicrosedale.org/upcoming-events/

Please scan the code with your Smartphone or other device to visit the Historic Rosedale site.

What's the deal with UFOs?

June 2021

L ike most kids of the Sixties, I grew up musing about Unidentified Flying Objects. I read sci-fi books, watched the night sky for Sputnik and marveled at meteors.

What if a spaceship landed with strange beings like the ones on *The Outer Limits* or *The Day the Earth Stood Still?*

Project Blue Book—the government program, not the TV show—collected information about sightings across the nation. Over the course of twenty years, thousands of incidents were reported and analyzed, but in the end, the Air Force claimed unequivocally that nothing reported to them was extraterrestrial or a threat to our national security. Furthermore, there was no evidence of technology beyond the range of modern scientific knowledge.

But reports of UFOs haven't stopped. In fact, they've become freakier. Some of the bogies have chased US spacecraft. Others have played cat-and-mouse with military aircraft and war ships. One recent incident involved an object matching the speed and bearing of a US destroyer. According to the ship's log, the episode went on for ninety minutes.

One of the most bizarre UFO videos was shot by Navy personnel off the coast of San Diego. Maybe you saw it on the news. The black-and-white video clip was shot in 2019 from the *USS Omaha* showing a sphere flying parallel to the horizon before disappearing into the ocean.

Meanwhile, American submariners have encountered mysterious objects traveling hundreds of knots per hour under water.

That's a new one on me.

As always, most anyone reporting a UFO has faced laughter—even if the person making the report is a seasoned commercial pilot, a sworn law enforcement officer or a respected Sunday School teacher. Such sightings are explained away as hallucinations, weather balloons, trick photography, the work of pranksters or natural phenomena such as swamp gas. Or something from China or the Soviet Union.

My family had a close encounter one evening in 1962. A mysterious light was hovering above our back yard. The culprit: a plastic bag attached to a metal frame with a lit candle inside. Some neighbor's idea of a joke. Luckily it didn't catch our house on fire.

As a pilot, my Dad witnessed unusual phenomena over the years. One was St. Elmo's fire—the rare electrical discharge that can be seen as blue light on the exterior of aircraft. It happens under certain atmospheric conditions.

In the days of tall ships, St. Elmo's fire was seen on yardarms and spars, a forewarning of a lightning strike. Some sailors regarded the odd light as a good omen.

Dad saw at least one UFO in his flying career. It was a cigar-shaped object that hovered above the horizon one fall evening. Colored beams of light could be seen pointed toward the earth When he took off from the remote airport where he had just landed, the object quickly shot out of sight at a speed he could never explain. It was as if the object was observing him and knew when to hurry off.

Most laughed. It was a weather balloon, some said, or swamp gas. The same people who had never flown a plane, much less knew about weather balloons or swamp gas, when there were no swamps to create it.

A couple of years ago, a friend saw a doughnut-shaped object in the night sky. His neighbors called him to look out the window. Several people saw it, and were baffled by its erratic flight path and speed. Photo images from that night closely resemble "flying doughnuts" that have been recorded as far away as China and Ireland and as near as Robeson County, North Carolina.

Closer to home, the late George Fawcett owned a sandwich shop on Main Street Lincolnton, for many years. The walls were decorated with pictures of UFOs, which seemed odd unless you knew that Fawcett was a long-time UFO investigator.

He spent most of his life wondering about the mysterious craft, collecting data and enduring countless jokes. North Carolina chapter of the Mutual UFO Network, a nationwide organization of volunteers to investigate UFO reports. He was MUFON's North Carolina director for eleven years.

Fawcett was written up in the *Los Angeles Times* reporting that of the 1,000 sightings he had investigated, all but twenty-two percent could be explained by natural phenomena, manmade objects or hoaxes. Still, that left 220 as unexplained.

The article, published in 1985, didn't count the additional incidents Fawcett investigated up until his death in 2013. Along the way he wrote books about UFOs and taught UFO courses through Gaston College.

It's a pity that George and many other witnesses won't be around for the next chapter in UFO history: a federal reveal due later this month. Written into the $2.3 trillion COVID relief package of 2020, the law mandates the director of national intelligence and secretary of defense to provide a report to Congress on everything they know about UFOs. I hope the report won't be as redacted as many such documents in the past.

Director of National Intelligence John Ratcliffe has already revealed there are "a lot more sightings" than the public knows about.

Luis Elizondo, former Pentagon intelligence officer who has had access to UFO data kept by the agency, has stated that UFOs do indeed have "transmedium ability." They can freely travel in space, water, and air.

Which brings me back to that weird round object photographed by sailors on the *Omaha*.

It would be stunning to know that humans possess such advanced technology. If they do, let's hope they're on our side.

PARINGS AND PEELINGS

What to take, what to leave

August 2018

California's fire season has been a record-breaker. This latest wildfire, dubbed the Holy Fire, has had me keenly interested. Photos of a suburban neighborhood showed thick smoke billowing from hills overlooking the area where our son and family lived less than two years ago.

Thanks to an arsonist, the streets and buildings we visited near Corona were evacuated as firefighters moved in and aircraft dumped water and fire retardant on homes and lawns. I'm trying to imagine that subdivision with its palm trees and irrigated lawns covered in ash and soot and a pink coating of Phos-Chek.

When the alarm came to move out last week, most people scrambled to collect their pets and valuables. Residents loaded vehicles with their cherished possessions, deciding quickly what to save and what to leave behind.

I remember an exercise in school in the 1960s. Suppose you have a bomb shelter and the alarm has sounded. You can only bring so many things with you. What do you take? What do you leave behind?

Pets of course, are the top of the list, along with jewelry, money, wallets, birth certificates, diplomas, passports—stuff that's a hassle to replace.

It amazed me that news reports said that once a mandatory evacuation order was issued in my son's old neighborhood, residents were not allowed to return to retrieve small animals. Maybe some people were stuck in traffic and couldn't get home when the evacuation order came. I can believe that. Southern California traffic can be bumper-to-bumper at any given hour.

What many forget is that some valuables are automatically secured in a safety deposit boxes. Computer services such as iCloud and Carbonite back up digital records and photos that have been scanned and saved. Most all financial records are available online.

If I had an hour to grab things from our house and had just one vehicle to drive, my husband and I would first round up the dogs, then I'd grab my jewelry box.

My next quandary would be the cabinet full of family files that took forty years to collect, most of which are not scanned. I would grab our wedding album, photo albums and scrapbooks though I'll admit so many bulky items would occupy half the space in the vehicle.

Paintings, signed books, memorabilia, Grandpa's clock, family silverware, Grandma's dishes. Sometimes I think we live in a museum instead of a home.

And what of the family quilts? One of them went from Illinois to a Kansas homestead in 1868, and great-great grandma isn't around to stitch another.

Like my ancestors packing a Conestoga wagon, there's no room for pianos or heavy chests of drawers or desks. Very little furniture will make it out the door.

Going through such a list does separate the valuable from the clutter.

I probably wouldn't pack my wedding gown and veil that occupy boxes as big as half the back seat. I wouldn't bring many clothes, either, which makes me wonder why I have such a full closet in the first place.

Almost none of the attic contents would go with us, the stuff we've saved because we've never gotten around to a thorough weeding. What I'd grab in each room would be minimal because I have only two arms and little time.

All said, I'd probably wind up with an odd mix of stuff to go with my memories—things that wouldn't hold much monetary value, necessarily: the family christening gown, the handwritten cookbook my Dad gave his mother in 1937, the framed photo of my grandmother in 1904.

I wouldn't be like the die-hard homeowners in Corona who chose to stay behind and listen for helicopters with gigantic water buckets and low-flying aircraft spewing fire retardant over roofs and palm fronds. I'm not brave enough to hunker down and stand my ground on dry-as-bones grass, and turn on the sprinkler system, hose down the roof and pray.

As it turned out, Corona appears to have escaped the inferno with about half of the wildfire contained, as of this writing. Residents can return to their homes.

I wonder about my son's former neighbors as they unpack what they whisked away. I wonder if last week's nightmare showed them what to value. It would me.

No joy? Off it goes

February 2018

Recently my pastor posted a photo of his overflowing office bookshelves. "Marie Kondo has no clue."

The person he was referring to is the queen of neat. Kondo's bestselling book is subtitled, "The life-changing magic of tidying-up," and it has been a worldwide best-selling guide for those who want to be better organized.

Kondo's de-junking test sounds simple. Consider any object you own. If it doesn't spark joy, toss it out, re-gift it or donate it to charity, but above all, get it out of your life.

Ideally you should have no more than thirty books, she says. Surely she can't be thinking of pastors or professors or writers. I'm thinking more like thirty books per shelf instead of the entire house.

Kondo hails from Japan, a small, crowded island. That may explain her approach. Still, I know that Kondo's method is appealing. Who among us isn't intrigued by magic or having our life changed? Well, OK, maybe the magic part sounds good.

You will feel a pulse in your body, sometimes big, sometimes not so big, Kondo says. The feeling will be different for each item, but in some way your body will let you know. If you feel nothing, then you have your answer, she says.

OK, I don't get trembly about ink pens swiped from conferences and hotels. Even if they're from exotic places, they become less joyful when they stop writing.

Little hotel soaps don't do much for me, either. I've heard that homeless shelters can use them. Reuse, recycle, repurpose.

A friend in Texas recently made a suggestion for Lent: throw out one thing from your closet for forty days. I messaged back, why not ten per day? That's basically all I really use anyway. Ten pieces of clothing.

Pilled acrylic sweaters don't bring me any more joy than the pair of green slacks that never did fit correctly. The short zipper should have shouted "Don't buy me," but the voice wasn't loud enough. I thought I'd feel great with a dropped-waist pair of slacks. Besides, they were on sale and the fabric had "give." In hindsight (and I do mean hindsight) these green slacks give new meaning to the term "muffin top." Bread loaf would be more like it.

Yes, these slacks have to go.

Speaking of clothes, I have a few on hangers that are sentimental: a commencement robe, some skirts that fit OK last year, a red top I bought in Mexico that looked better there than it ever will in Catawba County.

And there's that pair of white pumps I could wear if I go rogue and break my own fashion rule about white shoes: namely, don't wear them. White shoes make my feet look gigantic. But I won't likely ever wear white dress shoes even if it is after Memorial Day and before Labor Day.

And then there are the loose tops that have oversized necklines that shift around and remind me of Jennifer Beals in *Flashdance*. Flattering for Jennifer, not me.

Unused belts hang and curl like stretched serpents. Are thin belts in or out? I can't remember. What about cotton or linen things that have to be ironed, for heaven's sake?

And oh, the gloves! I could start a dating service with my spare gloves that have been widowed every winter. Pity the spares that can't be paired with the single earrings. Send them on their way. That would make Marie Kondo proud.

My jewelry box contains costume mixed in with the good stuff. Is that allowed? Maybe those should be separated. I should isolate earrings that have languished alone and mate-less for years.

Let's not even look into the pantry. One shelf has more flower vases than a florist shop. And I wind up using mason jars because the mess on the shelf is too cluttered to see what I've got.

The books have multiplied since we moved to a bigger house, proving that stuff fits the space allotted, which brings me back to Marie Kondo and her rule about books. Thirty wouldn't even cover the children's books I have from my own childhood, much less our son's. Nor the signed copies, collections from favorite authors, books I'm keeping in case I ever run out of something to read.

Books are friends. Maybe I can re-gift some... except the ones I want to keep, which is at least 500.

If pastors are exempt from the book rule, so are writers. My shelves shall continue to runneth over and I shall be joyful in the abundance.

Take that, Marie Kondo.

Where have all the lost things gone?

Ma Brittain's egg plate.

July 2019

The chance of losing something is directly proportional to its value. Say you have a $50 bill and the picture of a $50 bill on a piece of junk mail. Which one do you think will get lost?

OK, it wasn't actual money. It was a $25 gift certificate printed from the Blue Cross/Blue Shield website. I printed out the certificate and clipped it to my paper calendar. (Yes, I'm old school; I still use paper) and carried it around with me for two weeks. At some point, I removed the certificate thinking I might lose it, and guess what? I lost it.

The paper vortex in our house always sucks away the good stuff—such as a $25 certificate—into nothingness, and leaves behind every other piece of junk mail, receipt and expired coupon.

I know, it's just twenty-five bucks, but it's the principal of the thing.

I phoned Blue Cross. Nope, once printed from the website, it cannot be reprinted.

I have looked everywhere for this missing gift certificate: the recycle bin, the garbage, the car, my endless stacks of paper near the phone, my stack of scrap paper by the computer, the "catch all" hutch. I do not know where things go in this house; if I were that woman in the Gospel of Luke, I'd still be hunting the lost coin.

I shared this disgruntling news with my friend Candace. She could immediately relate. "I could give you $25 in Cash, and it wouldn't be the same, would it?" she said.

No, I said.

Then she told me her egg plate story. Years ago, she found the piece in an antiques store. She was delighted with the white china and the delicate old-rose design on the front and the bit of human history on the back—a strip of masking tape with "Ma Brittain" written on it.

Candace didn't know who Ma Brittain was, but removing the tape would have ruined part of the plate's provenance. Obviously, the plate had been a family piece for someone named Brittain.

Over time, Candace used the plate for various occasions, but took care to not let the label disappear. Maybe because of an imagined story about Ma Brittain, where she'd used the egg plate, Candace couldn't part with that shred of history.

And then came the move in 2016.

If you haven't moved, you have no idea the kinds of odd goings on that will grab the wheat from your chaff. In this case, it was the Ma Brittain plate. Gone.

After months of searching, Candace gave up, then happened to find an identical egg plate at a tag sale. She was delighted, but not ecstatic. I can relate; someone giving me $25 cash wouldn't be the same as finding the Blue Cross certificate. A substitute is not the same thing as the original that we've longed for and cannot have.

This spring Candace looked one more time into an empty box in her attic and behold, there was "Ma Brittain"!

"Now what do I do? I don't need two egg plates," she said.

I haven't advised Candace what to do, but her choice should be simple: Keep both. If one plate breaks, she'll have a spare, which is the reason we have so much stuff to lose in the first place. We can't pare down and be happy about it. We can't be pared down even by accident.

Seek and you may eventually find

May 2021

An old friend I'll call "Maria" was lamenting the fact that she cannot find her topaz necklace.

It's a beautiful stone, she said. She had looked in every hiding place she and her husband could think of.

I told her not to give up. Maybe the saints can help.

It was a strange suggestion coming from a Protestant, so let me explain. Earlier this year, I discovered that my cache of "good jewelry" was missing. Not cheap costume stuff. There was plenty of that lying around. No, these items involved precious stones and 14 K gold—pieces that I hope to hand down to family members someday.

The last place I'd seen the jewelry was at the dining room table, sorting pieces that had become tangled. In the cache was an opal ring that's too delicate to wear every day, a necklace my father gave me after he went on an overseas trip, my sorority pin, my engagement ring. I'd lost it all.

In early February, when I realized the pieces were missing, I dove into search mode, checking all the obvious places and the non-obvious ones: cabinets, closets, the deep freeze.

I checked my safety deposit box. Nothing.

I searched every purse I own, carefully peering into the zippered compartments. I rifled through the luggage.

The thing about losing treasured possessions is that the loss never really leaves your conscience. It remains like a nagging toothache as you drift off to sleep and as you wake up in the morning. It goads you to mentally scan every nook of the house while you take a shower, vacuum the floor, fold laundry.

I tried to trick myself into thinking maybe I had imagined the whole thing. I would peek inside my jewelry box and there everything would be. This had all been a bad dream like in some cheesy sitcom.

After a few weeks of befuddlement, I started mentioning my frustration to friends and relatives. Sympathy might help. Maybe they could suggest places to look.

They couldn't.

"You'll eventually find it," my cousin said.

Easy for her to say.

Maybe I was getting to be like my aunt when her memory began to slip. She claimed that staff members were breaking into her apartment and stealing things, which was unlikely. She was missing family history files and emails.

If I could sleep on it, that might help, except I'd already slept on it for months. All that did was keep me awake. If all else failed, maybe I could be hypnotized, maybe hire a psychic.

My son said the problem was that I have too many hiding places.

He was absolutely right. How many times had I said "I know where it used to be in the old house"?

Every time after I'd cleaned out closets and reorganized.

I checked my vehicle to make sure my lost pieces weren't left inside the armrest or in the glove box or under the seats. Crazy, I know.

For a while I wondered if I'd placed the things in a box and somehow mistook it for trash. Maybe my treasures were in the Blackburn landfill.

In the world of self-torment, this situation was fast turning into a Rubik's Cube or one of those metal knot puzzles I hated in elementary school. Or me, trying to unknot the fine chain of a necklace with two sewing needles as I was doing last fall, when all this started.

Last Sunday, I decided it was time for intervention, and St Christopher was my guy.

Within minutes of asking for help, I envisioned a book safe. Yes, of course! I'd bought one , but I hadn't seen it lately. I immediately thought of the book shelf near the TV. I rushed to the living room and sure enough, there was my missing jewelry in the hollow book safe, where I'd left it last October.

I shared this story with Maria, who was raised Catholic. She wanted to know if I'd prayed to St. Anthony.

No, to Christopher, I said.

It was then I realized my mistake. St. Christopher is the patron saint of travelers, not lost objects.

My cousin, who predicted that I'd eventually find my jewelry, wondered if I'd asked the saint of lost causes to help.

"No, that's St Jude," I said. I knew that from his association with the research hospital in Memphis. "Turns out St. Anthony is the patron saint of lost things."

"Anthony? Isn't he the one you bury in the yard to sell your house?"

I'd read about that. To sell a house more quickly, a Joseph statue is to be buried upside down, 12 inches deep near the For Sale sign. It's unclear how this custom began, but it's been a thing since about 1990.

I checked Amazon. One can buy St. Joseph Home Sale kits for $4.99, while a tandem kit of Joseph and Jude (extra-challenging properties, obviously) can be had for $7.99. Saints do indeed work together.

So, did St. Christopher team up with St. Anthony?

All I know for sure is that after searching and stewing over it for months, I asked for help and solved my jewelry mystery in minutes.

Call it mind over matter, an interesting coincidence or divine intervention. I'll take it.

I'm a material girl

After much hem hawing, I finally said yes to these red bowls.

February 2018

Recently my friend—I'll call "Mrs. T"—and I went on another of our infamous shopping forays out of town. I'm usually the buyer, she is usually the partner in crime, the bad influence when it comes to gratuitous buying.

This past week, I was tempted to purchase a pair of cherry-red serving bowls. I didn't know that I wanted them until we stopped by a pottery shop, and there they were in their crimson splendor, sitting on a lower shelf with other members of their crimson family: pitchers, vases, plates...all hand-turned, signed and brilliant, lustrous red. Each had a decorative handles. These bowls were begging to go home with me.

"I know what you're going to do," Mrs. T said. "Just get it over with."

I hem-and-hawed. I didn't really need them. They weren't on sale. They weren't even available on a quantity discount. I try to subscribe to Mrs. T's philosophy; own only what gives you joy. I imagined how joyful those red bowls would look amongst Blue Willow dinnerware, or as accent pieces on a side table, notching up the holiday décor when Christmas rolls around.

Two days later we were having lunch near the "red bowl store," still considering the possibility of my owning them.

"I'm not going to be party to this any longer," she said. "Just do it so I won't hear about those blessed bowls forever."

It's not usually the things we do that we regret; it's the things we don't. At that point, I still had the chance to act by returning to the store. Instead, I practiced restraint. We went on our way until I stopped in my tracks. "All right, let's go get them."

She rolled her eyes.

I had violated my own rule: if you see it, and want it, you'd better get it. Those bowls were signed, hand-thrown in an unusual squarish shape. And when we returned, the store was closed for winter hours. They wouldn't re-open for two more days, when we were long gone home.

The episode reminded me of what happened a few years ago at a Hickory consignment shop. Both of us spotted four prints of delicate French pastries. The framed set enchanted us both. We aren't particularly fond of tarts, choux, canelés or petit fours, but the prints spoke to us. Neither of us needed four. Neither of us needed two for that matter, and in the end, we didn't buy any of them. Later, suffering non-buyers' remorse, when we returned, they had been snapped up by another customer.

When an object "speaks" to you and you can afford whatever it is, it's best to not ignore that small voice. Between the two of us, we have regretted not buying various pieces of clothing and household accessories, special note cards, a bear folk mirror, and for her, a house with a brass fox head door knocker. Actually, it was more about the door knocker than the house. "But I could never find a door knocker quite like that vintage one," she said.

Those "buy-me" moments define us as consumers. Mrs. T and I both agree with Madonna. We do live in a material world, and we are material girls.

Over time I have made some rules about shopping. One is if you see it, and you want it, you'd better buy it. Secondly, is if you don't buy something, someone else will, and its corollary, everything worth buying is already bought.

I have no doubt that I would be a bit more joyful I had not broken my own shopping rule, bought those red bowls and shut up about it.

Mrs. T then quoted her favorite Sheryl Crowe lyric. It's not having what you want; it's wanting what you've got.

Will we ever be satisfied? Not so long as there are deals to be had and cool stuff to buy.

Good luck shopping local

February 2017

Life perks along until that you realize the awful truth: time has passed you by.

It happened two weeks ago. Three things on my shopping list could not be had: a glass egg plate, a Christmas card address book and a recipe box. Over the course of ten days, I tried to buy each of these items locally. I went to eight retail outlets—small shops, discounters and three department stores.

Every time I asked for help, salespeople looked as befuddled as I was.

"We used to carry those (recipe boxes)," one clerk said, "but we don't have them now."

My search for a simple glass egg plate was just as difficult. One store had two—a metal version for $50 and an Easter version with a ceramic bunny in the middle. "A glass egg plate? We have a hard time keeping them in stock," the salesperson told me.

That, I suspected, was because they were never stocked in the first place.

The address book proved equally scarce. Rifling through the stationery section at one local store, I noticed several blank notebooks. Apparently, folks are heavily into journaling and poetry but no longer need to write down mailing addresses.

I explained my exasperation to a good friend.

"Addresses are kept on Smartphones now," she said.

I expressed my frustration at how times have changed, not necessarily for the better. There was a time, I told her, when you could go to a nice gift store or card shop and buy all three of these things.

My friend looked at me as if to say, "Bless your heart."

I keep an address book so I'll know where to send birthday and Christmas cards, a quaint exercise I learned from my mother. Never mind that Mom's list was a scribbled jumble on envelopes and scrap paper that had to be deciphered every year. The point was, she wrote them down.

In a fit of organization, I began my card career with my own list recorded in a Hallmark booklet that used to sell for $1 at the checkout counter. Every five years, I graduated to another booklet and then another, each time paying more for the same thing until about 2012 when the booklets disappeared from store shelves along with fill-in-the-blank party invitations, nice ink pens and other remnants of finer living. Why waste time writing things down when one could waste more time and paper jamming a printer with thick card stock? Or simpler yet, send an impersonal email?

I am coming to realize that Christmas and birthday cards are going the way of bridge tallies, but nothing says a touch of class like a hand-written note or a hand-addressed envelope.

As for the recipe file box, I wanted a nice sturdy one made to last, but I know I'm part of a shrinking minority. Apparently metal and wooden boxes are no longer worth space on store shelves. The cutesy ones we grew up with—recipe files with illustrated pots and pans and painted lobsters and cakes and such—are considered novelties that fetch upwards of $15 a pop on eBay. I know because that's where I wound up shopping.

The Christmas card trackers sell for $9.99 these days. They're still being distributed by a specialty outlet in a place called Bean Station, Tennessee. My new glass egg plate is coming from a warehouse in Pendergrass, Georgia. The recipe file is being shipped by an eBayer from an undisclosed place in "the United States."

Like Mom, I resorted to mail-order as she did back in rural Illinois, where the nearest department store was thirty miles away. Instead of thumbing through a five-pound catalog and phoning in an order, I logged on to eBay.

My point isn't to show how shopping local can be frustrating—which it can—but how my holding on to some tangible basics from the past are impossible to buy without technology. I could not have located any of these things without the Internet. Apparently, few save recipes now; it's so easy to Google them. Few keep an address list when it's so easy and cost-free to record the information on their phone, or just skip the mail altogether and send
email greetings.

And why have an egg plate when one can serve them from a plastic deli container?

Society has changed, but some of us still thirst for something personal and elegant. I know I do. It's 2017, but there are pieces of 1957 in me that are worth preserving.

Tax file purge recreates 2012

March 2021

E very spring I conduct a search-and-destroy mission for old tax records. This year, it was 2012. Those papers had been kept for more than the required seven years, so it was time to strike a match.

In the process, I came upon two check registers. For you young folks, a check register is a wallet-sized paper ledger that you record activity in and out of the account. Checks, by the way, are small hand-written documents used to pay debts—an old-school version of the debit card.

As I thumbed through this record of my spending, I saw how some things haven't changed.

I use the same bank. I support the same church and most of the same causes. I still subscribe to *Poets & Writers*, both local newspapers and Netflix, though I no longer receive DVDs in the mail. Programs are streamed now.

I still use the same nail salon. I use the same computer tech guy who makes house calls and the same pet sitter, though I no longer have "Kitty Frank," as noted for veterinary care.

I've had to switch physicians twice, thanks to insurance networks, though it meant circling back to the same practice I had in 2012.

So, was that a change? Maybe not.

I no longer receive direct deposits from the Library System. I retired from there in 2015.

In 2012, I wrote a check for tickets to see author David McCullough in Winston-Salem—back when hundreds could gather in an auditorium without people freaking out. Is McCullough still writing books? I hope so.

I bought my aunt a Dairy Queen gift card for her birthday in 2012. It would be her last. She passed in 2013. She was 98, but still loved her Dairy Queens.

I purchased a handmade birdhouse from "Clifford Wagner" down around Lillington. I was on my way to Topsail Island and spotted a front yard display of intricate birdhouses for sale. This one had several apartments. A friend came over with his posthole digger to install the thing in the back yard. It was fine until the bird apartments filled with nests and were later abandoned like a derelict apartment block.

I wrote a check to Harris Teeter in Lincolnton. By 2012, I was still bemoaning the fact that the Newton store had closed in 2007. And if you ask me, things have never been the same, grocery-wise. You HT fans know what I'm talking about.

In 2012, I bought some sewing supplies at Hancock Fabrics, which no longer exists, anywhere. The company was liquidated in 2016.

Some other places I patronized in 2012 are no more. For instance, Bottom Dollar, the cut-rate supermarket in the Hamrick's strip mall. There were some decent bargains to be had at Bottom Dollar.

And what about Christopher & Bank? That ladies' store left Valley Hills Mall years ago. Last month they closed for good nationwide. COVID apparently did them in. Their core customers were Baby Boomer women, who were staying home last year instead of buying new apparel. I suppose this means my C&B labels are now collector's items.

I see that I purchased something from Sears. Probably for vacuum cleaner bags. They had the best ones to fit a Kenmore.

These days, Sears is on life support. Less than one hundred twenty-five stores remain, compared to the heyday when Sears and its acquired Kmart stores numbered 3,500. I knew that world. Both my husband and his brother retired from what became Sears Holdings.

Believe it or not, Sears and Roebuck was once the biggest retailer in the world. Its headquarters in Chicago was the tallest building in the world. It was the biggest employer in America, and was even the biggest publisher, thanks to its famous catalog. It's flagship station WLS (World's Largest Store) was where millions tuned in during the halcyon days of AM radio. If only Sears had gone online when it killed the catalog.

But I digress.

In 2012 I wrote checks to Belk, which was no surprise. I've shopped Belk for years, but the chain declared bankruptcy in February. Uh oh.

A. C. Moore is another blast from the not-too-distant past. I used to buy yarn there for various knitting projects. Note: used to.

There's no longer a Honey's IGA in Newton either. Honey's was once the go-to place for special order breads from the deli.

Speaking of Newton, I haven't written a check to Abernathy Laurels in over a year. Thanks to COVID, their CORE Fitness facility has been closed to non-residents.

Back in 2012, I was making bank deposits for book sales. I'd just released a collection, *Dining with Robert Redford & Other Stories*, and was giving readings hither and yon.

Oh, and I was earning some interest on my checking account in 2012. Interest, in case you've forgotten, was money credited by the bank for having money on deposit. Interest was more than a few pennies each month.

Which brings me to this point: You don't know how good things are until they're moved out, gone bankrupt, shuttered and discontinued.

ON THE ROAD

What I learned in Kansas

Tableware salvaged from the Arabia.

October 2015

There's nothing like a long road trip to put life in perspective. That's especially true for the Great Plains. I'm not talking flyovers, but driving an SUV across Kansas, feeling every turn and bump in the road.

Tym and I took this trek on our recent Western excursion. Kansas was our first leg of a three-week journey to San Francisco—1,500 miles as the crow flies. The Great Plains were the warm-up.

As we crossed the Kansas River, I imagined hardy, or foolhardy, tenderfoots with visions aplenty as they set out from Westport, Missouri. Once the jumping-off point on trails west, Westport is a Kansas City neighborhood full of restaurants and a bar known as Kelly's Westport Inn. In the 1850s and 60s, the Kelly's building was a store for provisioning wagon trains. No doubt it saw my ancestors, the Hart family, off on their attempt to homestead the Kansas wilds. The year was 1867. Things didn't work out. By 1870 they were safely back home in Illinois.

The *Arabia* Steamboat Museum in Kansas City was an excellent introduction to that period of history. The *Arabia* sank when it hit a snag on the Missouri River in 1856, laden with goods for the frontier. In 1988, a team of researchers excavated the boat from a farmer's field, as the river had changed its course and silted up. Inside the sunken hulk was a Victorian Walmart: tons of new old stock, from glass buttons to bonnets to leather shoes, chinaware, bolts of cloth, door hinges, nails, tools and horse collars were displayed as they might've been had the boat made it west of Quindaro Bend.

Mud is a preservative. I stood gap-mouthed in amazement at jars of pickles that the excavators claimed are still edible, along with every other thing one might buy in 1856.

§

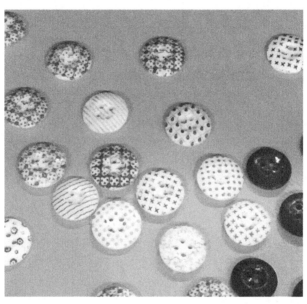

Glass buttons, a tiny fraction of items that sank in the Missouri River in 1856. The merchandise was bound for general stores on the frontier.

We headed west on I-70, and the landscape turned into rolling hills then grasslands, flat and treeless—four hundred miles—an entire day pondering life on the trail from the comfortable front seat of an SUV. We spotted faint remnants of wagon ruts on the Santa Fe Trail near Dodge City, reminding us of how America's story is as amazing as the ghosts left in its wake.

We considered the weeks it would have taken to make it across Kansas Territory at five miles a day, watching for the trail, fording streams and rivers, hoping the livestock didn't go lame or drown or fall ill. Praying that an axle didn't break and the horses stayed calm. Watching for signs of illness, safe water to drink, rationing supplies, on the lookout for hostile Indians, outlaws, foul weather; guarding against sunstroke, insect bites, rattlesnakes, fevers, infections and sprains—girding strength to endure the loneliness and the fear of moving headlong into a dry, dusty unknown.

Many didn't make it. An estimated 20,000 perished on the Oregon Trail alone. We don't hear much about those unfortunate souls, just as my family seldom talked about my great-great grandparents and how their dream of a Kansas homestead evaporated. They made the 400-mile journey from Illinois, but life on the plains proved too much. Within a year or so they pulled up stakes and headed home.

An odd relic handed down from the Harts is in an ox yoke. It rests in our attic as a reminder of something I should know. Was this the one used on the trek to Kansas? Maybe.

What I am sure of is how I admire them for dreaming of life beyond Westport, Missouri and for their determination to make the vision real. What I admire most is their courage to put one foot in front of the other, to keep going long after the dream vanished.

A bridge too far, over the Chesapeake

April 2019

By the time you read this, I will have once again driven over the Chesapeake Bay Bridge.

More than likely, I will have experienced a nightmare about the drive to and from Annapolis. This bridge is nearly 380 feet high—enough to clear the mast of a tall ship with two hundred feet to spare—and more than four miles long.

I'm not alone with my *gephyrophobia* (fear of bridges). Some motorists actually hire a service to drive their cars across. Nervous locals regularly pay $25 each way to hire Bay Bridge Drive-Overs. Yes, even folks who commute to Annapolis every day.

Tolls are $4 eastbound and, assuming you survive that trip, there is no fee westbound. Billed as the ninth scariest bridge in the world, I don't want to even think about the first eight.

For doubters, there are videos of the drive such as this one filmed in 2011. https://www.youtube.com/watch?v=QmbRRG_-D4s Yep, imagine me in that middle lane, vehicles passing, hoping I get across before the rainstorm arrives.

The height of the bridge bothers me, but the flimsy-looking guardrails don't help. They allow an unobstructed look across to the other span or a vertigo-inducing glance down to the choppy ocean surface.

But to be honest, if it weren't for visiting my friend in Delaware, I wouldn't ever drive that nightmarish span. The other options aren't good: the Chesapeake Bay-Bridge Tunnel at Hampton Roads—twenty miles across open water from Hampton Roads to the lower tip of the Delmarva Peninsula. Or, drive to the north shore of the Chesapeake Bay and back down again through Delaware, which takes at least three hours through Baltimore and Wilmington traffic.

Nope, I'll endure the six or seven minutes across the bridge. I've done it several times, but it's never fun. A friend whose son attended the U.S. Naval Academy at Annapolis knew exactly what I was talking about when I mentioned that I had to drive the Bay Bridge alone. Her recommendation: look straight ahead, focus on the vehicle ahead of you (there usually is one) and start counting one thousand one, one thousand two. It helps to listen to music, I've found. In less than seven minutes—or two songs—the ordeal is over. So far that has worked, but I pray there aren't high winds or bad storms during my trip over or back to the Eastern Shore. I've heard there are times drivers can't see land once they're in the middle of this breath-taking span. If you don't already have religion, that might give it to you.

Despite the white knuckles, the drives across the Chesapeake have never been as unnerving as what happened in 2015 in Zion National Park, Utah. Having cleared the lengthy Mount Carmel Tunnel, I was behind the wheel when we emerged from the other end like a pinball out of the chute, rounding a winding, narrow, mountain road with no place to pull off. I started yelling to my husband, "I can't do this!"

He said to keep my eyes on the road. That was the easy part; no way I was going to even glance down that steep canyon. I warmed up the brakes before we reached a pull-off, engaged the emergency brake, scooted across the seat while he got out and walked around the car to take the wheel.

I get my fear of heights honestly. I grew up one hundred miles from St. Louis, home of the legendary Chain of Rocks Bridge that crossed the Mississippi on Route 66. This spindly monstrosity featured a particularly terrifying twenty-four-degree bend halfway across the river. My mother, who was more gephyrophobic than I am, always dreaded that bridge, especially when she spotted a tractor trailer coming toward us at the bend.

The Chain of Rocks was decommissioned years ago and is now closed to all but foot traffic, so if you want to terrify yourself above the Mississippi, go for it.

I'm still coming to terms with the fact that a catwalk exists across the Chesapeake.

Please scan the code above with your Smartphone or other device to visit the YouTube video mentioned in the essay.

This world could use more Motown

This Motown museum is a must-see in Detroit.

October 2016

What do you do on a drizzly October afternoon in Detroit? For my husband Tym and me, it was a trip to the Motown Museum on Grand Avenue. A friend told us not to miss this museum, and she was right.

So much happened in that old American Foursquare at 2648 Grand Avenue. The year was 1959 when Berry Gordy borrowed $800 from his family and turned it into $20 million in seven years. His is one of the most amazing business success stories of the twentieth century.

Gordy, a songwriter, was inspired by the rhythmic sound of machinery at the Ford assembly plant where he had worked. His first business, a record shop, had failed, but he was determined to set up his own music publishing and recording business.

Gordy added a back room to serve as a studio and converted the kitchen into a control room. He came up with a catchy name, "Motown," and offered his co-written song "Money" to a young singer, Barrett Strong. The fledgling record peaked at number two on the rhythm and blues chart. Not a bad start.

Soon Detroit became synonymous with the "Motown sound," an

upbeat form of rhythm and blues featuring various black vocalists.

Motown offered a danceable alternative to the British Invasion started by the Beatles. In 1964, the band was told, "In Detroit, Michigan, they're handing out car stickers saying Stamp out the Beatles," to which Paul McCartney replied, "Yeah well... first of all, we're bringing out a Stamp Out Detroit campaign," thus launching a friendly rivalry with Motown.

Touring Hitsville, our amiable, guide broke into soulful song as she led us from room to room, pointing out the typewriter that Diana Ross used as a Motown secretary, the microphones used by the Temptations and the Four Tops, Stevie Wonder's harmonica, Michael Jackson's sequined glove and an orange vinyl couch that doubled as Marvin Gaye's bed.

Motown singers mostly lived within a few blocks—Smokey Robinson, Martha Reeves, Mary Wells, Diana Ross and Stevie Wonder. Gordy signed them all. Over time he bought eight properties along Grand Avenue to house offices for sound mixing, finance, shipping and public relations—and education.

Young wannabes were taught by Maxine Powell, a renowned modeling and staging coach who taught poise, grooming, etiquette and elocution. Motown was a class act—no disrespect, saggy britches or ragged t-shirts allowed.

Gordy's Hitsville, U.S.A. was Dreamsville for the young musicians who walked through those doors to become stars.

Was it magic? Sort of.

Gordy was a shrewd businessman who believed in turning negatives into positives. To get around the rule that DJs air only one song per label per hour, he created several labels to gain more airtime for his artists on Motown, Tamla, VIP, Gordy, Melody and Soul.

Motown songs focused on emotions that all of us have in common: love, heartache, ambition, loss, shame, pride. Music is the great equalizer, for who can resist tapping their toes to "Do You Love Me," "My Girl" or "Going to a Go Go"?

Gordy and his powerhouse of musicians experienced racial prejudice, but instead of accepting victimhood, they put their energy and talent to work and literally won over the nation and the world. Motown offered more than entertainment. Its music was a great equalizer, appealing to everyone, regardless of age, gender, race and social class.

Years later, Stevie Wonder teamed with Paul McCartney to record "Ebony and Ivory," that made Number 1 for seven weeks in 1982. McCartney paid homage to Motown when he toured Hitsville and noticed that the old Steinway grand was in bad shape. And so the piano that can be heard on so many Motown hits has been refurbished, thanks to McCartney's checkbook.

What goes around does come around. All of us would do well to take some cues from stories told inside that big old house in Detroit.

Sometimes you get lucky

August 2018

You fumble through pockets, bags and check your surroundings and suddenly realize the horror: your brand-new cell phone has vanished.

That happened on a recent trip to Boston. We returned our rental car at Logan Airport, and if you've ever flown in and out of there, you know what a challenge it is. The car rental center has twelve car rental agencies and is reached by shuttle bus that circulates among four terminals at Logan Airport.

So there I was at our gate, fifty minutes until boarding and I was phoneless. There was only one solution: leave my bags with my husband, take the shuttle back to the rental car garage and hope to find the phone and return before our flight left.

After a five-minute shuttle ride, I rushed to the lower level of the Rental Car Center to find myself standing among acres of cars. I hurried over to the Budget area, but nothing looked familiar until I spotted the attendant who'd checked us in less than an hour before.

She shrugged when I told her my dilemma. "Ask the man in the Avis shirt," she said.

Avis? He hadn't been involved. Panicked, I stepped up several rows to the man wearing a bright red shirt. He was busy haggling with a family who spoke only Portuguese. This was going to take a while. My heart raced. I glanced at my watch.

After a minute or two, I told Avis Man my predicament. I described the car, showed him my receipt and realized how many of these cars look alike. Ours was dark blue, almost black. A four-door Camry. Within a couple of minutes, I saw the familiar Massachusetts license plate. I opened the passenger door, scrambled into the front seat and checked the console. Nothing.

Meanwhile, Mr. Avis was checking the back seat. I knew that was a waste of time because the last place I'd seen my phone was in the front console. In the dim light of a parking garage and the black interior of the rental, finding anything is tough.

"I found it!" he said.

I couldn't believe it. My phone had somehow slid its way off the front console to the back floor. I thanked Mr. Avis profusely and rushed back to the shuttle. I made it to our gate with twelve minutes to spare.

The episode reminded me of another time, in 1995. My husband, our nine-year-old son and I spent a week in Europe. We were returning a Hertz rental car at the airport in Frankfurt, Germany. Somehow my wallet was dropped from my handbag. Again, we were in a dimly lit parking garage and dealing with the black interior of a station wagon.

Our flight was ready to board when I realized that my wallet was missing along with my credit cards, driver's license and cash.

The flight to Boston (yes, Logan Airport again) was the longest six hours of the entire trip. In that time, the car would have been cleaned and possibly rented to another customer who could have driven off to parts unknown.

In Boston, I reported the loss to Hertz and canceled my credit cards. At home, I used my passport to get a new driver's license and held my breath that no one had used my credit for a joy ride through Europe.

About two weeks later, a package arrived in the mail from the Hertz office in Frankfurt. It contained my wallet with all of my credit cards, every bit of my cash and my driver's license.

Also in the package was a British passport with a letter enclosed.

"Dear Mrs. Wilson," it read. They had found "your husband's passport." Incredibly, the same station wagon had been rented to a Scottish Mr. Wilson and his nine-year-old son who were traveling on the same passport. They were from Ayrshire, Scotland.

I don't know how these British subjects were able to return home without their passport, but I remember writing a letter of explanation and shipping it to the British Consulate in Atlanta.

Maybe that passport was reunited with its owners; I have no idea.

Over the years I've pondered the odds of the same car in Frankfurt being rented to two families named Wilson who were each traveling with a young son that July. And I've pondered the likelihood that both families would lose something important in that car.

I think the odds are pretty slim.

Our worn path home

Illinois farm country, flat as a skillet.

August 2019

Many of you know that Tym and I aren't from around here. We grew up in Shelbyville, a farming community halfway up the trunk of Illinois.

Leaving family behind in your home state means the burden of visiting has always been on us—the leavers, not the leavees.

Let's say that we've come to know the road well. Take I-40 West to Nashville and 24 North to Paducah, and 57 north. Just as well as we know I-40 to Knoxville I-75 to Lexington, 64 West through Louisville and across the toe of Indiana to Mt. Vernon, Illinois, and turn north up I-57. Both routes are about the same distance, give or take twenty miles.

The trip is a full day, counting breaks for gas and meals. We do it in twelve hours—the time it takes to drive seven hundred miles without getting a speeding ticket.

Over forty years, we've driven one of the routes at least sixty times both ways. Like long-distance truck drivers, we threw the roadmap away years ago, and drive by instinct, the highway sprinkled with memories of stops we've made, such as the Midway, Kentucky exit where our toddler locked himself inside the car with both sets of keys and laughed at us until a

269

kindly man with a camper loaned us his coat hanger to slip inside the driver's window.

A lot of the memories relate to food. There was the great discovery of Log Inn a few years ago, the "oldest restaurant in Indiana." It's now a popular eatery that's been featured on the Food Network. It's located inside an 1825 tavern that was a stagecoach stop as well as a stop on the Underground Railroad. Abraham Lincoln dined there. Seriously.

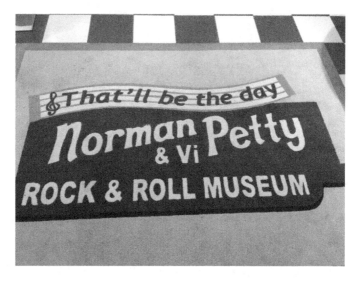

The Norman and Vi Petty Museum of Clovis, NM, honors Buddy Holly and other early rockers recorded by the Pettys.

We know to buy gas before we cross the Mason-Dixon Line, where state taxes rise with the latitude. We've learned that Cracker Barrel is our best choice other than fast food, at least until we cross the Ohio River, where grits give way to hash browns and iced tea divorces its sugar.

To break the monotony, we've stopped at some attractions over the years: Churchill Downs, Mary Todd Lincoln's home and the Kentucky Horse Park in Lexington, the Jim Beam distillery, Mammoth Cave, Nashville, Andrew Jackson's Hermitage and the birthplace of Kentucky Fried Chicken in Corbin. We've passed by Clarksville–the place the Monkees sang about during the Vietnam Era. And we've seen the Corvette Museum that fell into a sinkhole at Bowling Green.

We've toured the National Quilt Museum in Paducah and sped past the federal penitentiary in Marion, Illinois, built to replace California's famous prison on Alcatraz. We consider Marion's inmates: John Gotti and Pete Rose and, more recently, members of Al-Qaeda.

This year we were dismayed to see that the best pie place in Illinois has shut down: Austin's Broasted Chicken Restaurant in Dix, Illinois, the first exit north of Mt. Vernon. For forty years, it was our prime stop for homemade coconut meringue pie.

Every time we return to our childhood home, we notice how distances have changed. Familiar landmarks—farmhouses, windmills, weather-beaten barns—are thinning out, and in a land of flat, square fields, we see the world we used to know, but can no longer claim.

We can't return to Illinois farm country without speculating what it would be like to renounce our Carolinian citizenship. Could we ever belong in Shelbyville again?

There would always be that gaping hole of our history, the missing years down South. The toasted meringe has been our time here in North Carolina, a place we can never fully explain, even to people who've known us all our lives. You have to experience a place and love it, like that pie at Austin's with the toasted coconut.

Gone to look for America

Old Route 66 skirts I-40, the four-lane that bypassed many small communities, taking traffic and prosperity with it.

October 2017

My husband Tym and I spent most of October driving to California. We're retired, so we have the time. This go-around, we wanted to see a new route on our way to visit family near Reno. In a rented Jeep Compass, the road took us west on I-40, wound us through small towns and cities, past farms and ranches for 4,800 miles. Three weeks later, we were on a plane headed home.

People who've never done this have no idea how large our country is, or how varied. They cannot fully grasp the amazing things the United States has to offer: Nashville, Graceland, the mighty Mississippi River, Hot Springs bath houses, funky Branson theatres, The National Cowboy Museum in Oklahoma City, the Texas Panhandle, the Grand Canyon, a Nevada ghost town. Seeing all of this in sequence unfurls an unforgettable story.

Our trip played a musical theme. We saw the Country Music Hall of Fame and Studio B in Nashville, we toured Graceland and stood in Sun Studio where Elvis recorded "That's All Right," strolled Beale Street, toured the Gibson guitar factory, caught a show in Branson, stopped by the Buddy Holly Center in Lubbock, scouted out the Norm Petty Studio in tiny Clovis,

New Mexico, where Holly, Roy Orbison and Waylon Jennings recorded hit records.

We had a photo op at the Casey Jones home in Jackson, Tennessee; shopped the world's largest Bass Pro Shop inside a giant pyramid overlooking the Mississippi River, took the Peabody Hotel tour complete with the duck parade, saw the Sam Walton Museum in Bentonville, stopped by Baker Creek Heirloom Seed Company with more heirloom seeds for sale than you can imagine, in Mansfield, Missouri. We stopped at Jack Sizemore's RV Museum in Amarillo which was more amazing than the Cadillac Ranch. We visited the Route 66 Museum and complemented it with occasional stretches of the Mother Road. We marveled at huge petrified logs near the Painted Desert, walked the rim of the Meteor Crater (a mile wide) and the Grand Canyon (a mile deep), visited America's oldest house and church in Santa Fe, saw where the first atomic bomb was assembled in Los Alamos, and moseyed through the kitschy Neon Museum at Las Vegas.

The journey became one endless Burma Shave, which we saw an example of on Route 66 east of Kingman, Arizona.

Every trip offers some takeaways. Here are mine:

1. Most cashiers cannot make change.

2. Siri is more reliable than Garmin, unless you're in the mountains. I still want a map.

3. Mile-long freight trains form a steady stream from the port of Long Beach, loaded with double-decker ship containers.

4. Westerners worry more about drought and wildfires than Confederate statues.

5. Expect a steady diet of Mexican food when driving through West Texas, New Mexico, Arizona, Nevada and California.

6. The Oklahoma City National Memorial is a must-see, down to Timothy McVeigh's getaway car with no license tag.

7. Two weeks after the Las Vegas mass shooting, Route 91 Harvest Festival posters still hung around Las Vegas Village. Shooter Stephen Paddock sprayed bullets across a busy intersection. The news media somehow missed that detail.

8. Markers for "Historic Route 66" are too little too late. Most of the towns bypassed by I-40 are emptier than the Mother Road.

9. Thousands of cattle stand unsheltered, in stockyards in all kinds of weather. I shall eat less beef.

10. I can't forget two Arkansas gentlemen. One, an elderly white man, rushed to insist on holding the door for me as I entered a restaurant in Hot Springs. The other, an older black man, greeted me warmly as I passed him in Little Rock, the flashpoint of racial integration in 1957.

11. Having endured a Hot Springs bath, I know how it feels to be a lobster in a cookpot.

12. America's highways are full of trucks pulling ship containers and Baby Boomers pulling campers, looking for America.

We're from 'the good place'

May 2017

Wherever my husband and I went in Scandinavia last month, we were reminded how "American" the world is.

There's the expected Coca-Cola, McDonald's, Kentucky Fried Chicken and movies and popular music. You know that the minute you hear Harry Connick Jr. sing jazz in a Chinese restaurant in Bergen, Norway, which begs the question—what was I doing eating Chinese in Bergen on a blustery, chilly night? We had a choice of Asian with a menu we could not read, a McDonald's with $8 hamburgers, a Mexican taqueria, or walk several blocks in the rain to something more Norwegian.

We chose the Chinese place with English subtitles on the menu. And Harry Connick sang "One Fine Thing" on the music system while we dined on Drunken Noodles and fried rice.

We don't go overseas to hang out with Americans, though what constitutes "American" these days is hard to decipher. We're all over the news, for instance, though Brexit and Frexit were getting a lot of airplay along with the standoff between President Trump and North Korea's Kim Jong-un.

Our strategy to keep quiet and observe didn't mark us as rank American tourists. In fact, we fooled a few on the street who asked us directions in Norwegian or Danish.

It was not surprising, then, that as our train rolled into Copenhagen, a friendly young conductor asked for my ticket in Danish.

I showed him my Eurail pass.

"You are from…?" he said.

"The USA," I said.

"Ah! The good place!"

The comment startled me. The good place? Few places other than Normandy Beach consider the United States to be good these days. Or so I thought.

He asked what state I was from. "North Carolina, in the South," I said.

I knew better than to try to explain how north can be south.

"I have not been to the South. I will have to do that," he said.

He was all smiles. It happened that he had worked in Las Vegas, and had also visited Utah. That was the extent of his American experience, he said, but it had been a good one. He wanted to come back.

Danes are said to be the world's happiest people. With universal health care and free college tuition, subsidized child care, five weeks of vacation, great beer and a cushy retirement to look forward to, they have little to make them anxious. Not even the 56% income tax gets them riled.

With so much happiness, it stands to reason that the amiable conductor was only doing his job—making this visitor believe that Danes are truly joyful.

And, I believe the young man was genuine when he said my country was the good place. He'd been more than a tourist. He had worked here, lived the dream and paid half the income tax he was accustomed to. Maybe it was running with the big dog—321 million in America versus 5.6 million in a country the size of Maryland plus Delaware.

Maybe it was the wide-open spaces or the Vegas neon that impressed him or maybe the limitless sky.

I didn't speak with the conductor long—just a minute or two—but when I heard him call America "the good place," I knew I wouldn't forget it.

The odds can be pretty darned odd

May 2017

Life has its random moments, which brings me to April 10 in Iceland, the island in the North Atlantic. In recent years, Icelandair, WOW, and other carriers have marketed Iceland as a stopover, and thousands of us have taken them up on the chance to see volcanoes, glaciers and such.

Tym and I were on the first leg of a trip to Scandinavia. Nordic countries had been on my bucket list since sixth grade. Something about Scandinavia in my geography text attracted me, and not just the pretty sweaters and quaint fishing villages. Norway seemed like a homey place where I might belong if I were to choose a non-American home other than England or Ireland.

A prime attraction is the spectacular Blue Lagoon, a geyser-fed pool thirty miles outside Reykjavik. The water stays bathwater warm even when it's snowing, which it does a lot in that part of the world. They don't call it "Iceland" for nothing.

Jetlagged but determined, I was at the Blue Lagoon, ready to join the fools in bathing suits heading out into the wind and snow. In the crowded corridor I heard my name called. I turned around to see Phil and Barbara Barringer from Hickory.

"I didn't think you were one of the Scandinavians," Phil said.

So here we were, 3,100 miles from home, as the Arctic tern flies.

I said I couldn't get Tym to take a dip in the Blue Lagoon. He has more sense than to go swimming in such frigid, foul weather.

We three laughed, and after I turned to head on upstairs to the locker room, I pondered how odd it was to see familiar faces in a random meeting. There were hundreds if not thousands of people at the Blue Lagoon that day and I happened to walk into the corridor at the very moment the Barringers walked out of it.

I won't even consider the odds that you could meet anyone from home in Iceland. The population of 330,000—roughly twice the population of Catawba County—is spread over a land mass larger than the state of Virginia.

Meeting someone—anyone—takes work, especially in a crowded place like the Blue Lagoon, but coincidence can be awfully coincidental.

"We read your columns," Barbara said. "I'll bet you're going to write about this."

"You're right; I will," I said.

And then it struck me. Last month's other column was about me becoming a new parent. I first met Barbara in 1985, right before our son was born. She was our Lamaze instructor.

What I took away from Ireland

June 2016

U nless you are a Catawba Indian, your people came from someplace else. For me, someplace else is the United Kingdom and Ireland, where I visited last month. I know that people go there every day, but we hadn't been in many years and neither I nor my husband had ever set foot in Northern Ireland.

Our Irish experience began in Dublin where one of our must-stops was the Jeannie Johnston Tall Ship and Famine Museum. Docked on the River Liffey, the ship is a reproduction of a vessel that carried desperate emigrants escaping starvation and disease in the Great Famine of the 1840s. It was on such a ship that my mother's McGuirk family made their way to New York.

Northern Ireland or "Ulster," the place that used to grab headlines, has settled down since the Good Friday Agreement of 1998. After nearly thirty years of bloodshed the Unionists (Protestants) and Nationalists (Catholics) laid down their weapons.

Belfast is a bustling city, with tour buses, day trips to the Antrim Coast (did this) and a large exhibition to the building of the *Titanic* (did that too). It was once the shipbuilding and linen capital of the world, the latter an industry that occupied my 4th great grandfather John McElroy, a weaver. He brought his Presbyterian self to Philadelphia around 1800, leaving Ireland behind. It was a place my father, a private pilot, had puzzled over for much of his life. He had traveled many places in his seventy-nine years, but never to Ireland.

I have yet to learn exactly where John came from. Some say County Armagh; others County Antrim. As our train sped northward from Dublin to Belfast, crossing the now-invisible boundary between the Republic and the UK-controlled County Armagh, a small airplane soared alongside our train. I have never seen a small private plane anywhere in Europe, much less in Ireland, but for a few minutes on May 24, I thought maybe it was Dad giving me a Godwink as I caught my first glimpse of "home."

Once in Belfast, we noticed how many of the locals look like me— tall white people with fair skin that refuses to tan or even freckle before burning. Being so fair-skinned was the bane of my existence as a teen-ager. Being white-white was never cool. It occurred to me that some passersby might share my DNA. They were as suntan challenged as I am. Maybe we shared ancestors—Viking invaders from the 9th century or displaced Scots who drifted in a bit later.

Celtic music played from stores and bars with familiar bluegrass notes. I kept telling myself that this place with dark brick buildings and gray stone was home though there was nothing hospitable in the chilly, damp wind except for the incredible greens of the landscape—every possible shade from forest to lime and all of the Kellys in between. The greens are fed by daily doses of rain—not the deluging howlers we experience here, but gentle, quiet showers that turn turf into padded carpet and lilac bushes into waving perfume factories. The greens are almost as vibrant as the auburn hair. I took an informal survey one evening in our restaurant—of the eighteen diners in the room, three had those amazing Irish-red locks.

There was no doubt that I was "home" in Belfast; all doubts were erased when we flicked on the TV and saw the documentary, "Klansville, USA" featuring Catawba County's historian, Gary Freeze. I am not making this up. There was Dr. Freeze with his North Carolina accent, explaining the history of the divided society that produced so much violence in the American South. And the BBC commentator was, of course, appalled that such a divided society could exist.

Next day our tour bus took us around Belfast including the notorious walled neighborhoods of Protestants and Catholics and their murals and "peace gates" that remain closed on Sundays. Schools, our guide said, remain ninety percent segregated by religion. America, I learned, doesn't hold the franchise on divisions.

Overall, our trek to Ireland was a pleasant one overshadowed with the notion that I might meet my double at any turn. A woman who resembled my Aunt Loa greeted us at a pub. A lookalike of my Cousin Robert served us our meal. A dead ringer for my Cousin Gary stepped out of a crowd of tourists. That's how it feels to be the first to return to the old sod after more than two centuries. You think you belong, sort of.

Let's crusade for better taste

September 2016

Recently I had the good fortune to tour Israel with a group of Presbyterians. Pastor Whit Malone of First Church, Hickory led a flock of thirty for eight days of sightseeing, Bible referencing and exploring from the Negev Desert to Mount Hermon.

In America we consider something built in 1920 as "old." Over there, ancient sites are layered by as many as twenty-four cultures. Wars and earthquakes leave buildings to fall into decay only to be eventually leveled and rebuilt. For example, Jesus' "layer" in Roman times is roughly one story below street level—relatively new in this ancient world.

In Israel I was amazed at the human tendency to reuse and repurpose over the millennia. Buildings and entire cities rise from compressed layers of their former selves. Most everywhere is evidence of former powers—Assyrians, Babylonians, Greeks, Romans and medieval Crusaders.

Crusaders were Christian zealots who marched off to the Holy Land to rid the territory of Muslims. Over five centuries, from 1095 to the 1500s, they did a major number on the population of the Holy Land, not to mention the landscape. Ancient buildings sprouted European towers, walls and gates.

Consider the South Wall of the Second Temple in Jerusalem. A magnificent Herodian arch was cut in half by a clunky Crusader wall. Go figure.

Got a Holy Site? Build a church over it. It'll be more acceptable to Westerners.

Such buildings do shield what's beneath and they do draw attention to holy sites. But there's something about stained glass, brass and carved marble that distracts me from the lowly cave where Jesus was born. The place has been refashioned into the image the church wants to project, not what was there in 6 BC.

To reach the actual "stable"—or grotto—visitors descend steps of a basilica built during the 6th century. The reputed place of birth is marked with a large silver star attached to a marble slab.

A bit like the 1970s, I thought. I know, that's a weird observation to make during a fantastic tour of the Holy Land, but the Crusader's remolding of the Holy Land has been repeated to this day. Consider the Muslims who recently built homes over ancient Jewish tombs in Jerusalem.

Consider Downtown Hickory. For years I've heard long-timers lament urban renewal of the 1970s—the implosion of Hotel Hickory or the effort it took to demolish a tough old bank building on Union Square.

Tear town and rebuild is an age-old story, and what we lose can never be fully recovered. I thought of this as we visited ancient Capernaum—the fishing village where Jesus preached and St. Peter lived. It was abandoned long before the Crusaders arrived.

But never fear, the renovators eventually showed up. The foundations of Peter's house can be seen today beneath an ultra-modern church on stilts. This architectural abomination arrived in 1990, when church officials decided a 2000-year-old site would be best appreciated beneath a structure straight out of *The Jetsons*.

St. Peter's house with a flying saucer covering it? I rest my case.

Sometimes it's best to put up and shut up

January 2019

We fly more miles than the average couple, so our luck was bound to run out. It did, on December 27 on a flight from Los Angeles to Charlotte.

If you think that jetting across the country is somehow glamorous and fun, let me put that notion to rest.

I'll admit that I wasn't in a good mood that day. Tym and I had recovered from a nasty norovirus while vising our son and family in California. We'd been up at sunup and headed home for three hours already. I'd just paid $15 for a soggy tuna sandwich, a bag of chips and a bottle of water at LAX.

The oversold flight meant there was no room left in the overhead bins, so I had the pleasure of cramming my laptop computer, medicine and breakables into my large purse and gate checking my carry-on duffle bag.

To top it off, I was in the last boarding group along with a couple and their two unruly girls. While we were preparing to board the plane, these kids were rolling on the floor, literally punching one another. As their parents fumbled with their bags, the girls ran ahead, screaming. I silently pitied whoever had to sit next to this family.

I followed them into the front galley, past the first-class seats, through the main cabin and on to row 24. There they were, one row behind us.

Tym was already settled into his aisle seat. He'd been assigned to an earlier boarding group.

"Get ready," I told him. "You have no idea what you're in for."

He shrugged that off until he felt the kids kicking his seatback. By takeoff, he didn't look happy.

"What age are they?" I overheard a woman ask the mother.

"Three and six."

"Oh, how fun!" the woman said.

I rolled my eyes.

"Mom, I 'm scared. We're going to take off. I hate it when we take off," the older girl yelled.

"Madison, we gave you your anxiety medicine. We did, didn't we?" Mom asked the dad.

Dad, dressed in sweats and a hoodie, wasn't sure. They were dealing with different time zones. Maybe he hadn't given her the medication at the right time.

The screaming and yelling continued nonstop for the next five hours—parents yelling between one another, the kids poking and hitting one another, the parents shouting back at them. The kids wanted this or that, or a toy, "A T-O-Y. No not that one, a new one."

To add to their misery, the girls' cellphones weren't charged.

"Sorry, Baby, can't do that. You'll have to wait until we land," their mother replied, all the while swiping her own phone.

"I want my cellphone," the older girl whined.

"It needs charging, sweetie," Mom said.

"But I want it now!"

"I'm hungry," the other one wailed.

Dad, exasperated, became testy with the flight attendant for not having the food-for-purchase they wanted, blaming the wife for not having ordered the correct lunch online.

The parents got into a heated argument. They had aisle seats—the Dad next to the girls who occupied the middle and window seats.

When the yelling grew especially loud, I turned around to give them the stink eye. The kids proceeded to talk back to their parents and be the bratty selves they'd learned to be.

"Mom, McKenzie is hitting me."

"Am not."

"Make her stop."

"Madison, leave your sister alone, baby."

"But she's bothering me."

"McKenzie, honey. Won't you be nice to your sister? Please and thank you."

"She's still bothering me."

"Madison, sweetie, you're beautiful, but put a lid on it."

Any sensible parent would have separated the girls, but Dad didn't want to take charge. He let things accelerate to screaming. Mom had no interest in intervening. She had seated herself safely across the aisle, close enough to bark orders but far enough to leave the heavy lifting to her hapless husband.

Tym said the mother never stopped looking at the phone during the entire flight, but I know that's not exactly true. She put it away three times to take the kids to the bathroom—the only times that the cabin was calm during the five-hour flight.

Flight attendants made their way past the melee, but never once bothered to comment. The lady next to me was saying how "sad" it all was. I wasn't sure if she was sad for the kids or sad for everyone else whose flight had been ruined by this obnoxious drama.

Ninety minutes out of Charlotte, a fellow passenger finally asked the parents to quiet their kids.

The Dad turned around and proceeded to hurl curses at the man, telling him to mind his own business. Then the kids resumed yelling.

In hindsight I could have summoned a flight attendant. Yes, I could have done that, but I didn't. If this hostile father had been confronted by anyone in authority he would have likely started swinging. Things could have easily escalated. The captain could have diverted the flight. All 175 passengers would have been inconvenienced. Instead of five hours, this hellish flight could have lasted seven or more, waiting for authorities to come on board and handcuff the dad.

We might have made the news, but fellow passengers would have no doubt given me the stink eye, blamed me for causing trouble. If I'd keep quiet and let this family provide all the drama, we could all get to Charlotte on time.

What did happen was the captain came on the P.A. and asked everyone to prepare for landing. And then Madison announced, "I think I'm gonna throw up."

"From now on, fly first class,' one friend suggested later.

But she doesn't realize that I follow Passenger Shaming on social media. I already know that rudeness and bad parenting aren't confined to the main cabin.

When room service wears thin

February 2020

Ordering room service isn't necessarily glamorous. Trust me on this.

On Jan. 29 I found myself in the medical clinic of a cruise ship. That day I had no energy and was experiencing chills as we visited sites around Cozumel. I'd asked the bus driver if he could adjust the air conditioning.

That evening I was administered an IV and given the nasal test for flu. Turned out I had a strain not covered by this season's vaccine.

Two hours later, an attendant wearing a face mask pushed me in a wheelchair back to my state room. I'd just been issued a five-day prescription for Tamiflu and instructions to use room service.

It was a good thing that I had my e-reader and crochet hook. For the next day, while coughing and taking flu meds, I watched the continuous loop of TV reports on Brexit, impeachment and the coronavirus. Footage showed travelers confined to a cruise ship off Japan and travelers from China being bussed to an isolation unit in the United Kingdom. The bus driver clearly wore no mask; while the escort seated next to him wore full hazmat gear.

Back on my ship, word spread that a guest in cabin 7031 was contagious. Room service attendants arrived in full mask and gloves. By the next day, some refused to touch the door, much less come inside. One meal was delivered on a tray wrapped in layers of plastic, accompanied by an orange bag labeled "biohazard." Later that same day, a waiter brought breakfast. Inexplicably, he wore no mask or gloves, which may explain how germs can spread.

Illness on a cruise ship is serious business. Cruise lines want healthy ships. The last thing the captain and his staff want is an outbreak of illness.

For the next two days, my cabin mate went about her business, religiously taking her precautionary supply of Tamiflu, as I busied myself with my e-reader, crochet hook and yarn I'd brought along for the sea days. I gazed at boats in the harbor, thinking about excursions I was missing in Honduras and Guatemala. This trip to the Caribbean had been planned for more than a year, and here I was, confined to my quarters, ordering room service: croissants, tea, salads, fettuccine, fries, more salad. Hardly glamorous.

This wasn't the first time that illness spoiled a trip. Last Christmas I was introduced to the dreadful Norovirus in Reno. The absolute worst, though, was back in 1974, holed up in a London hotel room with a bad case of food poisoning. My room service consisted of dry toast, hot tea and Vichy water—at the insistence of the house doctor who was summoned twice to give me injections in my stomach. To this day I don't know what he gave me, but at that point, I couldn't have cared less.

I'm happy to report that the ship medical staff had me back on my feet in two days—until I read my medical bill: $2,900. I caught my breath and felt even sorrier for myself. And then I remembered those poor travelers quarantined off the coast of Japan, facing the threat of coronavirus. My two days of room service pale in comparison.

Diary offers glimpse of wagon train life

John Wesley Cooper, after his legendary trek to the gold fields.

July 2020

Every once in a while, a dream comes true.

Last month I opened an email, and there it was: a complete transcription of a diary written by a young man heading west from St. Joseph in 1850. But not just any wagon train; this one involved my great-great grandfather and his brother on the adventure of a lifetime.

I'd heard about the trip from my own grandfather who told of two young brothers heading west on a wagon train from St. Joseph, Missouri. John Wesley Cooper was twenty at the time; his brother William was twenty-two.

The brothers were legendary in my family. The lure of gold, the notion that two young men would travel 2,000 miles by horse and wagon, braving wind, rain, blazing sun, snow, treacherous trails and rushing rivers! Over the years, I'd mused about the possibility of one of them keeping a diary, but I could only dream that such a document actually existed.

Thanks to a chance contact on Ancestry, a kindly genealogist sent me the complete transcription—thirteen pages, single spaced. It had been written by William Cooper using a hard-lead pencil. He took care to record the weather, the mileage, and landmarks along the way—the Platte River,

Chimney Rock, Independence Rock, Soda Springs, the Humboldt Sink.

The saga picked up on May 12, 1850, as the wagons were headed toward the Big Blue, a river in Nebraska Territory. The brothers followed the well-traveled Mormon Trail to Salt Lake City in Utah Territory. They sold their wagon on July 3, then packed mules and horses to make the rest of the trek to the gold fields near Placerville, California, on August 8, a month before California became a state.

Their party stayed a week in Salt Lake City, which must have looked heavenly after three weeks on the trail littered with misfortune.

On July 13, they came upon a man who had died of smallpox.

The next day, the horses got sick. "Gave them some tartaric acid and black pepper," William writes. And I am reminded how these men not only had to bring everything they needed with them, and what they didn't have, they could make-do. These men were used to working with animals, and taking care of their horses, which of course they depended upon. After an arduous stretch, they made sure the animals were rested before pressing on.

Every entry mentions water and grass—essentials for horses and mules traveling on dry, desolate trails. Their route followed creeks and rivers that make up the modern alignment of Interstate 80. I have no idea how they traveled a twenty-eight-mile stretch without water or grass.

Near Ft. Laramie, they passed two Sioux villages. "They wanted bread, tobacco, matches, handkerchiefs and fishhooks," William wrote.

Did they make a trade? The diary doesn't say.

Most mornings, the travelers were well on their way by 5 a.m. to avoid the heat. Breakfast was always mentioned, lunch rarely. They burned wood when they could get it, even if it meant fording the Platte to reach a wooded island. Buffalo chips and sagebrush came in handy for campfires, too.

Their diet isn't mentioned except to say they caught fish and shot prairie dogs and rabbits.

To be sure, the journey was rife with danger: runaway horses, sickness, hostile Indians, broken axles, vicious storms in which they had to turn their wagon "sternwise" to keep it from blowing over.

One day alone they shot three yellow rattlesnakes.

Another day, a fellow in their party chased his hat for seven miles. It sounded funny until I figured how essential a hat was for protection from the elements. There were few trading posts on the trail.

There were constant reminders of death: old graves, new graves of travelers who perished along the road. They came upon the grave of a Wisconsin man who had been shot by Indians.

One day near Ft. Laramie—a settlement of sod buildings—a member of the party lost $150, worth about $5,000 in today's money. The cash was never found. I wonder how the man survived such ill fortune out in the middle of nowhere.

Fording swift-moving rivers required a ferry or a raft for the wagons or swimming horses across the current. At one point in Northern Utah, a raft capsized, taking one poor fellow's supplies, clothes and money.

A later entry captures the desperation and grit of anyone able to make the grueling trip across Nevada in the heat of summer:

Tuesday, July 30th. Started at 5 o'clock across the desert. Stopped at 12 o'clock. Built a fire of a wagon box. Fed our horses some grass that we brought along. Ate a lunch. Rested the 1-1/2? hours. Then started and drove till morning. Stopped and cooked our breakfast and fed our horses the last of our grass. Packed up and started. Reached Salmon Trout River. Distance of 45 miles from the Sink. The road is good exc some small sand spots and 10 miles of the last of it is v. sandy. The desert is generally covered with sagebrush. It is covered with sand hills from one 1 to 4 feet high and 10 feet across.

We counted 172 dead horses and mules 50 dead; oxen some teams gave out and left their wagons and pushed for the river. I saw a man driving his mule to water and it was like to give out. He took his knife and cut its throat right in the road and pushed ahead.

We reached the river at 11 o'clock with our horses as good as when we started on the desert. We watered our horses carefully with a little branch in the water. Cooked our dinner and drove 2 miles and camped on the bank of the river. Forded our horse across the river, on to splendid feed and cut grass for the night. There [are] several trading posts here. Flour is 1 1/2 dollars a pound; beef 25 to 40 cts; bacon one dollar.

By the time they reached the Truckee River in California a few days later, they had to brave August snows, no doubt reminding them of other Illinois travelers four years earlier: the ill-fated Donner Party that had perished on the slopes of the Sierra Nevada.

The diary ends on August 8 with mention of great pines 150-200 feet tall. This was surely a place we now call Yosemite.

I've long known the rest of the Coopers' story. The brothers lived in a mining camp along the American River, and later in Sacramento, where John Wesley made well for himself selling groceries and other supplies to the miners.

By 1853, the brothers returned home by sailing from San Francisco to the Isthmus of Panama (there was no canal yet), and then crossing one hundred twenty miles of mangroves and undergrowth rife with yellow fever, malaria and cholera. Once they reached Panama's Caribbean shore, they boarded a revenue cutter for New York. They then took a steam locomotive west to Illinois. Of course William's diary would have made the trip, too.

My Dad told me that John Wesley's vest existed into the 1920s, retaining the imprint of coins that had been sewn into the lining. Even though the vest and its treasure are long gone, I have their story for keeps—all of it, including that rich, dreamed-about middle part.

More lessons from the Oregon Trail

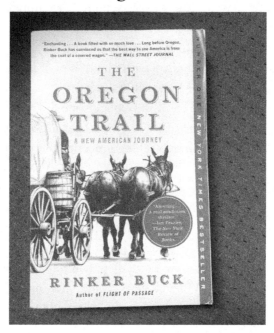

This book explained what William Cooper's diary could not.

August 2020

Recently my friend Candace suggested I read *The Oregon Trail: A New American Journey* by Rinker Buck. It's really good, she said.

She remembered the column I wrote a few weeks ago. It was based on an old diary about my Great-Great Grandfather John Wesley Cooper and his brother William who went west during the Gold Rush. In 1850 it took three months to travel from Will County, Illinois, to the jumping-off town of St. Joseph, Missouri, and on to Placerville, California.

William Cooper's firsthand account included runaway horses, capsized wagons, lost money and constant worry about water and grass for the horses. But his entries were short and cryptic. The day-to-day grind of cooking, cleaning and searching for water and grass along the trail had to be a tedious regimen of drudgery and filth.

The Oregon Trail filled in many of the gaps. It's the 2011 account of Rinker Buck and his brother, Nick—middle-aged adventurers who sought to fulfill a dream of journeying by wagon from St. Joseph, Missouri, to Baker City, Oregon, to make history of their own: be the first to cross the Oregon

Trail in a hundred years. Their adventure would take them on remains of the actual trail as narrow as the wagon itself or as wide as a quarter mile.

The Bucks studied the map and knew something about handling draft animals and making wagon repairs. Their father had been a covered-wagon enthusiast, and they'd taken a few trips by wagon as children in New Jersey and Pennsylvania. Their conveyance this time was a Schuttler wagon—boxy, lighter and more maneuverable than the sweeping Conestogas we see in paintings and movies.

Theirs was a solitary journey, unlike what the Coopers would have experienced when the Oregon Trail was crowded by endless, white-topped wagons of religious zealots and gold seekers.

Overpacking was a common problem for the pioneers. Approaching the Platte River in Nebraska or the steep grades of the Rockies, sections of the trail became a dumping ground of trunks, furniture, dishes, books and casks of supplies. Like pioneers before them, the Bucks lightened their load, tossing out a barbecue grill and other cargo they could live without.

Along the way, the Bucks met ranch families who offered water and corrals for the horses, and hospitality for the men.

Out of cell phone range and confused about which set of ruts to follow, the pair became lost once or twice, a situation that would have been less likely for pioneers traveling in large groups with experienced guides. That's not to say the westward journey was blissful. American pioneers grumbled. Fights broke out. Serious offenders could face frontier justice as his grave was being dug. Within an hour or so, the wagon train would move on.

By 1850 cholera ravaged travelers. It was a disease that had found its way into the port of New Orleans and up the Mississippi in time for the west-bound travelers to carry along the Oregon Trail along with measles, diphtheria, dysentery and typhoid fever.

And then there was hypoxia, "altitude sickness." Lack of oxygen affected Ricker Buck, who wrote of becoming forgetful, a hazard of thin air. He started forgetting things along the trail, like one of their water buckets back at a spring.

The more I read *The Oregon Trail*, the more I came to appreciate how incredibly lucky my ancestors were to make the 2,000-mile journey without a serious illness or accident. Many a traveler died from falling off wagons and being run over by the wheels. Any cut or scrape could cause a deadly infection, but the trail itself posed its own dangers. Other common accidents involved firearms and stampedes. What did a pioneer do if the team got spooked by a herd of buffalo and ran away? Good question.

One of the Bucks' most hair-raising episodes was at South Pass in Wyoming. It involved a steep, narrow passage in which the wheels of their wagon were within a foot of the edge of a deep gorge.

Many sections of the original Oregon Trail are historic sites with visitor centers, parking lots and hiking trails built around former encampments, defunct trading posts and Pony Express stations.

The Oregon Trail is also referred to as the Mormon Trail, a nod to thousands of Latter Day Saints who fled persecution to settle in Utah Territory. Once Salt Lake City was established, the Saints enabled later followers to make the journey, publishing maps, setting up ferries and other businesses to assist travelers. The ferry that my Cooper brothers used to cross the Bear River in Wyoming was undoubtedly a Mormon-run enterprise—one price for Mormons, a higher price for Gentiles. The wait for the ferry would have taken hours. The white-tops were lined up for as far as the eye could see, according to pioneer accounts.

The road west has left its mark on our national history, quite literally, at Independence Rock in Wyoming. The gargantuan granite bears carvings of the thousands who stopped to inscribe their name and hometown. Maybe someplace on that rock is "William and John Wesley Cooper, New Lenox, Illinois."

COVID TAKE-AWAYS

Life in the time of Covid-19

The morel that popped up in my flower bed.

March 2020

Life in 2020 is a lot like the plot of a science fiction movie: Mysterious virus marches across the world that halts in its tracks, the stock market crashes and millions lose their jobs as humanity hunkers down to hide from a dreaded bogeyman. In this case the bogey is way more than the virus. He is fear, paranoia, and the loss of control that all came crashing down on Friday the 13th. Hollywood couldn't devise such a plot.

The week prior, I sensed something was awry. I and a host of others found myself at Walmart, cruising the pharmacy aisles. I stopped a clerk to ask for hand sanitizer and wipes. She gave me an incredulous look until she searched the opened carton on her cart. One 20-ounce bottle left. "It's the last one in the store," she said.

I bought it.

In hindsight (no pun intended) I should have snapped up some toilet paper too.

I never envisioned myself wearing latex gloves while pushing a shopping cart, but germophobia has taken over. Is COVID-19 lurking on the door handle? How about the canned goods? The credit card reader?

I get more anxious seeing gaps on the empty paper goods shelves, the absence of cleaning products, the vacant egg cooler. It's a taste of what life must be in Cuba or Venezuela, where shopping is a game of strategy.

Days tend to run together with no rhythm of a normal week—no eating out Friday night, no shopping on Saturday, no Sunday services. It's no longer necessary to check the calendar because there are no meetings to miss or gatherings to attend.

And then, something delightfully unexpected happens.

This past Saturday I came upon a four-inch morel mushroom in my flower bed. I gasped. Morels, one of the few edible wild mushrooms, are more than rare. I grabbed my phone and took a picture.

That specimen was one of maybe a handful I've ever found, which is a pitiful admission for someone who grew up in morel country.

It took me back to my days as a reporter for the *Shelbyville Daily Union,* that celebrated mushroom culture maintained by bragging rights and closely guarded secrets. The parade of morel mushrooms into the newspaper office was a rite of spring—who could find the biggest morel, the smallest, the most in one patch—all collected from lucky wooded spots known only to the hunter who expected a photo and coverage in the local news section.

Science has never figured out how to raise morels commercially. Whoever does it will be wealthy indeed. A pound of fresh morels fetches as much as $90.

Saturday I put my prized shroom in the refrigerator. On Sunday morning I split the handsome morel in half, dipped it in egg and milk, then a bit of flour; sprinkled it with a bit of salt and pepper and fried it up.

For all the fuss about morel mushrooms, I admit that this one didn't taste like much. To be honest, they never have. Morels are all about longing and deprivation. The rarer the find, the greater the prize.

As humans, we crave something more when we can't get it, and we have a lot of can't-get-its these days.

I didn't go hunting mushrooms; it happened to find me, nested there in the hosta lilies as a reminder from my past, a double dare to stop and savor what's left of the magical and the ordinary.

COVID poses more questions than answers

May 2020

COVID-19 is a novel virus, so by definition it's learn-as-you-go. I get that, but nothing drives me crazier than inconsistency and condescension, and these days we have plenty of both.

A few weeks ago, I ventured out on a grocery run. I wore a mask and wiped down the grocery cart handle. Immediately, I was fussed at for shopping the "wrong way" down the grocery aisle. Then a checkout clerk scolded me for placing items on the belt before the customer ahead of me had moved completely away from the cash register. That was the rule and rules must be followed. Couldn't I read the sign?

That masked, gloved clerk was only doing her job, but it made me feel like I was back in kindergarten.

The very next week at the same store, staff did not wear masks. There was no pausing for a wipe-down at the checkout, no static about moving too close to the next customer.

It was as if the virus was no longer a big deal.

This spring we've grappled with a kind of paranoid confusion. Raleigh officials have exhibited baffling concepts of what is "essential." ABC stores and golf courses are apparently essential; state parks and trails are not. It was fine for delivery people, grocers and health care workers to risk their health to serve the rest of us, but not cool for us nonessentials to walk outside the front door.

Some lockdown warriors say they haven't left the house for X number of weeks. They have supplies delivered. If I were cool, I'd get with that program.

Meanwhile, a few are having too much fun. A woman I know was rattled about her neighbors playing corn hole in their backyard. She threatened to call the cops.

Far-fetched? Not really.

Consider the surfer who was handcuffed for riding the waves off Malibu or the Texas beautician who was jailed for seven days as punishment for opening her salon.

The snitch mindset may be the creepiest takeaway from this pandemic. Home-grown informants make it their business to police their neighbors. They watch; they take notes. Instead of calling the neighbors to talk things over, they immediately contact law enforcement.

When I hear about such overreaction, I think of East Germany, whose secret police thrived on intelligence from citizens willing to spy on fellow citizens. We're far from that, thank heavens, but the stress of lockdown brings out the unsavory urge to rat on the neighbors.

Criminalizing normal behavior such as surfing or cutting hair is like killing ants with a sledgehammer. It seldom goes well, especially for the ants.

Meanwhile, I've tried following "the science" and "the data," and I'm finding the equation unsolvable as variables keep shifting. Should I wear a mask? If so, what kind? Should I ditch the latex gloves? Now I see that hand sanitizer can catch fire in a hot car, maybe I should use gloves after all?

Life has become one giant conundrum. In spite of all we've done to stop the spread of the virus, more than 100,000 have reportedly died in the US from COVID. But that headline is only half of the story.

While we "flattened the curve" to save our hospital capacity, Great Depression II came calling. More than 36 million Americans are currently unemployed. A record number now depend on government assistance. Seeing cars lined up for food is more than troubling, especially when the lines are blocks long.

The stress of joblessness is spawning mental health issues. We've already seen spikes in substance abuse, domestic violence, child abuse and suicide. Each of these stories is a family heartbreak and a community tragedy.

Lockdown orders barred patients from elective medical procedures. A lot of folks delayed joint replacements, cancer screenings, immunizations and checkups. That may be no big deal for many, but bad news for those with undiagnosed illness.

Thanks to coronavirus, some sick people are now too frightened to get medical help for fear of catching the disease. Some have put off seeing a doctor, making their conditions worse. Others have waited until it's too late.

Are these people any less important than those with COVID?

On becoming a maskmatician

COVID turned me into a "maskmatician."

April 2020

I hopped onto the mask-making bandwagon about two weeks ago.
Now, thirty-six masks later, I realize that I will never catch up
with my son's mother-in-law who has made 300. But if more people made
masks—even a few—there wouldn't be such a shortage, especially now that
the CDC recommends that all of us wear cloth face coverings in public.

I'm making cloth masks because it's the right thing to do and
because I have the time, the ability and a lot of fabric scraps. I've given the
finished products to neighbors, family members, friends and a nurse who took
eighteen of them to the hospital.

These homemade masks don't meet N-95 standards, but they are
better than nothing for medical staff who have run out of surgical masks.

I rifled through boxes of scraps from sewing projects. The sight of
them is like visits from old friends: floral chintzes, nursery calicos, white
cotton spangled navy stars. One sample of polished cotton was the border of a
nursery quilt I made back in 1985.

Green striped remnants came from bathroom curtains crafted in 2008.

A scrap with fish swimming across a blue background was what remained of a pillowcase sewn for my son more than twenty-five years ago.

One unique cotton print depicted supplies for a crab boil with printed images of paper towels, graniteware pots, tongs, tins of seasoning, crab mallets and corn on the cob. It was the perfect choice for my friend in Delaware.

A honeybee calico was trimmings from a dress I made my granddaughter last year. I used it for my own mask as a kind of defiance; I'm allergic to bee stings.

My scraps have followed me through several moves and purges. Crafters know the drill. Tote assorted fabrics from place to place because you can't part with cloth that could become something else—maybe a quilt, doll clothes or trim for a future garment. Or face coverings in a pandemic.

A mask starts with an eight-inch by nine-inch piece of cloth, an old t-shirt and interfacing—that material used to stiffen collars and such. Cut a rectangle of cotton fabric and a piece of interfacing and old t-shirt fabric of the same size. Make three pleats on the left and right sides of the fabric. Fuse the interfacing to the backside of the top layer, sew three pleats on the left and right side of the entire piece. Attach seven inches of narrow elastic on the pleated sides or, if elastic isn't available (it isn't) attach an eighteen-inch tie to each corner before you sew the right-sides together leaving a gap large enough to turn the fabric inside out. Press. Topstitch the entire piece and voila! A mask is born.

I've been creative with the ties. I've used everything from hem tape to single-fold bias tape to shoe laces and grosgrain ribbon.

Maskmaking requires a working sewing machine. Mine refused to sew just as I was ramping up production. Yes, this very machine that had seen me through thirty-three years of quilts, curtains, wedding attire, Halloween costumes, dresses and countless garment repairs, decided to lie down on the job. Bobbins threads tangled, sewing needles broke, feed dogs jammed.

I took the bobbin mechanism apart, cleaned the lint, lubricated the places that needed oil, just as I've done forever. No sooner had I asked a sewing friend about borrowing a machine, I heard that Joann Fabrics was about to be shut down because such stores are "non-essential."

Then along came the rumor about Walmart roping off its non-food/non-pharmacy aisles which would eliminate purchasing of sewing supplies. This news was particularly troubling to us maskmaticians.

Thankfully, the rumors about Joann and Walmart were only rumors.

Meanwhile a few naysayers have scoffed at my homemade masks. A cloth mask—even one with three layers of cloth—won't prevent Coronavirus, they say. Maybe not, but a little bit of something is better than a whole lot of nothing.

A mask reminds us not to touch our face, which is how we get Covid- 19—touching our eyes, nose or mouth. A mask will remind us where we are and when this is, as if we could ever forget.

The house dress comeback

June 2020

Many of us have adopted a simpler dress code during this COVID staycation.

Clothing was relaxed well before the pandemic—thank Casual Fridays for that—but the extended quarantine has prompted a state of perpetual dress-down.

With no meetings, church services, luncheons or dinner parties to attend, there's no reason to dress up. And if thirty days form a habit, we've had ninety days in sweat pants and t-shirts.

This is the longest I've gone without a wristwatch since fifth grade. And who needs lipstick when you're wearing a mask? I haven't. Zoom gatherings require little more than combed hair, a decent top and a smile, lipstick optional.

Recently a friend I'll call Bev said she was going to order herself a new "boardwalk dress." She described it as a simple cotton shift to wear around the house. The boardwalk name suggested something to wear at the beach, so I was naturally curious.

That evening we chatted on the phone for the better part of an hour as we compared notes on our computer screens. We perused clothing websites, looking at flowy shifts made of breathable fabric—what our mothers called a "house dress."

Today's versions are trendier than mumus or frumpy, snap-up-the-front housecoats. Boardwalk dresses are perfect for running errands. Think of a t-shirt that wants to be a dress, or a dress that wants to be a long, loose t-shirt.

By now, my friend had convinced me that I needed a boardwalk dress too, especially after I admitted that I'd already pushed my luck during this pandemic, wearing pajama bottoms and a jacket to water plants out front. There's little chance of someone unexpectedly driving up my driveway, but still.

I told Bev about "Swirl" dresses, a popular item at a store my mother frequented sixty years ago. Swirls were cotton wrap dresses that tied in front— holdovers from Hooverettes, worn in the 1930s, named for the President or the vacuum cleaner, I'm not sure which. Women on *I Love Lucy* were wearing these dresses into the 1950s.

Bev wasn't familiar with Hooverettes or Swirls, but she understood what I was talking about. Dowdy or not, true boardwalk dresses would pack well if by some miracle I might be able to take an overnight trip.

I knew we were onto something when, not two days after our boardwalk dress conversation, I spotted an article in *Southern Living*. "The House Dress is Officially Back and We Are Here for It," the headline read. An accompanying text was titled, "20 Comfy House Dresses Stylish Enough to be Spotted In (Even If You Won't Be)."

While we were locked down at home, the world reverted back to the 1930s—Hooverettes, unemployment, battered economy and all.

It's amazing how history repeats itself.

No, your senior portrait doesn't honor the Class of 2020

April 2020

Call it a symptom of COVID boredom. Recently older Facebookers have been posting youthful images of themselves for the world to see "in honor of the Class of 2020." But exactly how does this honor today's students?

I posed that question a couple of weeks ago on Facebook, and was told that I should lighten up. Vintage photos are meant to be fun.

Still, this fad doesn't make sense to me. OK, I'll call it what it is: a thoughtless reminder to students and their families who are being cheated out of their senior rites of passage, thanks to a world pandemic that's no fault of their own.

Recently Gov. Roy Cooper announced that public schools will be closed for the rest of the term to protect the health and safety of students and staff. I get that. What I don't get is how me posting my senior photo from forty-eight years ago will honor the current graduates.

Granted, teens aren't generally on Facebook, but some of their parents and grandparents are. My posting a senior photo would only rub it in that their loved one is missing out on what has become American tradition. The Class of 2020 will have no commencement or prom. No sports banquet, spring play, band concert or Honors Day.

If you're one of the Facebookers who has joined the senior photo trend, I realize I'm stepping on your toes. But like a lot of other silly games and fads that rip through social media, they're all about being part of the flock and harvesting information for potential hackers (though I'm sure my account can be hacked with or without my senior photo to entice them).

I'm sorry that this year's seniors are being left. I'm sure I would have resented not being able to dress in a cap and gown to receive my diploma. Most certainly I would have felt cheated if I had been asked to give a valedictory or salutatory address. I wasn't asked back in the day, but if I had been ….

I would have likewise felt cheated if I'd missed Honors Day or not been able to participate in the spring musical and band concert or senior trip, if we'd planned one. All of these give graduating seniors the privilege to revel in those waning days of high school.

I would have been bummed had I not been able to gather with friends and family to celebrate graduation. Such gatherings usually include more than ten people and don't involve social distancing.

That said, I haven't even mentioned those who will miss college graduation or ceremonies conferring graduate degrees. Imagine completing all that work and not being able to formally celebrate.

Some have suggested that students can have their graduation later. But exactly how would that work? Graduates, if they're lucky, have jobs or internships or other commitments. Some have signed up to join the military.

No, the time to graduate is when it's time, not on some arbitrary date in midsummer or early fall.

Yes, I may be overthinking this. I should take a deep breath and lighten up, but 2020 isn't a lighten-up kind of year.

Today's graduating seniors will be forever bruised by this strange period in history. I'm too much of a realist to not believe that isn't so.

Me posting my senior portrait on Facebook won't change any of that.

Closet purge begs fashion questions

October 2020

Between moving house plants inside and turning on the gas logs is a time-worn rite of autumn: the closet switcheroo.

Saturday's rain gave me the perfect excuse to swap my summer things for cold-weather gear. Rifling through sweaters and boots, it seemed a lot longer than seven months ago that I wore this stuff. That's how it is in this year of drama and contradiction.

I vowed to do some serious editing to my wardrobe which was fairly easy. And if there's one thing I've learned from 2020, it's how to edit my life. COVID has pared down our need for outfits—when outings amount to walking the dog or pulling weeds, we have little need for cashmere or formal wear.

I joyfully tossed out pants that no longer fit, figuring if I eliminate the larger trousers, I'll be less apt to grow back into them.

I checked my purses and found some dregs of my former life nestled in the zippered pockets: business cards, a tube of lipstick. (Who still wears that?) Inside one side pocket was a bottle of hand sanitizer. A year ago, I would have puzzled over the sanitizer. I wasn't a germophobe until last March.

I found my spare pair of glasses that went missing last month. Somehow, they had burrowed their way into the lining of an otherwise empty handbag. I have no idea how these things happen.

I sighed as I shoved my party clothes to the back corner. Last Christmas I purchased a dress in a candy cane print, a holiday number you don't dare wear before Thanksgiving or a day past New Year's. I wore the dress a few times last December, but something tells me this holiday season it won't see the light of day.

This summer I noted in a Walmart ad that the 1930s milkmaid dresses—dull prints, fitted waist, button front—were making a comeback, which made this COVID time warp even weirder. Looking to Walmart for fashion advice is one thing, but what those Walmart apparel buyers forgot was that Great Depression people actually dressed up. They still had places to go.

Reviewing what remained of my wardrobe, I asked myself which items are in style? Are angled hemlines still a thing? What about sweaters with drapey points? Tops with shoulder holes?

For my own edification, I Googled "fall fashion trends for 2020," so I'll be on trend when I do the drug-store drive-thru.

A few style statements and my notes:

1. Fringe—Nope. If I didn't wear that in high school, I'm not wearing it now.

2. Faux leather puff sleeve blouses—A blouse made of vinyl? Who thinks this is a good idea?

3. Jewel tones—Classic. Good.

4. Turtleneck sweaters—OK, turtlenecks tend to be hot and itchy, but at least they're not pretending to be a leather jacket. (See number 2).

5. Preppy plaids—Check.

6. Rhinestone headbands—Is this a joke?

7. Sherpa jackets—Only if it's freezing outside.

8. Shades of brown/beige—Nope. Those colors make me look dead.

Most of the fashion trends focused, more or less, on the top half of the body, and we have Zoom to thank. In a virtual meeting, all that matters is your head and shoulders. (If you're having a bad hair day, do as I do and skip the video feature altogether. Log on as a blank icon or point your computer camera to the ceiling.)

Which brings me to another point. Must your mask coordinate with what you're wearing? The other day I noticed Nancy Pelosi's mask was made of tangerine calico to coordinate with her orange ensemble.

So is color coordination important? What about masks that display slogans? Is it fashionably correct to wear a disposable sky-blue mask if you don't work in health care?

Don't ask me. I'm still puzzling over the faux leather blouses.

Zooming into the holidays

December 2020

Zoom meetings, Zoom church, Zoom Christmas.

Some authorities suggest that we pare the home holiday crowd to two or three and invite the extras virtually.

It's not a new idea. Several years ago, a gathering of friends on Thanksgiving included a Facetime session with a relative living in California. She watched us longingly as a dozen of us gathered around the dinner table three time zones away.

It was a nice try at inclusion, but all we did was tantalize the poor Californian who couldn't enjoy the turkey, dressing and pumpkin pie with us. We were having a great time, but for her, not so much.

Which brings me back to Zoom. COVID-19 is spiking. We shouldn't pass germs around, but let's not kid ourselves: Virtual anything is not the same thing as meeting in person. Compare a live concert to one broadcast "live." They're hardly identical twins.

At the same time, I know we should be happy that Zoom exists. Back during the Great Influenza of 1918, all folks had to rely on were party lines and hand-crank wall phones to communicate remotely. And letters, assuming germs didn't hitch a ride on the envelope.

The Zoom platform has rapidly moved into our lives. This year alone I've attended two national conventions, a state convention, hosted chapter meetings, taken workshops and attended board meetings virtually more times than I care to count. And I'm a retiree.

I'm not a Zoom fan. I cringe at the technological glitches, the pre-meeting chitchat, the unmuted mute buttons that create unearthly feedback. I'm annoyed by people who have barking dogs (such as me). those who leave TV on in the background or have family members ramble into the Zoom room unaware.

Zoom puts our living spaces on display. Since March we've all become familiar with the kitchens, home offices and living rooms of TV anchors, politicians and performers. While they're talking or singing or playing guitar, I find myself wondering why national figures choose to set up their laptop with their kitchen stove in the background. Meanwhile, I check the photos and book titles on their shelves, scoping out these once-private quarters thrust into the public eye.

Along the way, I've learned a few tricks of the Zoom trade. For example, if you don't use the video feature, it doesn't matter if you're still in your bathrobe or having a bad hair day. You can eat oatmeal, chew bubble gum, pet your dog or do needlepoint without anyone being the wiser. If you use a mobile device for Zoom, you can dust the entire house while others think you're glued to your computer. Shhh. Don't tell anybody.

Zoom does save time and gas. It frees us from worrying about rain gear and parking places. It allows us to multitask. It permits us to be there without being there.

I know Zoom is here to stay. It saves way too much time and money. Still, Zoom bothers me because it frees us from one another, and that may be a habit we cannot shake.

The bad juju of 2020

January 2021

If you listen to some forecasters, 2021 may turn out to be 2020's ugly sister. I hope not.

This COVID year brought one misfortune after another: shutdowns, layoffs, record downpours, Hurricane Zeta—even a rare Carolina earthquake. Bad juju run amok.

Last spring, when face masks were becoming a thing and were so hard to find, I sewed some for family, friends and area nurses. A few dozen masks into the project, I received a call from the friend of a friend. The caller suffered from COPD. Would I make her a mask?

Yes, I said. No need to pay me. Just make a donation to the Red Cross.

I really didn't care to meet a maskless person at my door. I said I'd leave the mask in my mailbox.

You mustn't do that, the woman said. Don't you know it's a federal crime to leave stuff in a mailbox?

I was a little taken aback.

I'm doing you a favor, I told her. It's my mailbox. If I get arrested, so be it.

A few months later, I found what looked like pink confetti inside my mailbox along with remains of a burned firecracker amongst the mail.

I called the Sheriff's Department. A kindly deputy came to investigate. Of course, I didn't know who'd done it, and of course Uncle Sam didn't send a posse.

So much for the federal crime.

But 2020 wasn't done with me. Aside from epic battles with cucumber beetles, horn worms and stink bugs, it was a wet year. Plants wilted and mildewed. Part of the yard turned into a waterway, taking newly planted sod and grass seed with it.

Gutters malfunctioned. The crawl space turned damp.

My rot-resistant cedar lamp post decided to rot anyway and lean precariously toward the driveway.

My built-in microwave oven died.

Do you have any idea how many sizes of microwaves and trim kits there are for a built-in microwave? Can you imagine how many of them won't fit my cabinet?

Such frustrations were all the more challenging because 2020 arrived four months after my intro to widowhood.

Tym's grave didn't yet have a permanent marker. That project resumed this past summer, after the quarry shutdown due to COVID. Tym's stone was set alongside mine, my full name and birth date carved like I might imagine in some nightmare.

Three weeks before the tombstones were to be installed, groundhogs came calling.

I reported the problem to the Newton maintenance department. By the time they had a chance to trap and re-home the varmints, the burial plot was beginning to resemble a prairie dog town.

Wildlife, I am told, is nothing new to local cemeteries. Foxes, groundhogs and the like show up from time to time.

A friend commented that maybe the groundhog was Tym's totem animal. Curious, I looked it up on the Internet. Totem animals are part of the Native American tradition. The designated animals "stay" with you for life, both in the physical and spiritual world.

Not juju exactly, but close.

Yet in forty years of marriage, I don't remember any connection to groundhogs. Not that there should be.

I consider the cemetery groundhogs as random bits of 2020 weirdness. Such stuff doesn't happen often. Otherwise, it wouldn't be weird.

Vaccine theories leave me exhausted

March 2021

Getting the COVID vaccine has become something of a test. My first shot wasn't until this past Friday, so obviously I lost the race. Most everyone I talk to had their shots weeks ago.

In late December the news was full of images of politicians, celebrities and other more-than-equal personalities "setting an example" by being first to take the vaccine.

I'm sure they meant well. Don't they always? But jumping ahead of the most vulnerable—i.e. nursing home patients and health care workers—struck me as insensitive.

On the day that COVID vaccine eligibility was lowered to age 65, I went online to set up my appointment and was assigned to get my first dose on February 26. That was before I'd been outdone by most everyone I know in my age bracket.

As if I should be shamed for not getting in line sooner.

And then along came the anti-vaxxers.

For weeks, an acquaintance badgered me with emails warning of the dangers of COVID vaccine. It's not thoroughly tested, she said. Taking the shots was taking my health into my own hands, which was true. Every day that went by without a vaccination, I was indeed taking my health into my hands.

But everyone can't know as much "science" as an anti-vaxxer.

After a while, I told the email lady to please stop. I'd already signed up to take the shot.

The fact is, she and anyone else over 65 should remember the polio days of the 1950s—the children using crutches and wearing leg braces. I know I do.

I was reared by parents who considered it unacceptable to not take advantage of modern medicine that's available.

My mother dragged us to the doctor's office each spring for our polio shots. Yes, this is how we were immunized in the days before sugar cubes in little paper cups. Real shots; real needles. Every year.

My Dad was all in with Mom when it came to vaccines against polio or any other childhood illness. Not one to mince words, he had something to say about parents who failed to get their kids vaccinated. Such people ought to have their rear-ends kicked.

When the time came for swine flu shots in 1976, I was in line with Dad and my brother. Refusing the vaccine was never considered.

I learned a valuable lesson from Dad. He contracted malaria while traveling in Mexico. The recurring illness was something he would have surely avoided had there been a preventive readily available.

Later, his brother was hospitalized with typhoid fever because he failed to be inoculated before traveling to South America. Skip your shots at your own peril.

Over the years I've taken tetanus boosters and DPT and hepatitis shots. I've taken typhoid shots, malaria meds and cholera injections and been re-vaccinated against smallpox before traveling to sketchy destinations.

I've taken an annual flu shot and had two rounds of shingles vaccines. Not that I enjoy being a human pin cushion, but I like it more than getting sick.

Which brings me back to COVID. The shots have become political, which is a shame. President Trump bent the rules last year to get the vaccine rolled out in record time, but anything associated with Trump is suspect. Meanwhile, anti-vaxxer Robert Kennedy Jr. has been back on the stump, railing against the vaccine and big pharma, like he does with every vaccine.

Meanwhile, some anti-COVID vaxxers assume those receiving shots are morons.

That shot will change your DNA, they say. Which got me to thinking. Could my blood type change? How about my eye color? Might I morph into a size petite? Wake up as a man?

Others insist that the COVID vaccine causes infertility, but I'm not fazed. I don't plan to start another family in my retirement.

And then there are the government conspiracy theorists.

The other day my brother told me he'd had his second shot. You know, he said, the one where the government puts that microchip tracker into your arm.

Of course, he was joking. We were raised by the same parents.

A LA CARTE

Any day can start a new year

September 2018

The coming year began months ago with a scheduled dental appointment, club meetings and conference dates. By early August, my notes for 2019 were bunching up.

It was time to buy a new calendar, one of those broad spiral notebooks with a vinyl cover and two pages of squares for each month.

For me, the year starts in January, as I was taught in first grade. Now, I learn, you can buy twelve-month calendars that start at different times. Last month I found calendars for sale covering July through June—catering to business people and teachers, I suspect. To my dismay, none began in September or October though a few were still available that started April 1.

Who starts their year on April Fool's Day?

When it comes to keeping time, I'm a purist. The proper year is January through December. It would be nice to have a few bonus months thrown in—maybe November and December 2018, or January 2020 to help us bridge to a new year of thinking.

I am fixated on a two-page spread of numbered squares to fill in because, frankly, if I don't have space to write it down, it doesn't get done. The squares need to be large enough—say, two inches by two inches.

I told a friend about my calendar dilemma. She understands my thinking because she also refuses to let her Smartphone calendar replace the old-fashioned paper variety.

Calendars are printed on a rolling basis, she said. Fiscal years—July to June—have shaken up the calendar world.

She advised me to check an office supply store. I did, but not without grief. The 2019 format I wanted came only with a gray cover, which makes me wonder what harbinger this color may mean. 2018 was a nice cheery red.

We haven't always lived a January-December existence. Until 1751, the old-style Gregorian calendar used in the English-speaking world, started each new year on March 25, roughly synchronized with the spring equinox, the time for spring buds and new beginnings. March 25 was also Lady Day, the festival of the Annunciation to the Virgin Mary.

The Julian calendar, adopted by Britain and its colonies in 1752, began the year on Jan. 1. That calendar was originated by Julius Caesar to honor Janus, the god of doors. Thus, January became the portal to the year.

The American election cycle used to be synchronized with the old-style calendar in a sense. Prior to 1933, we swore in our presidents in March, not January.

Still, I think it's wrong for a year to begin in April or July or any month other than January. I'm a creature of habit, and my habits began in the 20th century. And now that I have my 2019 calendar, I'm good to go.

Keepers and their keepsakes

February 2015

Recently I attended a writing workshop offered by Poetry Hickory. For those of you who aren't aware, Poetry Hickory is a monthly gathering of readers and writers at Taste Full Beans, a coffee shop in downtown Hickory. It's organized by Scott Owens.

That evening Jaki Shelton Green, a revered North Carolina poet, shared how objects can inform writing. She told us of a nail that has been handed down in her family since slave times. As the story goes, one of her ancestors was sold to another white family, and as the mother ran after the buck wagon whisking her daughter away, a nail fell to the ground. It was one last physical connection between mother and child.

The woman picked it up and sewed the memento into the hem of her skirt for safekeeping. The nail has since been handed down for more than 150 years.

Such a dramatic story gives me goose bumps. Later, the dozen or so of us shared brief stories of objects that we had brought with us. They were as varied and interesting as the people telling them. A plastic toy truck, a driver's license, an Air Force navigation computer, a diploma.

My object was a small pocket diary from 1965. At age ten, I recorded my daily comings and goings within its pages. Such unrelated events as "Made ant cemetery. Watched Johnny Carson. Had a milkshake."

The diary is precious to me because it was my first attempt at keeping a daily log. I get this honestly. My mother kept her diary from 1929 to 1963, a remarkable feat. Reading through her pages, I confront my younger self, the day I was born, and the days I progress up to age eight.

And then one day my mother stopped writing. Life got in the way, things got too complicated and knowing that she could never recapture all those lost days, she gave up.

In 1965, she hoped that she could pass the writing gene to me. For six months. I wrote what I was doing in fifth grade, of Girl Scout meetings, class assignments, playmates, piano lessons and a fantastic trip we took to California and back. The diary serves as a document, a personal and a family history. No one can argue when and where we went on that trip. It's all there in my fifth-grade handwriting.

And then on June 17, 1965, almost halfway through the year, I stopped writing. Keeping a diary requires dedication and discipline, two qualities I had not developed. And out of frustration and hopelessness, I gave up my diary.

My mother would be pleased to know that her effort wasn't in vain. I still keep a journal on my computer (with backup of course). I have done so since May 17, 2001. It has served to oil rusty memories and settle arguments. When did we buy that car? When was our niece born? My journal settles it.

It's also a historical document for me and my family. Someday someone may delve into my typewritten pages and learn what life was like in the early 2000s—not that my life is particularly important or exciting, but it, like all other lives, matters. My thing is to write it down.

Our stories are part of a greater narrative that connects us to everyone else who has ever lived or has yet to be born.

Talking herbs at Hart Square

Judy Sigmon (left) is the horticulturalist. I'm the dabbler.

July 2016

I received an invitation to time travel last month and of course I jumped at the chance.

For several years, Judy Sigmon and I have portrayed 1840s herbalists during the fall festival at Hart Square, Dr. Robert Hart's complex of log cabins near Plateau.

It's the largest collection of original historic log buildings in the United States and it's right here in Catawba County. The festival draws thousands and should be on everyone's bucket list.

This time the call came from Reggie Thomas, a friend and local photographer who's been recording the comings and goings at Hart Square for more than twenty years. He and a videographer have been working on a series of DVDs about the village. I'd been in an earlier one, portraying a surveyor's wife and a churchgoer, but Judy and I hadn't yet been filmed as the herb ladies.

That Friday morning I turned up in a long calico skirt, apron and bonnet. Judy and I set up a table of fresh herbs, lavender cookies and her special cordial "recipe." We chatted on camera about medicinal and culinary uses of herbs.

Both of us have grown them for years. She's the horticulturalist. I'm just a dabbler.

My first encounter with herb growing came in college when I bought a "grow your own" parsley kit for my dorm windowsill. I'd heard the Simon and Garfunkel song, "Scarborough Fair"—parsley, sage rosemary and thyme. What did those plants actually look like? What did they smell like?

By the time I had my own home, I had grown these and more. I quickly found out how slow rosemary grows and how mint can take over your flower beds. I learned parsley is a biennial and that chamomile produces the most delicate white flowers.

The aromatic qualities of herbs appeal as well as their direct connection to our ancestors. One of the first things a pioneer family did was plant a kitchen garden that included herbs not only for cooking but to repel pests, mask unpleasant odors and cure ailments.

How many of us know that sage, the herb used in turkey dressing, can help with digestive discomforts and memory loss?

Parsley, the garnish seen on dinner plates, is a breath freshener. It's high in Vitamins C and K.

Rosemary, a perennial evergreen shrub native to the Mediterranean, is used in meat dishes. It's an aromatic herb that makes a great air freshener. It has been used to treat skin irritations and digestive problems. Sprigs of rosemary are said to ward off mice and rats.

Thyme is an ingredient in cough remedies, acne treatments and is said to be a mood enhancer. The plant also has antiseptic qualities.

Most years since 2008, Judy and I have talked herbs at the 1782 Kahill-Dellinger House during the Hart Square Festival. The event occurs on the fourth Saturday each October. Some two hundred volunteers demonstrate crafts such as spinning, weaving, outdoor cookery, sand casting, distilling, corn grinding and more.

Make plans to go this year, but don't tarry. Tickets sell out quickly.

Mom was right. Skip white.

Mom and I, sometime between Memorial Day and Labor Day in 1959.

August 2015

L abor Day is this Monday, and my Facebook friends have already seen my alert. White-shoe season is over.

My tongue-in-cheek post underscores a rule learned back when women wore hats and gloves to church. Clothes have seasons, and you should know what time it is.

My mother taught me this Old School rule. White footwear should be worn from Memorial Day to Labor Day. Fudging at Easter was pushing it because where I grew up in the Midwest, spring weather was iffy. How ridiculous we looked wearing straw hats and white patent leather with snow flurries in the air! It happened on occasion.

My mother had other items on the summer-only list: straw accessories, white handbags, seersucker, linen, eyelet lace, open-toed shoes and spectator shoes—those two-toned saddle shoes for adults with white and navy, black or brown leather. And anything resembling resort wear—seashell jewelry, white costume jewelry, canvas shoes and handbags, brightly printed cotton skirts and so on.

White shoes, straw hats and seersucker suits announced that summer was in session. Swimming pools were open. It was sensible to serve lemonade on the porch or go on a picnic. White-shoe summers were part of a rhythm that we have unfortunately shunted aside in favor of seasonless blue jeans and t-shirts. We've become less churchy, less formal and less well-dressed.

I admit I'm not a fan of white shoes. First of all, they're difficult to keep clean. Secondly, they make your feet appear gargantuan, and what woman wants that?

Recently a friend shared an article about why people don't wear white after Labor Day. The author stated her reasons, including the history of white being a cooler color to wear in hot, sticky weather. She pointed out how white was reserved for weddings and resort wear by wealthy Victorians who made the rules to be snobby.

What did I think? the friend taunted.

My reply was simple: The reason people don't wear white after Labor Day is because it's wrong.

There are some year-round exceptions: nurses, sailors, brides, athletes, debutantes, pages at formal functions.

Obeying the white-before-Labor Day rule, like all other rules, can be liberating. Life is simpler with boundaries. Rules eliminate ambiguity and guesswork. You don't have to wonder what to wear and when to wear it.

Celebrate the rule when you switch out your wardrobe. Out with the old season, in with the new. Living in a temperate climate such as ours is much less boring than coping with the eternal summer of Hawaii or South Florida, for example.

Stowing warm-weather clothes after the first Monday in September is a sign of fall. Glorious fall! In a season full of russets and reds and burgundies and golds, forest greens and purples, there's no room for white shoes, much less sandals.

And so, dear readers, I urge you to listen to the voice in your head. It's your mother with sensible advice. Don't wear white shoes after Labor Day.

Fun with Merriam-Webster

May 2018

You word lovers out there: here's a website you won't want to miss. The folks at Merriam-Webster, the dictionary people, have added an historical component to their website. You can find it here: https://www. merriam-webster.com/time-traveler/2016

Scroll back on the years and see when certain words were first printed in the English language. Words may be used in spoken English for years or decades before they finally make it into the written word.

Being the history and word buff that I am, I couldn't resist. Many of the words are driven by technology. No surprise there.

Words we use all the time now, such as "unfriend," came into use fifteen years ago, in 2003, a result of Facebook, of course. It was the same year that brought us baby bump, binge-watch and electronic cigarette.

Crowdsourcing, another function of the Internet, arrived in 2006, the same year that brought us "bucket list," the year before the movie of the same name was released.

Photo bomb? 2008. Ransomware? 2005. Social media is a relative newcomer, birthed in 2004, the same year as waterboarding.

Words, the building blocks of language, change over time as do meanings.

Pick your birth year, your graduation year, or the year you got married.

I picked 1979. The results were surprising. Thirty-nine years ago, the year of the Iranian hostages and hyper-inflated interest rates, we first read adjustable-rate mortgage, backslash, California roll, frizzies, homeschooler, identity politics, la-la land, log off, laser printer and Lyme disease, outsource and self-publish.

The Miriam-Webster time machine goes as far back as before twelfth century.to list basic Anglo-Saxon words still taught in easy readers: apple, cheese, goat, foot, look, man, owl, see, wood.

Fast forwarding to the Shakespearean era, the year of 1598: attorney general, cusp, cockpit, stigmatize, retired.

Or consider 1620, when Pilgrims landed at Plymouth Rock: cryptic, curling stone, gusto, hyphenate, lambaste, merchant bank, sundown, trashy—

an eclectic list.

On further, to 1776 and the Declaration of Independence brings some predictable newcomers: bluejacket, first sergeant, Franklin stove, jungle, killjoy, regime, slaveholder, tolerant, unelected—but also some words that seem out of sync: keyboard, sour cream, totem, volcanic.

1861, the outbreak of the American Civil War, brought some terms that were half predictable: born-again, dialysis, fire drill, jamboree, kepi, Medal of Honor, piranha, raider, riflery, slaw, submariner, states' righter, untrusting.

Fast forward to 1912, the year the *Titanic* sank: air pocket, Bull Moose, Camp Fire girl, chemical warfare, family values, moviemaker, nosedive, pizzeria, pedophile, quantum theory, strip poker, TB, Thousand Island dressing.

How about the end of World War II? Predictably 1945 has some appropriate terms: A-bomb, bird colonel, cold war, Dear John, firestorm, hassle, ID card, press secretary, sonic barrier, target date, TV.

Or 1967, known for the Summer of Love? New words included anti-pot, automatic teller machine, doobie, dork, flower child, ego trip, flower power, jihadist, land yacht, love-in, minicomputer, networking, psychedelia, rip-off, speed freak, whacked-out.

If words are indicators of the times, Miriam-Webster's most recent entries show the unseemly state of affairs. Trending on the day I wrote this column were acrimony, charlatans, excoriate, kakistrocracy, lowlifes, oligarchy, salacious, slime ball, spurious, redaction, white lies.

Look them up. Then take a shower.

Scan the code with a Smartphone or other device to visit the site mentioned in the essay.

They only want your money

February 2021

Considering all the robocalls about my vehicle warranty, I wish I had an unlisted number.

No wait, I do, but the robocalls keep on coming.

If you have a pulse, you know the drill. The phone rings. Caller ID displays Hendersonville or Spruce Pine or Forest City so you'll think it's someone from this region.

For a while I thought the calls had something to do with my vehicle being fairly new until a friend told me that she gets the same calls regularly. Her car is ten years old.

There are days when I receive three or more of these nuisance calls. Invariably they ring when I'm doing something else: cooking or driving or taking a shower or while I'm on another call.

And don't tell me to be placed on a do-not-call list. I did that years ago, but the scammers keep ringing my phone.

There was a time when the unsolicited calls were all about selling cable TV service or phone plans. Those solicitations went the way of the telegram when the scammers figured out that people have cut the cable and the landline.

During election years, the calls multiplied. I'd hear from various celebrities recorded to endorse a candidate or a particular cause, such as the Second Amendment rights or abortion rights or immigration reform.

"Don't pick up until you see who it is," my husband would say.

He rarely answered the phone, even if it was for him.

Still, it was amazing to be "contacted" by national candidates or members of their family to be singled out by former officer holders. Having a listed number meant open season on our phone line.

I should have recorded these calls for posterity. I want to say that Charlton Heston might have "dialed" our number. I'm sure the First Lady did.

Back then I took it in stride, didn't catch my hair on fire. I saw some humor in it, comparing celebrity robocalls with friends. I'd heard from Laura Bush; they'd heard from Hillary Clinton. It was back when you could joke about something without the other person losing their cool.

These days the robocalls are as unentertaining as life is serious. Hearing a female robot telling me my car is out of warranty isn't quite the same thing as hearing from say, Ivanka Trump.

But it's not just the calls that make me crazy. Now that the election cycle is over, I'm still getting mailed solicitations including packets of mailing labels with my name misspelled or shopping lists or notecards. Are we supposed to keep this stuff? Throw it away?

And what about the coin in the envelope window?

To be honest, I hesitate to give money to any cause knowing that my mailbox will be full forevermore. How is it that I give to a cause and they are compelled to remind me that I haven't given to them this week?

Boys Town popped up in my mailbox a few times recently, no doubt linked to my ongoing support of Children's Aid Society of New York. Charities have long memories. That group has been on my gift radar since they helped locate a record related to my great-grandmother and her brother, who were helped by the agency back in 1860. An annual donation is my way to pay homage to the folks who helped these children escape New York as orphan train riders.

Years ago, I made a donation to a Humane Society in memory of a family member. I have no doubt that the society is a worthy cause, but I live 750 miles away and am not compelled to repeat the gift. It took them a while to figure that out.

Nonprofits are short on cash. I like to help when I can. But being bombarded by mailings is a turnoff. If they can afford to waste all that paper and postage, do they need my help?

If you want to get my attention, send me a handwritten letter—yes, with a cross-out or a misspelled word. Hand-address the envelope. Make me know it comes from a real person with a real heart, not some computer linked to a mega printer.

Make it personal, humble and genuine. Make it impossible to resist, like Publisher's Clearinghouse. I'll admit I've put a stamp on a couple of envelopes with my winner stickers and coupons to ensure I'm in the running.

PCH says there's no need to order, but they sure make you sift through a lot of ads to make you reconsider. I haven't ordered any magazines or magic slippers or deluxe cutlery.

Just two weeks ago I sent off the "final-final" response to make sure the Prize Patrol doesn't overlook me. I'm as avaricious as the next person.

Last February, a man named Marc Friedman of Irvine, California, became the 2020 winner of $5,000 a week for life. I looked it up. He overcame the odds of 2.4 billion to one of winning the super prize.

And then there's Lana Sandlin of Largo, Florida, who pocketed $1 million last August. Not bad for the cost of a couple of postage stamps.

This year's super winner will be announced February 28 on NBC. Wouldn't it be cool to put Newton, North Carolina, on the map?

I think so too.

EDITOR'S NOTE: Two months after publishing this column, I received a call from a scammer claiming to work for Publisher's Clearinghouse. The scripted caller sounded fishy from the first seconds. I hung up. Upon research, I learned that PCH never calls recipients; the Prize Patrol shows up in person. They should call it the Surprise Patrol.

Confessions of a cable cutter

June 2015

Don't ask Millennials about cable TV programs. Chances are these young adults don't subscribe. If they've seen a certain "cable" show, it's streamed off the Internet.

Millennials, born from 1977 to 1994, are opting to not buy into cable bundles, but rather to tailor their viewing, and it's provided by social media companies rather than satellite or cable TV companies.

My husband and I are not Millennials, but we became cable cutters before it was trendy. In 2008 when we moved, we discovered that Charter would not hook us up. I spent well over an hour discussing this with Charter management in Washington State. That was in October 2008. We haven't spoken since.

Charter's answer was that they wouldn't provide service to our property. Can't or won't, I don't exactly recall. And never mind that our neighbors have had cable service for years.

What I didn't realize at the time was the big favor the cable company was doing for us by not allowing us to subscribe. I know. We could install a dish or wait for another cable provider. In 2015 we are still waiting, which brings me to the crux of the matter.

We stuck with retro rabbit ears. Don't laugh. You really can bring in several channels without an aerial antenna. We joked that our house was a throwback to the 1950s. Growing up, we had three TV channels, maybe a fourth if you counted the educational TV channel. We survived quite well.

Without cable, we quickly realized the savings of not paying the bill and using our time for other things such as…reading. What a novel idea, pardon the pun.

We did buy a Roku box a couple of years ago to stream some shows, but outside the Internet and our trusty rabbit ears, we're media deprived. Visitors consider our place quaint and refreshingly boring. Well, no, they think it's downright odd, but not as odd as they did in 2008. In fact, a few have cut their own cables.

We are not tied to a TV screen. We can't ever seem to pick up ABC, and if the weather is bad, there goes PBS, CBS, and NBC, too. So we read, work on a hobby, walk the dogs, work in the yard, entertain, write a letter. You know, stuff people did in the 1950s.

Did we ever need a prepackaged TV bundle for $70 or more a month in the first place? Probably not. Our Netflix subscription is about $8.50 a month, or roughly $100 per year. In eight years, we would have spent $6,720 for cable or $816 for Netflix. Do the math.

It's not just the money. It's about time and what we allow or don't allow media to do with our lives.

I'm not the world's best time manager, but given the choice of a good book or a cable program, I'll take the book. But I'm a lousy conversationalist when it comes to television. Cable cutting has its price.

Jolene the dog and other naming riddles

Lovable Jolene.

April 2015

I don't know where the Humane Society finds names for adoptable pets. In 2012, our corgi mix moved in with her medical record, a sweet disposition, and an impossible name: "Angelea."

I know the Humane Society folks mean well, and giving them human names makes these hopeful family members seem more like family. But my husband and I decided that we couldn't handle four-syllable dog name, much less "Angelea." The only human we knew by that name, or remotely close, was actress Angelina Jolie. The Angelea name got things rolling, and soon it morphed into "Jolene."

Yes, we had to notify Petfinder and the veterinarian. Angelea was now Jolene, the Dolly Parton song notwithstanding.

Our Jolene wouldn't steal anything but your heart. She looks at you with one blue eye and one brown eye (she has one of each) as if you hang the moon, which of course you do.

With our pets it never matters what the official name is on a vaccination record, the pet will invariably acquire a nickname or two or three. Jolene, for example, is now "Queen."

Several years ago, we adopted a chow from the Humane Society who had named her "Bambi." There was no way I would own a dog with such a frou-frou name, so she became "Bamboozle" or more simply, "Bam."

Eventually, she became "Spam." Rhymes figure heavily in the process.

Other dogs have experienced the same misnomers. Our first corgi, Winnie, was known to us as "That Little Girl" which was shortened to "That."

"Where's That?"

"She's on the couch."

"Has That been fed?"

"Yes, twice."

That also rhymed with fat.

Christine, a beagle we had once, became "The Teen." Spotty, our beloved beagle, was known as "Paté." Mildred, a basset-chow mix, was "Dutch." Cappy, another rescue, is often called "Roon." Frisker, our border collie/lab mix, is now "Furry" or "Mr. Fear."

I know. Don't ask.

Some people hate nicknames and refuse to call their dogs anything but "Jack" or "Ruff" or "Spot." Good for them.

But others share our penchant for "pet" names. Some friends' cat started out as Sweetie and became "Teeter Man." My brother's dog Buddy became "Butter."

If I've inspired you to adopt a rescued pet, the number for the Humane Society of Catawba County: 828-464-8878.

Me, after the fall

April 2016

Last Wednesday I took a tumble on a hardwood floor. I had never fallen on my face before, but there's a first time for everything.

The resulting goose egg bruise over my left eye evolved into a swollen purple eyelid and splotch toward my nose and cheekbone.

Then vanity set in: How to conceal the growing bruise (difficult), how to explain (equally difficult) and whether to become a hermit or face the world. After all, I can't see the raccoon eye without a mirror.

In the big scheme of things, I should be thankful that I wasn't injured badly, and I am thankful. I have no broken bones, no memory loss, no paralysis.

Still, there's nothing funnier than somebody falling, is there? I laugh. You probably do too. We laugh unless the joke's on us, and then we feel ridiculous and embarrassed. We want to press the rewind button and skip this next chapter.

I remember my fall in slow motion. I lost my balance, pitched forward, the slick flooring coming closer and closer.

Falls are no laughing matter. According to the Center for Disease Control, falls account for more than 25,000 deaths each year in the U.S. and most of the 250,000 hip fractures.

My lopsided "eye shadow" will work its way through blue, green and yellow as my face presents a story that others are itching to hear.

Some onlookers will joke to pull it out of me. You were drunk, weren't you? Who beat you up? Ha ha!

It may be simpler to begin the conversation with an explanation. "I had an accident…."

In time the bruise around my eye will fade, but what if it was a permanent scar or birthmark or a skin disorder that couldn't be treated? On a scale of one to ten, raccoon eye barely registers.

So, over the course of the next week or so, I will walk in shoes that are uncomfortable. And I will learn to empathize a bit more. In the end, I can let my shiner take center stage and stay home or I can go about my business and let "it" be someone else's problem.

I vote for the latter.

My close encounter with Buckingham Palace

Sharing lunch with London pigeons near Buckingham Palace, March 12, 1974.

November 2020

Season Four of *The Crown* is a great diversion for chilly November evenings. Netflix debuted the most recent episodes last Sunday with installments focusing on the 1980s and 1990s. It's history most viewers know: Prince Charles, Princess Diana and Camilla Parker-Bowles.

I can't watch any portrayal of the Royal Family at Buckingham Palace without hearkening back to my own brush with royal stardust. The year was 1974; Season Three, if you will. I was a foreign student in the seaside town of Brighton, an hour's train ride from London.

That year Queen Elizabeth was scheduled to open Parliament on March 12. This would involve much pomp and circumstance, and with any luck, we would see the Queen in person, something to tell our friends and family. So, it was decided—four of us Americans would play hooky that Tuesday. We would pack a lunch to eat in one of the London parks.

Did I mention that 1974 involved the OPEC oil embargo?

The energy crisis that ensued did a major number on the West, including Great Britain. I remember spending my first week in an unheated hotel (I could actually see my breath while taking a bath). At night I slept in my coat, hat and gloves and still shivered.

We American students arrived in London January 1, and until classes began several days later, we spent a lot of time riding public transportation and touring museums just to stay warm. People could be fined for leaving a light on in an empty room, a solemn reminder of what life had been during the Blitz thirty-five years earlier. Back then, citizens could be fined for allowing even a sliver of light to show German bombers where to drop their payloads.

Life was austere in 1974 as well. As for our foray to see the Queen, we were oblivious to the fact that the usual fanfare would be curtailed. Her trip from Buckingham Palace to Parliament was by automobile, not coach. It was the most dressed-down opening of Parliament since the war.

By the time we arrived at the palace gates, the dreary weather matched our mood. We were late for a party that never happened.

After eating our box lunches on park benches, the four of us lingered around the palace perimeter, gazing at the immense sand-colored building while a few members of the queen's household staff strolled along the tall iron fence, chatting with visitors.

By this point, two of my friends had wandered off. Sue, another student from Illinois State University, and I remained at the fence, when one of the men, a stout older gentleman in a long gray coat, made his way over to us and struck up a conversation.

When I asked what it would be like to see inside the palace, he paused. "Would you like to do that, Luv?"

I assumed he was joking until he unlocked the gate and motioned for Sue and me to step inside. Stunned, we followed him across the parade grounds to an entrance where we had seen official visitors coming and going from chauffeured vehicles.

I don't remember what Sue said to me or exactly what the guard said to either of us, except to be quick about it. Obviously, he was bending the rules.

We were ushered inside to an ornate table in a vestibule. I peered down a long hallway with gilt mirrors and red walls, and, of course, the proverbial red carpet for guests visiting the Queen's residence.

"Sign here," he said, pointing to lines below other visitors' names.

I don't remember if we used a plumed pen or a simple gold one. All I know for sure is that Sue Barkley from Yorkville, Illinois, and Tammy McElroy from Shelbyville actually signed the guest registry at Buckingham Palace.

In the years since, I've pondered why the two of us were singled out among the random people milling around the palace fence that day. I know that we were not invited until we shed our companions. That freed the official to invite two of us—a permissible number, apparently.

But why did he choose us?

Maybe it's because we were friendly and nonthreatening. Maybe we reminded him of someone he knew. Or maybe he assumed that we were daughters of American GIs who had done the British people a huge favor during World War II.

All I know for certain is that bad luck can sometimes turn on a dime, or even a six-pence, when you least expect it.

Enough dying already

January 2016

First it was singer Natalie Cole who died right before New Year's. Then David Bowie, Alan Rickman, Glenn Frey, Paul Kantner. Big-name entertainers all gone within four weeks of one another.

So far, 2016 has been bittersweet.

If you're a Baby Boomer, most of these names are familiar. They rocked our world at one time or another. Rickman, a famed British actor, is best known for his role in the Harry Potter movies. Glenn Frey was co-founder of the Eagles. Kantner co-founded Jefferson Airplane and Jefferson Starship. Natalie Cole was Nat King Cole's daughter who created her own star in the recording industry. And Bowie was one of the wealthiest and most influential pop musicians of our time.

We've lost some lesser-known players, too. Robert Stigwood, former manager of Cream and The Bee Gees, died January 4. Craig Strickland, front man for the country band Backroad Anthem, was found dead on the same day.

This past Friday I attended *Tuesdays with Morrie* at the Green Room Black Box Theatre. The drama is based on the best-seller by Mitch Albom. It's a memory play about a student and his former sociology professor who was dying of Lou Gehrig's Disease.

Based on a true story, the drama is particular poignant in the midst of all this recent loss. Death and dying are great equalizers that few do well. The play offers good points about how to live life before the final curtain.

"Once you learn how to die, you learn how to live," Morrie tells Mitch, his former student.

A Jew who describes himself as agnostic, Morrie eventually steps into New Testament territory when he advises, "Above all, love one another."

It's very evocative of 1 Corinthians 13: "Now these three remain: faith, hope and love. But *the greatest of these is love.*"

Back in the day, we Baby Boomers thought we'd live forever, but the bitter fruit of 2016 should give us cause for pause. We don't like our pop icons getting old, and we especially don't like facing the reality that we, too, are getting old. I suppose we're no different from any other generation.

"Old" used to be thirty before John Lennon hit forty. Fifty looked old, until the Stones and McCartney and Dylan passed that mark. These days most Sixties icons have passed the seventy mark, that is those who haven't already succumbed to hard living on the road.

Seventy is the new fifty if we fool ourselves into believing it.

As I write this column it's January 31. We haven't yet completed a month of this new year and the news is already littered with the passing of pop heavyweights. At this rate, we're poised to lose sixty major entertainers before the year is out.

What does it matter?

Our culture thrives on entertainment. It's what's behind so much of how we spend our time—whether it's tinkering with a smart phone, watching TV, going to the movies, listening to music in the car. Entertainment has crept into other parts of life as well—politics, journalism, church services.

"Everybody knows they're going to die, but nobody believes it. If we did, we would do things differently," Morrie tells Mitch.

In light of this past month, we should all pay more attention to Morrie.

Winners: No gloating, please

I've followed election cycles to one degree or another for more than fifty years. I learned much of what I know at the family dinner table. My father was an unwavering Republican who wore his preferences on his car bumper.

As a kid I assumed it had always been this way until Dad let it slip that he had cast his first Presidential ballot for FDR, the Democrat he would later term "The Great Destroyer." Like Donald Trump, Dad used colorful nicknames for politicians he didn't like: Horseburger, Pipsqueak, Egghead and Hood, to name a few. To Dad, "R" beside a candidate's name stood for "right" as opposed to "wrong."

As one of the youngest Americans ever to vote in a Presidential election, I cast my first ballot for the Democrat George McGovern in 1972. I turned eighteen that August. The major issue for me was ending the Vietnam War. My Dad wasn't for it either, but nothing could bring him to scratch his ballot and vote for Senator McGovern. Or, if he did, he never admitted to it.

My McGovern bumper sticker distressed my Dad, but he didn't do much more than exchange tongue-in-cheek humor. That's what many people did back in the 20th century. When we disagreed over politics, we didn't hate one another or howl at the moon over who won the election. We didn't take to social media to ridicule and degrade our friends and relatives for the world to see or march around carrying vulgar signs.

From today's vantage point, that time seems refreshingly quaint. Though my parents and I disagreed on who we were going to vote for, I wasn't disowned for my choice, not even after I shook hands with McGovern during a campaign stop that summer.

Had I been more savvy, I would have realized how badly McGovern's campaign was faltering, especially after he shed his running mate, Sen. Tom Eagleton, when it was revealed that Eagleton had been hospitalized for depression, a fact that had been hidden from the public. Mental health issues carried a bigger stigma then than now, and the revelation made Eagleton an unacceptable candidate.

As idealistic as I was about McGovern's antiwar stance, I didn't realize how easily a one-issue candidate's campaign can be torpedoed, which it was, by Richard Nixon, who claimed that peace was at hand that October.

After the votes were counted, McGovern won only 17 electoral votes to Nixon's 520. It wasn't a landslide; it was a tsunami. I couldn't imagine how anyone could endure the public humiliation of such a trouncing.

My introduction to politics had come during the Nixon-Kennedy campaign of 1960, though I was only in first grade. The contest was discussed regularly by my parents.

Every fourth summer my mother tuned in to watch political conventions of both parties. I was intrigued by the crazy hats worn by delegates, the air horns, the imaginative ways state delegations introduced their votes for candidates.

During the 1964 campaign, one of the games my mother suggested for us kids was to count the Goldwater and Johnson bumper stickers on out-of-town road trips. Whoever got Johnson had far more work to do.

The morning after the 1964 election, my Dad was crouched in our driveway, removing his Goldwater sticker from the back bumper. A neighbor I'll call Mr. Jones, drove by and rolled down his window. "I guess you're not too proud of Goldwater now, are you?" he laughed.

Dad didn't know Mr. Jones well, so he knew it wasn't a joke. The gloating comment took him aback—the idea that this man would go out of his way to make fun of Dad's choice, Barry Goldwater, who had endured a humiliating defeat only hours earlier.

The incident taught me how mean it is to make fun of a loser's supporters, especially so soon after the defeat.

Kids at school took the side of their parents which caused some schoolyard bullying as well. The conventional wisdom was that a vote for Goldwater was a vote for a bigger war in Vietnam.

My parents voted for Goldwater and sure enough, the war escalated, though Goldwater's opponent, Lyndon Johnson, was Commander in Chief. As we all know, the Vietnam Conflict grew to a staggering level through the 1960s. Our military involvement didn't end until 1975, more than ten years after the landmark election of 1964.

George McGovern overcame the debacle of 1972 and went on to serve in the U.S. Senate eight more years.

I crossed paths again with him at Lenoir-Rhyne where I worked in the 1990s. He was on campus to discuss his role as president of the Middle East Policy Council. By then my political affiliations had shifted, but I told the former senator that I'd voted for him in 1972. He smiled, no doubt used to being drubbed as one of the biggest losers in the history of the Electoral College. There weren't many of us who voted McGovern in the first place, much less would admit it.

There is a graceful way to win and a graceful way to lose. Gloating and bullying is never a class act. Through the years I've been on both sides of political contests, but through it all, I've never wanted to be like Mr. Jones or be shamed like my Dad was.

That was fifty-six years ago.

You may not remember what was said, but you'll always remember how a gloating comment made you feel.

Four-Way Test appeals to our better angels

January 2021

By now we're all familiar with the images of January 6 when a mob stormed the U.S. Capitol—the broken windows, the angry rioters on a rampage threatening Vice President Pence and other officials. Five people died in the melee, including a policeman.

The nation was outraged, and rightly so.

Such calamities light up social media, and this one has been no exception. A friend recently posted a notice on Facebook: if anyone among his friends supports Trump, please leave. "I no longer want you in my life," he wrote.

This friend has a lot of company. Minds are made up. There is no backing down.

But I choose not to engage. I don't need more heartburn. No one has the corner on truth. There are bits of truth on both sides of every argument. There are always gray areas.

This is why I find absolutism so troubling. Absolutists are always right because they think they're never wrong. Such a posture leaves no room for negotiation or reconciliation or forgiveness.

Joe Biden says he wants to unify the country. He's chosen the theme, "America United" for the inauguration. I didn't know inaugurations had themes, but I hope our new President succeeds in appealing to the better angels of our nature.

We should all take a deep breath, refocus and find ways to work together. With a raging pandemic, unemployment, lockdowns, runaway debt; there's plenty of work to be done.

Sadly, the U.S. Capitol has been turned into an armed camp. "Civil war," a term once bandied about by the fringes of society, is now being speculated by mainstream media.

A house divided against itself cannot stand. American history teaches how true that was back in 1861. Yet in spite of the books and movies, there was little glory in the Civil War, a conflict that left more than 650,000 dead, created 200,000 widows and a half million fatherless children. Four years of war left large parts of the country a smoking ruin. Half of all Southern wealth evaporated.

Let's hope we don't have to learn that lesson again.

The angry mob on January 6 reminded me more of Parisian revolutionaries storming the Bastille in 1789. Last week's rioters, like their French counterparts, were all about deposing their rulers, taking control of a system they believed to be oppressive and corrupt.

The Paris insurrection led to a ten-year Reign of Terror known as the French Revolution, during which tens of thousands were publicly executed, including the king and queen.

I don't want to go there either.

When I think of reconciliation, I remember my days as a Rotarian. At the close of every meeting, members recited the Four-Way Test, a reminder of the importance of leading an ethical life in a free society. Something of a riff on the Golden Rule. It goes like this:

The Four-Way Test of the things we think, say or do:

First, Is it the TRUTH?

Second, Is it FAIR to all concerned?

Third, Will it build GOODWILL and BETTER FRIENDSHIPS?

Fourth, Will it be BENEFICIAL to all concerned?

Much of what we do—and post on social media—would be more civil if we first asked ourselves those four questions

President Abraham Lincoln once said, "We must not be enemies. Though passion may have strained, it must not break our bonds of affection. The mystic chords of memory will swell when again touched, as surely they will be, by the better angels of our nature."

Lincoln included this paragraph in his First Inaugural address delivered on March 4, 1861, on the East Portico of the U.S. Capitol. As some 30,000 gathered, Lincoln made his way through a boarded tunnel for added security. Soldiers lined the streets. Riflemen were poised on rooftops, watching windows.

As Lincoln stood on the dais, he no doubt pondered the growing division in the country. The ongoing rift between free and slave states, North and South. Surely there was time to mend the nation before things boiled over.

Five short weeks later, on April 12, the first shots were fired on Ft. Sumpter.

The lessons of loss

May 26, 1979. A month later, we arrived in Catawba County, NC.

October 2019

September 5 was a day I hoped would never come. That Thursday, my husband Tym died.

Over the course of a year, he had experienced a progressive weakness and shortness of breath. He lost a lot of weight. There was no diagnosis until August 28, when we learned that he had ALS, Lou Gehrig's disease. Since there's no cure, maybe it was best that we didn't know for very long.

Tym had never spent a day in the hospital and forbade me to talk publicly about his failing health. He was a private person. He would hate me telling his story in the newspaper, but it's one that needs to be told.

During the exhausting days and nights, hurrying to and from the hospital—and later, the funeral home—I kept the car radio tuned to 1940s tunes, my musical comfort food. I didn't want to tattoo a popular song with this nightmare.

A month later, people ask me how I'm doing, and I don't know how to answer. Some days are less awful than others. Nothing feels truly normal unless I get lost in a book or my writing or a task that takes me out of where I am and when this is.

I've learned to accept help. My first week alone was a short course in home repairs and endurance. I began to worry about stuff I didn't know: how to change the water filter, how often to rotate the tires on the vehicles, when and how to change the HVAC filters, what to do about some dead trees out back. Some things had been left undone because Tym didn't feel like doing them, and I wasn't comfortable tackling the list that kept growing: rescanning the television channels, lighting the pilot light, hoisting cumbersome boxes to the attic.

In the middle of the upheaval, the coffee maker quit, the well ran dangerously dry, one of the dogs had to go to the vet, and the other began running over to the neighbors, no doubt looking for Tym.

I tried to be dutiful, notifying the agencies that needed to be told of Tym's passing: the bank, his pension plan, Social Security, credit card companies.

Utility companies were a test. Upon learning my husband had passed, I was told I was now a "new customer" though we'd written them checks for decades. A security deposit and a credit check were mentioned.

While informing the phone company that my husband had died, my Internet and email service were cut off. It was a coincidence, they said. That day I spent four and a half hours on the phone, being passed from one "technician" to the other. One of them pitched me a year's repair subscription. Another said it would cost me $49 to reconnect my service, and I began to wonder if they'd ever dealt with a bereaved customer before. I broke down in sobs as my cell phone battery lost power.

Other companies were more accommodating. Hotels.com refunded "nonrefundable" reservations for a trip we couldn't take. American Airlines allowed me to cancel flights and re-credit frequent flier miles, all the while offering profuse condolences. You see, Tym passed the day after we were to start a three-week drive to visit our son and family in California. We were to visit Mt. Rushmore and Crazy Horse and Yellowstone. Thank God we weren't on the road when things turned bad.

Our son booked a last-minute flight to hurry home and say goodbye to his Dad, explaining that since we couldn't go west to visit him, he would come to us. If Tym knew the real reason Lantz had come home, he didn't let on.

Loss can bring out the best in people. My cousin took an overnight flight from Los Angeles so he could be here. A neighbor spotted me walking the dogs one evening. She came out to offer condolences, then insisted I take home some sourdough bread she had just pulled from the oven.

Yes, I get teary when I see Tym's favorite foods at the grocery store or find notes he left around the house. I want to scream when I have to identify myself as a "widow," the sorrow-laden term that conjures up black veils and poisonous spiders.

Along the way I've learned about gratitude. I am grateful to have spent forty years with such a kind and gentle man. I am grateful to have a son who dropped everything and traveled 2,500 miles the minute I called him. I'm grateful to have loyal dogs to watch over me, blessed to have good neighbors and supportive friends.

Finally, I'm grateful that Tym and I chose to live in Catawba County. We moved here sight unseen as newlyweds in 1979. It was one of the best decisions we ever made.

After attending Tym's memorial service, family members from out-of-state told me how impressed they were with our adopted family of North Carolinians who have stood by me as I lurch into this new, ill-fitting chapter of life.

Lately I've been finding feathers in my path—blue ones, white ones, black ones and spotted ones. They've been resting in the grass, flower beds, along the roadside and sidewalks. A white down feather appeared inexplicably on my car seat.

They say feathers mean that angels are near, and I know this is true. Many of these angels are the good people of Catawba County.

And the most valuable lesson I've learned so far is this: Don't put things off. If there's something you want to do, then do it. If there's somewhere you want to go, find the time to go. As the cliché goes, this life is no dress rehearsal. Looking forward in hope will always beat looking back with regret.

About the Author

Tamra Wilson is an essayist and fiction writer whose work has appeared in *North Carolina Literary Review*, *Our State*, *storySouth*, and dozens of other journals and anthologies across the United States. She is the author of *Dining with Robert Redford & Other Stories* and co-editor of *Idol Talk: Women Writers on the Teenage Infatuations that Changed Their Lives*, which was a finalist for the Eric Hoffer Award. She has received two North Carolina Regional Artist Project Grants and has traveled the state as a Road Scholar for the North Carolina Humanities Council.

Tamra is a 2021 honoree of the Baker's Dozen Women's Society affiliated with The Corner Table, a nonprofit focused on providing meals to those affected by hunger in Catawba County. A portion of proceeds from this book will benefit that organization.

Made in United States
Orlando, FL
04 November 2021